ROMANTIC
Paris

THIRZA VALLOIS

Photography by Juliana Spear

ARRIS
BOOKS

An imprint of Arris Publishing Ltd
Gloucestershire

First published in Great Britain in 2003 by

ARRIS BOOKS
An imprint of Arris Publishing Ltd
Unit 1a, Fosseway Business Centre
Stratford Road
Moreton-in-Marsh
Gloucestershire GL56 9NQ
Telephone 01608 652012
Fax 01608 652235
www.arrisbooks.com

British Library in Cataloguing Data
A catalogue record for this book is available from the British Library
ISBN 1-84437-000-3

Permission to reprint copyrighted material is gratefully acknowledged:
From *Life with Picasso* by Françoise Gilot, with permission of A.M. Heath & Co, Ltd.
Quotations about and by Rodin, from *Rodin: The Shape of Genius*, by Ruth Butler,
    ©1993, with permission of Yale University Press.
From *L'hymne à l'amour*, lyrics by Edith Piaf and music by Marguerite Monnot,
    with permission of Editions Raoul Breton.
Eric Satie's letter to Suzanne Valadon, on page 50, from *Correspondance Presque
    complète*, edited by Ornella Volta (Paris: Fayard/IMEC, 2000) 42–43, with
    permission of Archives Eric Satie.
Les Prenoms de Paris, lyrics by Jacques Brel and music by Gérard Jouannest,
    ©1961, with permission of Éditions Gérard Meys.
Les Amoureux des bancs publics, by Georges Brassens, from Paroles et Musique de
    Georges Brassens, translation ©1999, with permission of Projet Brassens.
The letter to Gustave Moreau, with permission of the Musée Gustave Moreau
    archives (Arch. 6M 269.1). His own letter, on page 191, was published in
    Maison d'artiste maison-musée, le musée Gustave Moreau (Paris: RMN, 1987) 44.

*Author's note: All listings and prices were updated as close as possible to date of
publication. If some places have since disappeared, and some prices have changed,
please bear with me. Remember, the new euro may lead to some inaccuracy and
confusion. Please forgive me! We are all suffering its birth pangs together....*

Printed and bound in Korea

TO AMIRAM

who alleviated the suffering and preserved the lives of so many,
and helped give life to many others; who, despite his meteoric
race through life for the sake of the world, took the time to
pause and prove an amazing friend, and to share with me
his passion for Paris.

$\mathcal{C}$ONTENTS

⟨A⟩CKNOWLEDGEMENTS

ATHANIEL AND HILARY, WHILE STROLLING WITH ME on the flowery side-streets of South Kensington, London, gave me the idea of celebrating the romance of Paris. A loving thank you for the inspiration and for your patient help with the manuscript. And loving gratitude to my mother for teaching me how to look and how to travel, to my father for giving me loving support, and to Linda, who, unwittingly, sowed the seed of travel writing in me back in 1969.

Special thanks are also due to Juliana Spear, who enhanced my manuscript with gorgeous photos. Courtney Kolar wore out her feet in freezing weather in order to add some beautiful winter shots to the project. Judith Moore helped me translate and polish some of the verse. Project Brassens allowed me to use their translation of *Les Amoreaux des bancs publics*. Martin Gamet brought to my attention Jacques Brel's song *Les Prénoms de Paris*, which says it all....

I would also like to thank all my friends and professional contacts who gave me their support, in one way or another, and helped this book happen: Denise Acabo, Anne and Valeria Arella, Jacqueline Bayard, Alain Beausire, Caroline Belfort, Claudine Bertin, Philippe Bourguignon, Danielle Bruneau, Georges Brunel, Mireille Etienne Brunel, Louis Gerald Canfaïlla, Yann Canu, Michel Chaudun, Carole Chretiennot, Toni Cointepas, Christian David, Marie-Pierre Delclaux, Christine Durosier, Edmond Ehrlich, Pascal Fauvel, Pierre Ferchaud, Eve François, Gabi Gafni, Marie-Noëlle de Gary, Gogo, Mohanjeet Grewal, François-Xavier d'Halluin, Peggy Hancock, Anne Hoguet, Raymond Howard, Capucine Juncker, Elisabeth Jung, Arnold Klaassen, Henri and Maïté Laborde, Geneviève Lacambre, Juliette Lacote, Fabienne Laredo, Véronique and Thierry Le Cocq, Claudie Lepeltier, Sophie Le Tarnec, Romi Loch-Davis, Dominique Maillard, Vanina de Mallmann, Jérôme Manoukian, Guy Martin, Véronique Mattiussi, Marie Mercié, Pascaline Noack, Olivier Nguyen-Huu-Chieu, Jean-Luc Pahau, Ross Pipas, Marc Porthault, Pierre-Michel Rainon, Odette and Georges de la Rochebrochart, Barbara and Jeff Rogers, Dominique and Laszlo Rollet, Susan Rosenberg, Béatrice Ruggieri, Alain Schiedé, Kathleen Spivack, Philippe Tabourel, Claude Terrail, Jean-Philippe Testud, Christian Vergès, Jean Vendome, Catherine Vernoux, Vannina Vesperini, Ornella Volta, George Whitman, and Ywona Wolski. If I have inadvertently left out anyone's name, please forgive me.

PREFACE

F YOU ARE LOOKING FOR A DIRECTORY TO PARIS, close this book and put it back on the shelf. The only aim of this book is to turn your romantic dream of Paris into a reality. Armed with my experience as both a lover of Paris and a lover in Paris, I have let my heart be my only guide, and romance my only guideline. What I have put in this guide is what I love the most and without reservation; what I recommend is what I would adore experiencing with my lover. My only occasional concession was to quintessentially Parisian landmarks, which had to be included in a book that strives to epitomize the Paris of romance, even though, admittedly, some would not have made it onto my own priority list.

Of course, your special visit must be as hassle-free as possible. With this in mind, you will find some practical advice and tips. I cannot shield you from a routine French strike or bad weather, but I can definitely spare you the average guidebook's never-ending listings. You are not going to visit all the city's 150 museums or 140 gardens, nor are you going to eat in its thousands of restaurants. Rather than torment yourself with a plethora of choices, why not enjoy the selection of an expert who knows Paris's most intimate and special corners? My restaurant section, for example, has aroused particular interest among my friends. Dining out is for many a favorite form of entertainment, and often by no means cheap. I was therefore particularly careful with my choices for that section. Of course, even the best of restaurants have their days, even the best chefs are fallible, and a change of cook, in any restaurant, may have in store a happy or unhappy surprise. This may apply to your hotel or night out as well. Nevertheless, my deliberately limited selections were designed to satisfy as wide as possible a spectrum of tastes, ages, and financial means.

And one wonderful piece of news: Parisians of late have learned to speak English, and likewise to smile. You may still meet some hardcore surly, grumpy Parisians, but these belong to the old fast-disappearing stock. Today's Parisians are global dot-commers, which rubs off a bit on their elders—they have become a generally friendly, welcoming bunch. But if all does not turn out as planned, be sure to throw in your own share of sunshine, so that no cloud may cast a shadow over your bliss.

Bon voyage and have a wonderful stay!

INTRODUCTION

T WAS EARLY SPRING WHEN MICHEL AND I BEGAN TO spend less and less time in the university library and more and more time at the corner café on rue Bonaparte and rue Jacob in St-Germain-des-Prés (the very Pré aux Clercs where Hemingway dined with Hadley back in 1921, as I was to find out many years later). As the weather warmed up, we shifted our headquarters to the quais of the Seine, plying at random either of her banks, day in day out, and well into the lingering twilight and the night. There were no freeways then, no crowds of sun addicts, just the odd wino or fisherman… and the two of us, alone in the world. By early May, oblivious to end-of-year exams, we called the Seine our home. It was my first Paris spring, immaculately cloudless and coated with the wonderfully green sheen of untarnished youth: rows and rows of chestnut trees, drooping under the weight of their new pulpy leaves and graced, for a moment, with tapered clusters of pink and white blossoms. The air was filled with the song of birds and with unfamiliar, inebriating scents, and before I knew it my blood quickened and I was head over heels deep into a romance that ultimately changed the course of my life and turned me into a Parisian. Things came to a head on the first Saturday of May, when we raced up the Eiffel Tower for the fun of a bet, followed by the bliss of a midnight kiss on the western tip of the Ile St-Louis, across the water from Notre Dame.

We whiled away the entire spring by the river, carefree and happy, engrossed in each other, indifferent to the hordes of American tourists who, drifting past us aboard a fleet of *bateaux mouches*, intruded upon our privacy through their camera lenses. We must have cut an exotic figure back home when our photos were shared with their friends and relatives. Some may have even reproved (and secretly envied) us, the shameless hedonistic citizens of a modern-day Babylon.

Some thirty years later, my late American and French-born friend Guy was visiting Paris. It was a crisp December night and we too walked along the Seine, wandering about from bank to bank. Paris was no news to Guy, yet he marveled like a young first-timer at the bewitching reflection of the floodlit monuments in the gray wintry water and the curved silhouette of the stark leafless trees that line the quais.

All of a sudden he turned to me and exclaimed, "Paris is the most romantic city in the world! There is just no question about it. What is it about Paris that does it?"

After years of observation and exploration I still have no answer for Guy. Yet people are always asking me this question, in every television or radio interview and in every piece I am commissioned to write, always with that embarrassed half-smile of the self-confessed rascal caught red-handed, always with an unmistakable twinkle of excitement and desire. Nobody escapes it. Everyone wants a share of the dream.

For nearly a hundred years now, Hollywood has astutely (perhaps maliciously) kept the dream alive. I was the first to be fooled in my silly teenage years, when, carrying some vague recollections of *Funny Face*, I braved the Latin Quarter in a bulky black jersey as a prelude to falling in love with a Left Bank intellectual. Audrey Hepburn would end up in the fashion houses of the Right Bank, and in the arms of Gary Cooper at the Ritz, in some other life. I, of course, didn't—and wouldn't for the life of me have deigned to: as a worldly Sorbonne student my Paris was clearly marked on the Left Bank, the only one conceivable. And I could think of no better place for a home than a tiny cozy garret huddled up against a Parisian sky. Hollywood avoided mentioning the shivering cold winters and stifling hot summers under those picturesque tin roofs, when delivering their papier-mâché sets for the tap dance of some charismatic American. Nor was I forewarned that those cupboard-size *chambres de bonne* had no running water. And, of course, I was so uplifted by Rodolfo and Mimi's love duet that I overlooked the fact that it was in one of the leprous garrets of St-Germain-des-Prés that TB-ridden Mimi had given up her ghost. Those lofts had barely been upgraded when I was a student.

I have known others like me who have risen to the bait—the charming student who flew his unsuspecting girlfriend all the way from San Francisco in order to propose to her at the foot of the Sacré Coeur upon break of day; the nightly coachloads of lecherous old men who file into the lewd dives of Pigalle; the sedate retirees strolling hand-in-hand down memory lane; the millions of ordinary couples looking for some glitter for the celebration of a special occasion, the millions of vaguely hopeful singles, and the many infamous sinners in search of illicit adventures. Lovers and potential lovers the world over come to Paris with their store of anticipation and fantasies.

For decades I tried to figure out why Paris is shrouded in such mystique. Granted, walks at night along the Seine are enchanting, but that alone cannot explain why the very mention of Paris had always conjured up tales of romance, well before it was blessed with gas or electricity, well before its exquisitely lit street-corners were replicated the world over in black-and-white print. After all, medieval Paris was a dark den of filth, reeking with nauseous stench, and the two sinister prison fortresses that jutted out of its skyline could hardly have been conducive to romance. Not to mention the 32 rotting corpses dangling in the offing when the royal gallows was used to full capacity.

Yet the myth has been perpetuated for a good thousand years. Although occasionally there is the odd disappointed visitor, most cling to their image of Paris; if necessary they mishandle the truth for its sake, and understandably so—who cares to be reminded that everyday Paris can be blatantly unromantic, grumpy, tight-lipped and dour, filled with nerve-racking drivers, smeared with graffiti and explosive with social unrest, a far cry from the red-and-white checkered tablecloths and dainty white aprons that welcomed us to the Café de Paris in Medora, North Dakota, where Michel and I, the incarnation of the Parisian couple, were given the royal treatment by the sheriff.

Contrary to the myth, French men rank far behind their Anglo-Saxon counterparts as far as sexual activities go, at least according to a recent poll. Even worse, it seems that Parisian men have lost the knack of seduction. A new school has opened in Paris on their behalf, l'Ecole de Séduction, which offers training to improve their skills. The London papers, which never miss an opportunity to bring the French down a peg or two, were quick to report this piece of news. Yet in the face of all those waiting to dethrone it, Paris remains the mystifying city of love.

I racked my brains, I dug into the past, I traveled into my own psyche looking for an answer, but I came back empty-handed. There simply is no answer. There lies the beauty of the enigma. Paris is poetry, Paris is mystery, Paris is beauty—an exasperating decoy that never quite delivers, all the more compelling for its imperfection, the archetypal reservoir of all our passions. We come to Paris as to a stage on which to enact an episode of our love life, but before we know it we are caught under the spell and find out, to our astonishment, that it is Paris herself that has gotten under our skin, the one love that has no rival and that even time will never erode.

It was when I realized that Paris was my one source of inspiration, the object, in turn, of both my celebration and desecration, that I understood that Paris herself is a tale of passion, full of turmoil and fury and dazzling charm, the very essence of romance. I stopped questioning, and awed by the mystery, I succumbed.

1

LOVE HISTORY OF PARIS

Love is the poetry of the senses.

—Honoré de Balzac

ARIS EMERGED OUT OF THE WATER OF THE SEINE like some Venus rising out of the waves of the sea. And it was Venus's protégé, Paris, the dashing young son of King Priam of Troy, who founded the city and bequeathed to it his name, a task equal to this exemplary lover who had set ablaze the ancient world, all for the love of Helen the Fair. You may have read elsewhere that Paris was named after the Parisii Celts who settled on its little island in the third century BC, but this is only the historical version of the tale. In truth, Helen's lover came here first. It all started when, presiding over a beauty contest between Juno, Minerva, and Venus, his vote went to the Goddess of Love, to whom he also offered the Golden Apple of Discord as a prize. In return, the enchanted goddess offered him her protection and incited him to seduce Helen, the most beautiful woman of his time—but also a married woman, alas!—the wife of King Menelaus. The Trojan War and the ultimate fall of Troy were the disastrous outcome of Venus's terrible blunder. By some good fortune, however, Paris was unharmed by the fiasco he had provoked and, having made a successful escape, ended somehow sailing down the Seine and landing on the future Ile de la Cité, where he founded the new city.

Some pedants may object that Paris died in Troy, as reported in Homer's *Iliad*; others may argue that in French his name carries a little circumflex, which the city doesn't... But I for the life of me cannot think of a more suitable pedigree for the city of romance.

Before long, a city of splendor covered the little island, a match to its ravishing godmother Venus, though not necessarily a place of amorous bliss. As you embark on a 1,000-year flight over the love map of Paris, dear pilgrim, be forewarned: the map is crumpled in despair and drenched in the tears of many a thwarted love. Even in the world's most romantic city, Venus always seems to bungle things.

By the year 1118, a multitude of church steeples pierced the little island's sky—an exquisite sight. The cathedral of Notre Dame was in poor repair, soon to be leveled and replaced by a glorious monument that would take nearly 200 years to complete. Thirty-seven enlightened canons served this house of God, each allotted a neat dwelling where he lived serenely, waiting to be called back to God. It was in one of these dwellings, with its lovely grounds extending north down to the river, that the most famous love story of medieval France was enacted. And this time the tale is no fiction. Here Canon Fulbert took in his 17-year-old niece, Héloïse, so that she could benefit from the excellent education provided by the school of Notre Dame. The appointed tutor was 39-year-old Pierre

Abélard, the greatest scholar of his generation, whose reputation drew students to the Latin Quarter from all over Europe. He was also an accomplished poet and musician. In other words, Pierre was irresistible. Before long, Héloïse had to be sent back to Britanny to have her child away from the public eye. Her vengeful uncle, not content to keep the lovers apart, had Pierre captured and castrated, thus thwarting definitively their earthly love. Compassionate death, however, united them once more, as it often does for true lovers. For nearly 1,000 years now they have been resting next to each other, more often than not sharing the same tomb.

When Héloïse died at age 63, her body was placed in his coffin, where they remained together for over 300 years. But in 1497, some prudish nun, upset by such indecency, had them placed in two separate tombs. In 1792, more progressive authorities thought the better of it and united them again in one coffin, but with a leaden partition between them. In this coffin, the celebrated lovers were translated to the new Musée des Monuments Français, where they were honored with a neo-gothic monument designed

especially for them. In the early years of the 19th century, when the new Père Lachaise cemetery was trying to lure upper-crust tenants from western Paris to its huge grounds lying on the unappetizing, eastern edge of the city, someone came up with the brilliant idea of transferring the prestigious couple and their monument to Père Lachaise as a publicity stunt, and sure enough it did the trick. Everyone began buying plots at the new cemetery, which explains why the medieval pair now rests among the smug bourgeoisie of 19th-century Paris.

ᕬ

By the end of the 12th century, a wall girdled Paris north of the river. On its westernmost point, the fortification of the Louvre, surmounted by a tall tower, stood guard by the Seine, just west of the little island. In 1210, when the city walls were completed south of the river, another tower was erected across the river from the Louvre, to help stave off a potential attack by the perfidious English. This was the notorious Tour de Nesle, which changed hands for several centuries before finally landing under the quill of Alexandre Dumas. It was still standing in 1663, when it was replaced by the Collège Mazarin, and surmounted by a beautiful dome (now the Institut de France and home to the Académie Française.)

Named after the Lord of Nesle, who incorporated it as the Hôtel de Nesle, the tower became the property of the crown in the early 14th century. Although the English threat had by no means abated, it seems that the tower gained notoriety for feats other than military. Apparently the royal household's female members had been left pining away by their husbands. Understandably, they sought outlets elsewhere, in hide-and-seek sprees and similar frolics, all of which took place in the formidable tower. When the frolics escalated into outright adulterous liaisons, in which all three daughters-in-law of Philip the Fair were implicated, the princesses' lovers were tortured, castrated, decapitated, hanged by the armpits and then left to rot, while the two guiltiest of the princesses, Marguerite and Blanche de Bourgogne, had their heads shaved and were jailed in the fortress of Château-Gaillard overlooking the Seine, by Andelys, in Normandy. Marguerite was later suffocated to death between two mattresses by order of her husband; Blanche ended by perishing in her humid cell, apparently pregnant, after having been left at the disposal of her jailer. Both were in their twenties when they died. Jeanne de Bourgogne was kept in the Château of Dourdan, southeast of Paris, but having never been proved guilty, was released and allowed to accede to the throne as the wife of Philip V. Even better: between the years 1322 and 1329, good fortune granted her seven years of merry widowhood, of which she made good use once more in the formidable Tower of Nesle.

Rising conveniently above the Left Bank, the tower's window served as an excellent lookout for a student who would be called up to serve her needs and who, once exhausted, would be tied up in a sac and hurled down the tower into the Seine—or so reports the 17th-century chronicler Brantôme. In 1461, the renowned poet François Villon also alluded to these goings-on in his *Ballade des dames du temps de jadis* (*Ballad of the ladies of yore*), which was put to music by Georges Brassens, as any of his aficionados is sure to know. Villon even specified the name of the victim, though not the name of the queen, which led to a lot of confusion regarding her identity and enabled Alexandre Dumas to replace her with Marguerite.

Semblablement où est la reine	Similarly where is the queen
qui commanda	Who ordered
que Buridan	Buridan
Fut jeté en un sac en Seine?	To be hurled in a sack into the Seine?

Buridan, a quick-blooded fellow, actually managed to survive, having landed on a boat piled up with hay, and soon after got himself involved in another relationship, which came to a head in a duel and the near death of his rival. Some twenty years later Buridan was to be appointed the Rector of the University of Paris. As for his opponent, he reached no lesser heights as Pope Clement VI.

ॐ

On the other side of Paris, way up north on top of the hill of Montmartre, stood a graceful abbey surrounded by exquisite grounds. No less exquisite were its shapely tenants, even if they were hidden under veils and gowns. In 1590 the lustful Henry of Navarre and future Henry IV of France arrived here at the head of his army to besiege the "good city of Paris." His military mission proved impossible, due to the Parisians' heroic resistance, and after three months he had to order his troops to retreat. But in the field of love, he met with much less resistance from the beautiful brunette Claude de Beauvilliers, the abbey's seventeen-year-old Mother Superior. Once she unveiled her charms, her example was soon followed by the other chaste inmates of the nunnery, and the scandalized "good people of Paris" began to refer to the Abbey as the "depot of the army's harlots."

King Henry, a notorious philanderer, soon forsook the nun for her blue-eyed cousin, Gabrielle d'Estrée, apparently the one true love of his life, the mistress he wanted to make his wife, though this was a breach of royal etiquette. In the kingdom of France one separated the sheep from the goats: sex and fun were bestowed upon the mistress, royal reproduction upon the queen. Only Gabrielle's untimely death in 1599—by God's hand, the "good people" believed—thwarted the king's calamitous design, which, undoubtedly, would have plunged France into yet another civil war, for the young king had already scattered some 70 illegitimate children throughout his kingdom, among whom were some pretenders to the throne. The threat was removed only when the childless legitimate wife, Marguerite de Valois,

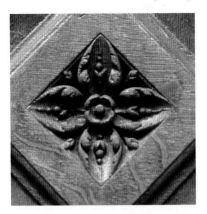

was replaced by Marie de Medici, who bore him a legitimate heir, the future Louis XIII.

Marguerite de Valois was delighted to be rid of her husband and get on with her own amorous ventures, for which she had been banished from Paris for eighteen years. In 1605 she celebrated her 52nd birthday and was allowed back to the capital, since her family assumed her sex life was over. Little did they know. While waiting for her new palace to be built on the quai Malaquais, across the river from the Louvre, she took up residence temporarily in the exquisite Hôtel de Sens in the Marais. Of course she was no longer a shapely beauty, but face powder—which she introduced in France and turned into a fashion—did help patch up some blemishes. In any case, the fire still burned inside her, and the ardent 20-year-old Comte de Vermond responded. He, however, was soon superseded by the even younger 18-year-old lackey, Julien Date, whom the Queen called playfully Date de St-Julien: it sounded so romantic! This was more than the count could bear, and before long he set out to kill his rival in front of the Hôtel de Sens. The next day the Comte de Vermond had his head removed on the very site of his crime by order of his mistress Queen, who watched his execution from the window; after which she carried her grief to her uncompleted new dwelling on the Left Bank, on the corner of rue de Seine and the river, never to set foot again in the Marais.

The Marais soon entered its golden age as the aristocratic hub of the city, and as such the center of its love life. Place des Vosges was the main outdoor stage, where many a passionate duel was enacted—for real. At the time it was known as place Royale, the first public square of Paris and the most prestigious part of the Marais. As the duels were in progress, the object of the rivals' desire would watch the action from one of the

square's balconies, and once the show was over, would pair off with the survivor. The more intimate love scenes took place offstage, in the boudoirs or bedchambers of the square's mansions, where the notorious courtesan Marion Delorme did all she could to offer a declining Cardinal Richelieu a foretaste of a different sort of heaven, and where the no less notorious Ninon Lenclos spiced sex with a touch of culture and a sprinkling of wit, Parisian-style, and dished the mixture to the greats of France, among them the Prince de Gondi, the Prince de Condé and the Maréchal d'Estrées, not to mention the Sévignés, both husband and son of the famous Marquise (see page 185).

A neighborly square, in the 18th century too, if we are to believe the tenant at 21, place Royale, the Duc de Richelieu, the Cardinal's great-great-nephew, who claimed to have slept with every single one of its female residents. Born prematurely at six months, he lived to the ripe old age of 92 and married for the last time at 84; he was said to be the most sexually active man of his epoch. Despite the wealth of opportunities available in the Marais, the Duke carried the chase to the new fashionable territory of Faubourg St-Germain, where he first had a taste of the Regent's daughter, then her sister, then her cousin, before proceeding to carry off three of his mistresses. Upon which this cumbersome personage was removed to Vienna, where he was appointed ambassador to France.

Off place des Vosges, at 56, rue de Turenne, still stands a modest 17th-century corner house, once the home of satirical poet Scarron and one of Paris's most brilliant literary salons. It was "the meeting place of the most polished members of the court and of all the great minds of Paris," according to Ninon Lenclos. Molière, La Fontaine, Lully, and the Duc d'Orléans (future Regent) climbed the narrow crooked staircase, bringing along their own food and drinks, as Scarron was too poor to provide for his guests. But he did provide entertainment, and that was worth all the luxury in the world.

Besides being poor, Scarron was a 41-year-old, deformed cripple—but his wife, Françoise d'Aubigné, was merely fifteen and attractive. She also knew what she was after. Widowed in 1660 at age 25, she was introduced to Madame de Montespan, Louis XIV's mistress and the mother of eight of his children. How unwise to have offered Françoise the post of her children's governess! The Montespan even threw in the domain of Maintenon as part of the package. So Françoise became the Marquise de Maintenan. When her charges were legitimized, the household moved to Versailles, along with the foresighted, patient, and determined Françoise. In 1788 Louis XIV was widowed, and before long was married to Françoise, the only case in French history when a king wedded his mistress. The fact that he called her "my solidity," speaks for itself.

ॐ

The narrow down-at-the-heels alley of rue des Oiseaux, on the northern edge of the Marais, may seem an unlikely shrine to Venus, yet this was the home of Mademoiselle de Scudéry, the meeting place of one of Paris's most famous literary salons, where love—and nothing but love—was the essence of the conversations, and conversations only. Every Saturday such eminent members of society as the philosopher Leipzig would climb up her modest staircase (she paid roughly the same rent as Scarron) and gather around *la carte du tendre*, a map of a land of platonic love, which Scudéry had drawn with the help of her friends. The place became the laughingstock of Paris, its members the target of the satirical quill of Molière, who derided its female *bas bleus* (blue stockings) in *Les précieuses ridicules*. Ninon Lenclos had little patience for those "who spend their time talking about it, but never put it into practice" and preferred to frequent the neighboring residence of the Prince de Conti (by the present square du Temple), a sumptuous palace built by the great Mansart, where a happy mix of cultural brilliance and merry debauchery was always on the menu.

For during the second half of the 18th century, this was that other court of France: the court of the illegitimate branch of royalty, such as Philippe, Duc de Vendôme, whom the beautiful Gabrielle had borne to Henri IV. The Prince de Conti was held in utter contempt by Louis XVI, who referred to him as "my cousin the lawyer." His female friends appreciated his company much more—or so suggests his ring collection of 4,000, each reported by him to have come from

a different mistress. (Though some envious wags contended that he had added a good number himself.) The prince was as much of a snob as his royal cousin, for though he admired immensely his mistress, the Comtesse de Boufflers, he refused to marry her because she did not have the proper pedigree.

Ninon's visits to the Prince de Conti's palace ended abruptly when the puritanical Queen Anne of Austria, Louis XIV's widowed mother, had her locked up at the nearby Madelonnetes, a convent-turned-prison for repentant whores, appropriately named after the Magdalen. The queen turned a deaf ear to Ninon's protestations that she was "neither a whore, nor repentant," even while her own conduct was not above reproach: a secret door in her Palais-Royal dwelling allowed her to steal to nocturnal rendezvous with her next-door neighbor, the Cardinal Mazarin.

Until the Revolution, rue St-Denis had always been the royal high street of Paris, the festive route of the king's entrance to the city after his coronation at Reims, and the mournful route along which his remains would be carried from Notre Dame to their burial site in St-Denis Basilica, north of Paris. It was a busy street that ran close to the central market of Les Halles and drew various trades, not least the trade of love. Few streets in Paris can boast 1,000-year economic continuity. As a matter of fact, rue du Faubourg-St-Antoine with its woodcraft is the only other example that comes to mind. Carnal love sprawled into the streets east of rue St-Denis and was commemorated by such forthright street names as rue Troussevache (jade-mounting), Transnonain (trancenovice), rue Trace-Putain (whore's trail), and the ironically named rue des Vertus, which runs in the 3rd arrondissement to this very day.

The Sentier neighborhood (so called after rue Sentier) west of rue St-Denis, is now the stronghold of Paris's rag trade, supplemented of late by Silicon Paris. Before that, in the 19th century, it was the stronghold of the press. But back in the latter part of the eighteenth century, it was home to Madame Gourdan's most distinguished brothel. Here, at 12, rue St-Sauveur, the last royal mistress of France, the Comtesse du Barry, was tracked down, to be introduced to Louis XV. The plush establishment provided for its select clientele a wealth of costumes in which to hide their identities, as well as a hidden staircase that led next door.

Jeanne Bécu had already acquired a certain notoriety under her trade name Mlle Lange before she was married off to Comte Guillaume du Barry, in order to make her acceptable in higher social circles. The count, having received a substantial sum of money for the deal, was content to retire to Toulouse with no further demands. The new countess, enchanted at being introduced to the highest echelon of the kingdom, in turn introduced the king to the highest spheres of her own realm—delights that were, surely, all the more appreciated since he had long stopped having sex with her predecessor, the Marquise de Pompadour. The Comtesse du Barry soon surpassed even the Pompadour in her outrageous spending (see page 18), and both women were hated and referred to as the "king's whore." In 1774, the dying king, terrified at the prospect of retribution, banished her to Louveciennes, where she lived for her last twenty years. Despite time's passage, the revolutionaries did not forget her depraved life of luxury and dispatched her to the guillotine at place de la Concorde.

❦

At 1, rue St-Florentin, and the corner of rue de Rivoli stands the American consulate, a gorgeous mansion enjoying one of the most stunning views of Paris—the Tuileries gardens, place de la Concorde, and the Hôtel des Invalides across the river. In the early 19th century this was the sumptuous home of Charles-Maurice de Talleyrand, one of France's most fascinating statesmen, the only one who managed to slither through all the brief regimes that rose and toppled during his lifetime. He died a natural death here in 1838, a content old man of 86. There were no flies on Napoleon regarding his right-hand man's machinations, as Talleyrand methodically spun the web that would bring about the emperor's downfall, but all Napoleon could do was diagnose him as "a piece of shit in a silk stocking."

The amorous career that he led in parallel with his political one was as prolific and as colorful, especially since he initially trained as a priest. It was during his student years in the Grand Séminaire next to the church of St-Sulpice on the Left Bank that he first noticed fourteen-year-old fair-haired Julienne at her window. Talleyrand himself was barely sixteen at the time. After an initial exchange of love messages in huge characters displayed in their respective windows, Talleyrand started going over the wall: "Climbing down the high wall of the garden at night did not seem to me impracticable because I was very much in love. Only going back was awkward. In order to return to my prison, I had to make the carriage draw near the devout fence, then climb from the seat to the upper deck, then from

the upper deck to the wall and reach the branches of a lime tree and let myself slide down to its foot." Talleyrand's feat was all the more remarkable since he was a cripple, but there is no stopping candid love: the two lovers did nothing but roam by moonlight through the city's boulevards, chaperoned by one of Julienne's girlfriends. This was love at its purest, but it was short-lived: five months later he was in the arms and bed of 25-year-old Luzy, an actress at the Comédie Française who confided in him that she hated the theater. Not to worry, he replied; he hated the church just as much. The nocturnal double life he led while training to

become a priest proved an excellent school in diplomacy and duplicity, as he implicitly acknowledged in old age to one of his lady acquaintances: "If I told you how I had spent my youth, you would be less surprised by many things."

By the time Talleyrand died in 1838, Paris was on the way to becoming the world capital of hedonism—with its intensity crescendoing as the century progressed. Energy surged along the *grands boulevards* (initially the city's northern semi-circular boundary, but by now its main thoroughfare), which sizzled with sensual and often depraved delight, and occasionally, spurts of sanguinary fury. Occasionally there were bloodstains on the pavement, but only the keen observer noticed them. Most Parisians were too busy merrily plying this glittering pleasure-strip, which grew ever more desirable and expensive the further west one went. Foreigners too joined in, including the Prince of Wales (the future Edward VII), who led the dance.

The enticing *lorettes*, those young poor women of easy virtue who lived in the vicinity of Notre Dame de Lorette (hence their nickname), were well aware of this as they descended on the boulevard in search of a loaded, and preferably pedigreed, catch. One such "magnificent *lorette* of the tall sort, all clad in black satin and velvet" enchanted the painter Delacroix, who wrote to George Sand that "when alighting from her *cabriolet*, with the nonchalance of a goddess, she let me see her leg up to her belly."

This was the age of new money, as fresh as the paint that covered the façades of Haussmann's new Paris. Paris became the new Eldorado, where men staked their future on the stock exchange and women on their venal beds. (Women did not have access to the Paris stock exchange until 1967.) Both sexes often ended in ruin, but at least there was no age limit set on the men. The women, on the other hand, could do nothing to stop time. In their rage for a modicum of fairness, many a vengeful courtesan set out to ruin the men (and their families) who had once been their lovers. "No money, no thighs," Cora Pearl warned Prince Napoleon on one occasion. Caroline Otero, on the other hand, upon closing a 20,000 gold franc deal with the Belgian king, showed more flexibility and agreed to throw in breakfast.

Few could resist blackmail. With temptation all over town, it seems the poor fellows were permanently aroused, be it on the boulevards, in the theater, at the opera, at the races, on the Champs-Elysées, and especially at the Bois de Boulogne, the parade ground of the *demi monde*, where the city's *amazones*, *cocottes*, *horizontales*, and other *belles de nuit* filed daily in their sumptuous carriages, flashing their scandalous finery. The emperor himself took the lead as he rushed about town, from one boudoir to the next. Cora Pearl, the very same who had blackmailed his son and whose carriage had, in its impudent magnificence, offended his wife Eugénie, reports how he arrived at her place late one night, after an official dinner, took off his pants instantaneously and pounced on her without uttering a word. Before she knew it, it was all over and he was fast asleep by her side.

Keeping an expensive mistress was part of one's social status, a necessary frill if you were to keep up with your neighbors. Whether the man was motivated by vanity or desire, his poor wife had no choice but to live with it. After all, the queens themselves didn't have it any better. Nor did the wives of composers. Poor Offenbach's wife! According to the Goncourt brothers, she had to run the household's budget on the money that dropped out of her husband's pockets or that she took stealthily out of his waistcoat while he was asleep. When Offenbach became besotted with the notorious Valtesse de la Bigne, he was ready to abandon his wife for the flamboyant red mane, milky skin, and voluptuous mouth of his new mistress, but Valtesse did not believe in marriage. She was a radical feminist before the term had even been coined and was determined to preserve her independence. She had no objection, though, to eloping with her lover to a hotel in Italy, where Offenbach's wife landed one day and provoked a tremendous scandal. Haughty and indifferent, the courtesan abandoned the battlefield and returned to France, leaving the spouses to settle their accounts.

Valtesse had also started out as a *lorette*. At first, she went by her birthname, Louise Delabigne. But just when the curtain was about to fall on the Second Empire, she staged her own social rebirth and emerged with all the splendor of a Venus, with the pompous new name of Valtesse (a contracted form of *votre altesse*, your highness) de la Bigne. The title of Comtesse, a pure fabrication, was prefixed to the whole. Since marriage had been ruled out, audacity was the only way to obtain a title. How astonishing that she should have served as a model for Henri Gervex's painting *Le Mariage civil*! Commissioned for the town hall of the 19th arrondissement in 1879, it has decorated its wedding hall ever since. As successive generations of brides and bridegrooms are about to take the solemn vow of marital fidelity, I wonder how many are aware that the model of respectability and chastity hanging on the wall was one of the 19th century's most notorious high-class prostitutes.

Prostitute for sure, but a cultured and sophisticated one, who befriended writers and especially painters, hence her nickname *l'union des peintures*. The above-mentioned Gervex, her lifetime lover Detaille, Meissonier, and Manet all celebrated her beauty in several paintings. Writers have left less flattering portraits, notably Emile Zola's upstart *lorette* Nana, perhaps his best known heroine, whom he modeled after Valtesse. Both Nana and Valtesse lived by place Malesherbes (the holy of holies, now place du Général-Catroux, north of Parc Monceau), in a staggering palatial residence now gone. The highlight of the place, the throne of this goddess of love, was her bed, a masterpiece of wood and bronze that cost its owner 50,000 francs and can now be seen in the Musée des Arts Décoratifs on rue de Rivoli, by the Louvre. "Nana had dreams of a bed that would be utterly unique, a throne or altar where all Paris would come to worship her in her naked, equally unique beauty," we are told by Zola. His depiction of the society of the time is to the point: "…an entire society making a dash at an arse. A pack behind a bitch who is not in heat and who mocks the dogs that follow her." And what dogs! "Semi-senile, debauched males ready to abandon everything for an arse," Zola jotted down in his notebook before writing his novel.

This was the revenge of the downtrodden streetwalker, when she had what it took to rise in the world.

❧

World War I put a stop to the fun for a while. The streets of Paris were deserted. While soldiers fell like flies in the trenches, the city dwellers went hungry, and the poorer their neighborhood, the hungrier they went. It was in such a place, on the eastern edge of Paris, far from the privileged northwestern *beaux quartiers*, that Edith Gassion (better known as "Piaf," meaning "sparrow") was born on December 19, 1915, in the heat of the war, and according to legend, on the curb of rue de Belleville. Officially, she was born in Belleville's hospital, l'Hôpital Ténon. Whichever way, she was named after the English nurse, Edith Clavell, who had been shot by the Germans two months earlier—

a name, really, that points to the patriotic and free spirit of Belleville. "My music school is the streets," Edith Piaf declared, and even in later life, when she was living on one of the most expensive streets of Paris, overlooking the Bois de Boulogne, in her heart she remained in Belleville. As with all Bellevillois, her life was about freedom, passion, and intensity. Life was lived right from one's guts, fully and without any concessions, just the way she sang. Her volcanic love life and her repertoire, sung with that flamenco-like voice, were one and the same thing, as best exemplified in *L'hymne à l'amour*.

> *Le ciel bleu sur nous peut s'écrouler*
> *Et la terre peut bien s'ébranler*
> *Peu m'importe si tu m'aimes*
> *Je me fous du monde entier...*

> The blue heavens may crash upon us
> And well may the earth shake beneath us
> Who cares, as long as you love me
> I don't give a damn about anyone...

Piaf dedicated this song to her lover, the boxer Marcel Cerdan, who died in a plane crash in 1953, along with the famous violinist Ginette Neveu. It is the favorite love song of the French!

Casque d'Or (golden helmet), so nicknamed because of her golden-reddish mane, was another of Belleville's legends, who later made her way to the screen via actress Simone Signoret. Back in 1902 she made all the headlines when she became the object of desire of Leca, the Corsican, and Manda, the "Man," the leaders of two of Belleville's enemy street gangs. A full-scale bloody battle followed, leading to the arrest and sentence to deportation and hard labor of both men. During the trial Manda told the prosecutor: "We fought each other, the Corsican and myself, because we love the same girl. We are crazy about her. Don't you know what it is to love a girl?" How far a cry from those emitted by the cynical society that moved about on the opposite side of the city.

❧

No one will contest the prime position of the Champs-Elysées, "the world's most beautiful avenue," as the French like to refer to it proudly. This is where the Bastille Day military parade takes place, where all heads of state begin their official visits, where the Germans paraded during the Occupation, and Charles de Gaulle at the Liberation. In short, this is the showcase of Paris, in particular the lower Champs-Elysées, the lovely gardens that lie between the Rond-Point-des-Champs-Elysées and place de la Concorde, where young Proust played hide-and-seek every Thursday with his freckled sweetheart, Gilberte, and where some of the city's best restaurants nestle in graceful pavilions.

To the north lies rue du Faubourg-St-Honoré, the aristocratic neighborhood of Paris in the 18th century, together with Faubourg St-Germain across the river. Magnificent townhouses (*hôtels particuliers*) still line the street. The Hôtel d'Evreux (so called after its landlord, Henri-Louis de la Tour d'Auvergne, son of the Duc de Bouillon and Comte d'Evreux) was the most gorgeous one of them all, which was why the Marquise de Pompadour had set her heart on it and bought it in 1753 to lavish frivolous entertainment on the decadent aristocracy when she wanted a Parisian break from Versailles. Playing shepherds and shepherdesses was their favorite pastime, while the true shepherds and peasants of France were starving under the yoke of overwhelming taxation. On one occasion a flock of sheep, decorated in pink and green ribbons and led by a gilt-horned ram, was herded into the mirrored hall to enliven this pastoral scene. Mistaking his own reflection for a rival, the ram began to charge, ransacking the place and causing a lot of swooning among the skittish shepherdesses.

The Pompadour's expenditures for the decoration of the Hôtel d'Evreux were as outrageous as her lifestyle: each set of curtains alone was estimated at 5,000 gold louis, to be multiplied by that many windows. Although the Champs-Elysées belonged to the public domain, she encroached on them in order to expand her own grounds, as you can still see if you walk along avenue Gabriel. She even had the avenue's trees chopped down, simply because they obstructed the view overlooking the Seine and the Invalides. The people of Paris were scandalized and called her the "king's whore." She caused no lesser outrage among the courtiers of Versailles, for being a lowly commoner. As a matter of fact, Jeanne Poisson, her real name, was born to an unknown father and a high-class prostitute, who "walked the Palais (e.g. the Palais Royal), the city's center of high-class prostitution during the 18th century.

The Hôtel d'Evreux is better known today as the Palais de l'Elysée. How apropos that the home of the president of France should have once been the *pied-à-terre* of France's most notorious royal mistress. After all, the very symbol of the Republic is a woman, the beautiful Marianne. Brigitte Bardot and Catherine Deneuve both served as models for postage stamps, and more recently Laetitia Casta sat for her bust. Ever since she guided the Trojan Paris to the Ile de la Cité, Venus has never wandered off its shores.

Paristory
11bis, rue Scribe, 9th arr.
Tel: 01 42 66 62 06

All visitors to Paris should start here, and so should all locals: I have never seen a more moving and spectacular introduction to the City of Light than the Paristory multimedia pageant. This show is not only a feast to both eyes and ears, but it is also amazingly accurate historically, edifying in its content and crystal clear in its presentation.

A FANTASY TRIP

She wanted to be in Paris, the city propitious to lovers, where policemen smiled absolution and taxi drivers never interrupted a kiss...
—*Anaïs Nin*

**HERE IS NO DENYING THAT YOUR BUDGET WILL PLAY** a substantial part in making this romantic trip a special one. If you both appreciate the hedonistic pleasures that a place like Paris has to offer, it is worth saving up for this visit. It will make all the difference in the world if you don't have to count your pennies during your stay.

That being said, don't let this put you off— Paris can be enjoyed on a shoestring, especially if you are young. Walking along the Seine costs nothing, and I can't think of a more romantic way to spend your time. Rest assured: you will find listings in this book in all price ranges, and for every age group.

PLANNING FROM HOME

When to go? Paris is special in all seasons, although spring and fall come especially recommended. My favorite is October, *la rentrée*, the time of year when the new cultural season takes off and the city is clad in the shimmering soft hues of a golden Indian summer. But since this is a romantic trip, spring should be your first choice, with its fragrant blossoms and lengthening days.

Advance Reservations

Unless you plan to stay at one of the very famous and luxurious five-star hotels, most of which are in the 1st or 8th arrondissement, on the Right Bank, choose a smaller hotel on the Left Bank, or in the Marais—these are the most delightful neighborhoods for leisurely strolling, and they have lots of charming small hotels, full of character and old-time feel. Their only drawback may be the smallish rooms, closets, and bathrooms, but that is the price to pay for staying in 17th- or 18th-century conversions. You will find plenty of hotels to choose from in this book. But for this fantasy trip, I have booked you into a lovely place in the 6th arrondissement, my personal favorite.

In addition to your hotel arrangements, make very advance reservations for top restaurants, and any special outing, venue, or popular exhibition. Note that most top restaurants have discounted lunch menus, which provide an opportunity to have a taste of an otherwise unaffordable establishment. When you are calling these places from the United States, drop the "0" at the start of the telephone number, and replace it with 011-33.

What to Pack

Even if your trip is scheduled for summer, take along some warm and waterproof clothes. The weather in Paris is unpredictable, although statistically sunshine outstrips the rain in most springs and summers. Whatever you do, don't bring too many clothes; try instead to have the right ones and combine them according to your activities. You can dress as informally in Paris as in any American city these days, especially while sightseeing. If you plan to dine in a good restaurant, or go to a show or a nightclub, bring the clothes you would normally wear for such events. And if you intend to shop or eat in expensive neighborhoods, you will probably be better treated if you are well dressed, although even in Paris there are no longer unbending codes. I always go for understated elegance when unsure. A tie and jacket are *de rigueur* in some restaurants, and never out of place when you are in doubt. I may even phone the restaurant beforehand to find out. No one takes offense these days. Don't forget you are also dressing for yourself and for your lover. Paris is the city of seductiveness: Why not join the club?

Maps & Guides

Always carry a street map divided by arrondissements. Locals are not always good at giving directions. I recommend in particular *Le Petit Parisien* (édition l'Indispensable), which integrates into each arrondissement its corresponding Metro plan and bus routes. As you consult the listings in this book and plan your trip, note that the last two numbers of the zip code indicate the arrondissement.

If you don't know any French, you may want to buy a small phrase book to ease your way, although most Parisians have at least some English these days, and some have very good and even fluent English. Don't feel paranoid about Parisians being xenophobic. If you meet someone who is unfriendly, it is not because you are a foreigner, but because he or she is unfriendly. Nothing personal. Parisians can be gruff and surly, but I have found tremendous improvement in recent years, especially among younger Parisians, who tend to be well traveled, open to the outside world, and keen to exercise their English. If you feel you are not being treated properly, don't be intimidated—stand up for your rights. You are most likely to achieve results by being diplomatic, yet firm, rather than confrontational.

ARRIVAL

You will land either at Roissy-Charles de Gaulle Airport, northeast of Paris, or at Orly, south of Paris.

Charles de Gaulle has two terminals and a direct RER (*Réseau Express Régional*) train to Paris, which links to the Métro system. The RER goes to Terminal 2 only, but a shuttle links the station to Terminal 1.

The RER is the fastest and cheapest way into the city, but also the least appealing and at times confusing. Unless you are familiar with it, I would avoid it at this early stage of your visit, when you also have to handle your luggage and a foreign language. Another option is the Air France bus, but you would then have to catch a taxi to your local destination from its drop-off at Porte Maillot. The local Paris bus, which would drop you at the old Opera House (le Palais Garnier at Métro Opéra) may be just as inconvenient.

Several private companies run shuttle buses between the airport and the individual passenger's destination, at under €30 for two (you can try the following toll free number upon arrival: 08 00 50 56 10). This service is convenient but you will have company and it can be slow. For €40–50, you can catch a cab and enjoy your privacy and a quicker ride to your hotel. You may be tired and jetlagged; and remember, this is a special trip. If you are young and backpacking, then by all means, take the RER. That's what your Parisian counterparts do! Otherwise smooth your way into the city of love.

Orly airport, south of Paris, also has two terminals, Orly Sud and Orly Ouest, but all international flights arrive at Orly Sud. It is much closer to the city and your cab ride will be cheaper.

I would avoid using the local bus for the same reason as the above. It drops you close to the Cité Universitaire or at place Denfert-Rochereau (in the 14th arrondissement), from where you still have to make your way to your destination. And I would forget altogether about the train from Orly: it is expensive and impractical, entailing a convoluted (albeit speedy) ride via the suburbs and ending in the gigantic and daunting station of Châtelet-les-Halles in central Paris.

GETTING SETTLED

Having checked in, there is no formula to what comes next. You may be jetlagged and need to flop on your bed. On the other hand, if your adrenaline is running high, you may be impatient to go out and paint the town red. Perhaps you'll want to start to check off the items on your list of must-see attractions.

If I were tired, I'd just go downstairs to the hotel bar. If I felt more energetic, I'd step out into the streets, stroll leisurely through the 6th arrondissement, just to get its feel, and then settle on a lively café terrace in a prominent position. People-watching from a street café is perhaps the most quintessential Parisian activity; much of French literature and painting has been sparked by it. Don't take offense if you become the object of someone else's gaze, for Paris is a stage where actors and spectators constantly swap roles.

You can stay in your café for as long as you wish. Some establishments may want you to order a second drink after a while (usually after a long while) and others won't mind if you spend the entire evening over one tiny cup of coffee. Whether the waiter is rude or friendly, don't feel obliged to move on. Make yourself at home. Although it is privately owned, the Parisian café is perceived as a public place, over which you have inalienable rights.

The trick to enjoying Paris is to be leisurely and soak up the atmosphere. "Doing" Paris fast is a sacrilege, like gobbling down a glass of fine wine, or mistaking a top-rate restaurant for a fast-food chain. The Paris experience is, by definition, in slow motion.

Dinner in Paris is served much later than in the US. You may arrive at your restaurant at 7:30 P.M., but in all likelihood no one else will be there before 8, at the earliest, which will make you feel miserable—there is nothing more dreary than dining in an empty restaurant. Since this is your first night, and you still have to recover from your trip, save your special dinner(s) for later. Many cafés offer light food, such as mixed salads (*salades composées*), but if you want to plunge down memory lane right away, head to carrefour de l'Odéon and settle at **Le Comptoir du Relais,** where the likes of Hemingway, James Joyce, and Man Ray once hung out. Order open sandwiches, made of delicious, warm *poilâne* bread, and good wine, which will ensure you a good night's sleep after so much excitement.

YOUR FANTASY TRIP

The listings in the following chapters will enable you to pick and choose and extend or shorten the trip, as you choose.

Day One

Your entire day will be spent in the 6th arrondissement—Paris at its best and its most unique. This area combines more hues, shades, and

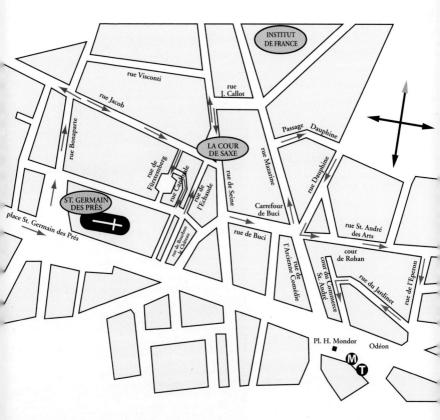

surfaces than any other, be it the old courtyards on rue Jacob, rue des Sts-Pères, or rue du Cherche-Midi, or the quaint ancient alleys further east, closer to the Latin Quarter; not to mention the dizzying proliferation of smashing boutiques and stylish shop windows, or the unspeakable beauty of the quais along the Seine, with their view of the city's two most romantic bridges, Pont Neuf and Pont des Arts. And, of course, the lovely Luxembourg Gardens, beyond which lies mythical Montparnasse with its artist studios. The 6th arrondissement is quintessentially sophisticated and quintessentially romantic. You could spend all your days here—which is what many of its residents like to do.

Morning

You have slept off your jetlag and have woken up in one of the exquisite hotels of the Left Bank. Hmm… To have breakfast in your hotel or dash into the city? If you happen to stay in one of the privileged rooms with a "made-for-two" balcony, you are the luckiest of lovers—both Paris and a private breakfast are yours.

But having breakfast in a street café is a Parisian experience not to be missed, just for the sheer pleasure of watching the indolent city make its way into a new day. Why not make your way to the **Café Flore** (see page 120) on boulevard St-Germain for your breakfast? During the Occupation, Jean-Paul Sartre and Simone de Beauvoir spent many a cold winter day upstairs, seated at separate tables, silently writing important works to help save a shattered world from utter ruin—this was no time for socializing and flirting. Today the Flore is exquisitely inviting, with its crimson benches, stylish waiters, and beautiful St-Germain clientele. What better setting for your first warm croissant and *café crème* or *café noir* in the French capital? (If you want it larger, ask for "*double*"; stronger, "*serré*"; or weaker, "*allongé*.")

After coffee, make your way to place St-Germain-des-Prés, the stronghold of the existentialists at the end of World War II. It is named after the one-time abbey of St-Germain, of which the church alone has survived. Its eleventh-century belltower is the oldest in the city.

Walk north into rue Bonaparte and left into rue Jacob. The corner café, the **Pré aux Clercs**, was the daily canteen of the honeymooning Hadley and Ernest Hemingway, back in 1921. They were staying at the Hôtel d'Angleterre across the street and dined here à la carte for six francs, (exclusive of wine). When Michel and I spent time here, instead of at the Sorbonne, it was still a very basic neighborhood café and looked much the same as it did in the 1920s.

At present, rue Jacob is one of the expensive and desirable streets in Paris, lined with fabulous antique, ethnic, and the odd clothing shops and charming hotels. It wasn't such a commendable address at the turn of the century, though, when the writer Colette lived here with her father. Her bourgeois aunt was living in a residential neighborhood to the northwest, and was appalled that her brother should live with his seventeen-year-old daughter on the dark and narrow rue Jacob, "where no nice people live."

Turn into the **Galerie Triff** at 35, rue Jacob. No need to shop— just walk into the paved courtyard and enjoy its lush greenery. Above are exquisite old roofs, one of the quintessential touches of romantic Paris. Keep looking for them wherever you stroll. At the end of the path is my favorite kilim shop, both for the beauty of each rug and for the trickling fountain inside (see page 152).

Retrace your steps along rue Jacob and turn right into the romantic rue de Fürstemberg, a must-see after dark. This is also the stronghold of wholesale designer fabrics, whose shop windows add a further touch of elegance to the place.

Just to your right, at 6, rue de Fürstemberg, is painter **Delacroix's last home and studio**, now a museum, and your next destination (see page 188). Like scores of small Parisian museums that were once the homes of artists, writers, and other prominent figures, this place has a feel of homely authenticity that brings the past to life. If you can make it early, you may find, as Delacroix wrote in his journal, "the sun shining in the most welcoming way on the houses opposite." The painter did not find much romance in this enchanting place, though: He was very sick and too weak to stand up to his willful Breton nurse, Jenny Le Guillou (a portrait of her by the artist can be seen in the museum), who made short shrift of any lady friend who wished to pay him a call.

Wander off into the picturesque side streets across the square—rues Cardinale, Bourbon-le-Château, and Echaudé, and make your way back to rue Jacob. At no. 12, tucked at the back of a wonderful courtyard, is the stunning jewelry shop **La Cour de Saxe**.

Turn left on rue de Seine, which is lined with excellent art galleries and some charming courtyards. On your left is the very narrow rue Visconti, where, in 1928, Henry Miller taught his wife June to ride a bike before they headed for the south of France on a cycling holiday. A little further, at 31, rue de Seine, was **the home of Aurore Dupin**, better known as George Sand, the one-time lover of Chopin and Alfred de Musset. She was one of France's first emancipated women who, at age 27, left her husband and settled here on her own. She traded her name for George (spelled the English way, without an "s"), and sported men's clothing, which took a lot of guts back in 1831.

Wander into rue Jacques-Callot, famous for its prestigious art galleries and for one of the area's most famous cafés, **La Palette**, a smoky hangout of bohemia and of Beaux-Arts students. It is also famous for its surly lack of hospitality—be prepared!

Retrace your steps along rue de Seine, and on past **carrefour de Buci**, to enjoy its colorful street market. Then walk along rue de Buci and enjoy its irresistible pastry shops. I also love the flower stall on the corner of rue Grégoire-du-Tour (next to the flower shop, Aquarelles), with its old-time vendor; in early summer he sells the loveliest of sweet peas—and they last. Carrefour de Buci is also a great place in the evening, especially on Fridays and weekends, when excellent jazz is performed on the streets, often by young Americans, who perpetuate the old traditions of the heyday of St-Germain.

Turn left into rue Mazarine. Ahead is the **Institut de France**, home to the five academies, whose members, the *académiciens*, are a venerated species—especially those of the Académie Française, who preside religiously over the destiny of the French language, and are fighting a heroic battle to preserve it from Anglo-Saxon contamination. Walk through the archway at no. 27, on your right-hand side, into the passage Dauphine. On your left is a charming *salon de thé* (tea house), **l'Heure Gourmande** (see page 116), a great cozy place on a dreary day. If the sun is with you today, settle outdoors and enjoy their impressive choice of excellent light food. Come back some other time for tea. A well-known language school, Eurolangues, on your right, conceals vestiges of the medieval city walls, as well as one of the formidable towers erected by Philip Augustus against the perfidious English.

Turn right into rue Dauphine and then left into rue St-André-des-Arts. For wonderful, tasteful, inexpensive accessories, step into **Kazana**, at no. 40. Low-budget lovers—this is a place for you! And high-budget ones too—I have astonished more than one high-flying acquaintance with jewelry bought here.

Continue along rue St-André-des-Arts, turn right into rues de l'Eperon and Jardinet and on into the 18th-century **Cour de Rohan**. Just stand and stare in awe, and come back after dark (hopefully the gates won't be locked). I shall refrain from saying more and let you unwrap the surprise on your own.

Step out on the western side of the Cour de Rohan, into the Cour-du-Commerce-St-André, a wonderful alley steeped in history and local color and lined with pretty eating places. Ahead is Paris's oldest

café (now a restaurant), **Le Procope**, opened in about 1685 by the Sicilian Francesco del'Procopio. He brought a certain beverage over from the nearby St-Germain Fair, where it had been brought from the east in 1672 by two Armenians. The beverage was an overnight sensation: Fans lauded its medicinal qualities and detracters claimed it caused impotence. That allegation carried little weight, for 40 years later Paris numbered between 600 and 700 cafés—a huge number, considering the very small size of the city and the fact that men alone frequented them.

The main entrance to Le Procope is on the parallel rue de l'Ancienne Comédie, named after the illustrious Comédie Française, which, between 1689–1770, stood across the street and helped propel Le Procope to fame. A century after its opening, Le Procope gained further momentum as the gathering place of the enlightened philosophers, the likes of Voltaire and Diderot, and also Benjamin Franklin, who drafted here the alliance between Louis XVI and the nascent American Republic.

Afternoon

Head south toward the boulevard St-Germain Métro. Cross over. Turn right along the island of carrefour de l'Odéon, past the metro station and Danton's statue, then left onto rue de l'Odéon, a splendid street when it was opened in the late 18th century as a route to the new home of the **Comédie Française** (now the Odéon Théâtre de l'Europe). It was the first street in Paris with sidewalks, the ultimate luxury in a city that resembled a cesspit prior to the start of Haussmann's cleanup in 1853. In 1921 Sylvia Beach opened the celebrated **Shakespeare & Company** bookshop at no. 12, a gathering place for expatriate writers, where Hemingway and Gertrude Stein first met and where Sylvia Beach published James Joyce's *Ulysses* in 1922. It was closed by the Nazis during the occupation.

Turn right into rue des Quatre-Vents and on to rue de Seine. Start your afternoon's shopping (or window-shopping) spree at **Gérard Mulot**, at no. 76 (closed Wednesdays). Get a luscious assortment of pastries—but save them for later—I have picked out the perfect spot for the end of your afternoon. Wander up and down the highlighted streets to see the best of Paris fashion. End your shopping where you started out this morning, on place St-Germain-des-Pres, where Emporio Armani, Cartier, Vuitton, and Dior reign, to the dismay of those who bemoan bohemian days gone by.

When you've had enough of shopping, head south along rue Bonaparte. The **Café de la Mairie** on your left at 8, place St-Sulpice, requires a stop. One of the city's great cafés, it lies opposite Visconti's spectacular fountain and is mentioned both by Hemingway in *A Moveable Feast* and Henry Miller in *Tropic of Cancer*. Other literati—Faulkner, Fitzgerald, Beckett—used to hang out here in the 1920s. Settle on the café terrace, sip your drinks, take your time like locals, and enjoy each other's company to the energizing sound

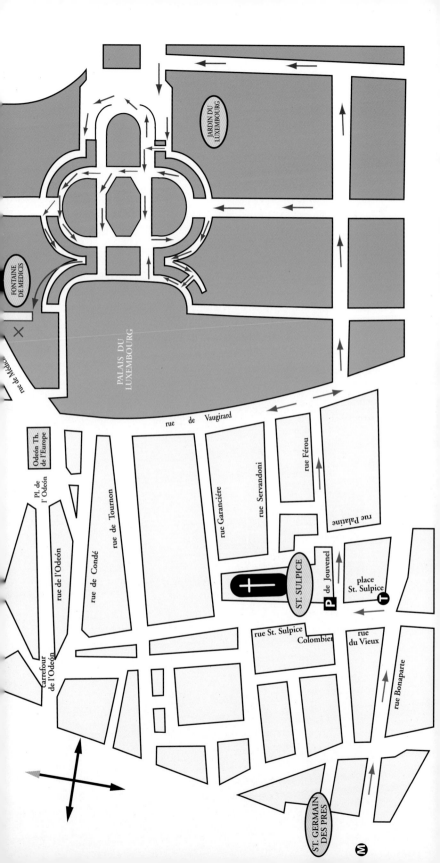

of the fountain's cascading waters.

Head south along rue Jouvenet, past the church, then on along rue Férou. Hemingway moved to no. 6 with his second wife, Pauline Pfeiffer, in 1926 (the very house of actress Luzy, for whose sake Talleyrand had gone over the seminary wall and was ultimately expelled), while Man Ray moved to no. 2bis with his wife Juliet upon his return to Paris in 1951.

Turn left into rue de Vaugirard. Across the street, the **Musée du Luxembourg** is located in the 19th-century orangerie of the Palais du Luxembourg, the one-time home of Marie de Medici, the queen mother of Louis XIII and widow of Henri IV. Today it is the seat of the **French Senate**. When the Impressionist paintings were first tolerated, they were housed at the Musée du Luxembourg, despite the protestations of those who still considered them "junk," and it was here that Hemingway first discovered them. The paintings were moved to the Musée du Jeu de Paume overlooking place de la Concorde in the 1920s, and to the Musée d'Orsay in 1986.

Walk into the **Luxembourg Gardens**, the playground of every true Left Bank denizen—toddlers, grandparents, joggers, tennis players, students, intellectuals, housewives, tourists... and lots and lots of lovers.

Note the 50 gorgeous statues of France's admired heroines who encircle its central pool. Sit down, watch the toy sailboats drifting in the wind and the delighted faces of those who own them for an hour, and unpack the pastry you bought earlier: now is the time to savor it and count your blessings. You have every reason to. If it's a hot day, you may prefer the greener southwestern section of the garden with its lush English-looking lawn, or, even better, the dark shady corner by the **Medici Fountain**, on the northeast edge of the gardens, unquestionably their most romantic nook, where Jean-Paul Sartre and Simone de Beauvoir had their first rendezvous.

Exit along rue de Médicis and back to place St-Sulpice. The **church of St-Sulpice**, begun in the 17th century but completed only in the 19th, claims to house the largest organ in Europe. It also takes pride in a couple of famous murals by Delacroix, and a beautiful statue of the Virgin and Child by Pigalle, who was a devout Christian, unfairly associated with Paris's seedy, sex-ridden neighborhood. The church's northern tower is the highest in the city, about 240 feet above ground and 13 feet higher than Notre Dame's.

Go back to your hotel, dump your shopping, freshen up, and get ready for your night.

Night

You are having dinner at **Le Toupary**, on the top floor of La Samaritaine department store, on the Right Bank end of the Pont Neuf, by the western tip of the **Ile de la Cité** (page 109). The entire riverfront of the 6th arrondissement is laid before you, including the magnificent dome of the **Institut de France** and the regal **Hôtel de la Monnaie** (the old Mint). Make sure to book a table with a view, preferably by the central window. And start your meal at the very end of twilight, to enjoy the mystery of the approach of night and the magical split second when all the bridges and monuments light up in unison. As you look at the **Institut de France**, remember that this is the very site of the ancient Tower of Nesle, from which the ill-used lovers of the widowed Queen Jeanne were hurled into the Seine.

Walk back across the **Pont des Arts**, perhaps Paris's most romantic bridge. Detour via rue de Fürstemberg, whose sole streetlamp holds up to the black night five globes of incandescent light.

Day Two

Today features some of the most famous sights of central Paris, including a stroll down the grand Champs-Elysées and a splendid twilight by Notre Dame.

Morning

Take it easy for a start: take breakfast in your room, or just roll downstairs to your hotel's breakfast room, or perhaps its charming patio garden.

After breakfast, head for rue de Médicis, along the northern side of the **Luxembourg Gardens**. Catch the Paris OpenTour double-decker bus at the stop at 4, place Edmond Rostand. Select the Grand Tour, which runs through the most glamorous sections of the city (ear phones are provided for a running commentary in French and English), with twenty hop-on–hop-off stops on the way. The bus runs every 10 to 30 minutes, depending on the season. (For more information, phone L'OpenTour on 01 42 66 56 56.) Get off at place Charles de Gaulle-Etoile. It was laid out by Baron Haussmann around the **Arc de Triomphe**, which was built to commemorate Napoleon's victories. Climb to the top of the monument for a breathtaking view of western Paris.

Stroll down the **Champs-Elysées**, preferably on the southern side. It is less sunny, admittedly, but more elegant and peaceful. I love walking past its string of cafés and restaurants all prettily framed by flower boxes and exuding an atmosphere of well-being. Notice at no. 99 the bright red awning of **Fouquet's**, the most famous terrace on the Champs-Elysées. When it first opened in 1901, the Anglo-Saxon possessive was added to the tail of its name to secure for it the same glorious success as the slightly older Maxim's off place de la Concorde. In no time it became a Parisian landmark, frequented both by the glitzy and the more modest literati, such as James Joyce, who is honored upstairs with a private lounge named after him. In the 1930s French writer Léon-Paul Fargues said, "Le Fouquet's was one of those places that could only go out of fashion in the wake of a bombing." Indeed, the same decoration and the same atmosphere have prevailed here for the past hundred years. And it's always been a magnet for actors. It was at Fouquet's that Ali Khan met and fell in love with Rita Hayworth in 1948, at the peak of her glory, and that Jean Gabin was first introduced to Michèle Morgan, before their collaboration as the mythical lovers of Marcel Carné's *Quai des Brumes* (Port of Shadows). It was the Paris meeting place of Hollywood stars—Cary Grant, Clark Gable, Gary Cooper, Kirk Douglas, Liz Taylor, Deborah Kerr.... everyone stopped at Fouquet's when in town. Today Fouquet's still upholds its show-biz traditions: Here the lists of nominations for the Césars (the more modest French equivalent of the Oscars) are compiled before award night, and here all France's film stars convene to celebrate after the ceremony.

> *We* dine in Fouquet's very frequently, in fact almost always. It has become a chic prize ring. The other night an advanced lady slapped a perfect gentleman's face on account of another perfect lady's being with him. The well-bred diners jumped up on benches and chairs. And the row went on. I refused to have any attention distracted from the business in hand, to wit, a carafe of champagne nature but I could hear a great deal....
>
> —Letter from James Joyce to his son, 1 July 1934

Continue down to the Rond-Point-des-Champs-Elysées. Avenue Montaigne, to your right, is the most elegant shopping street in Paris, lined with all the big names of high fashion, some of which spill over to neighboring streets such as avenue Georges V and rue François I. Avenue Montaigne is also home to the fabulous **Plaza Athénée hotel**, next to the bejeweled **Théâtre des Champs-Elysées**, my favorite concert hall in the city, where Diaghilev's Ballets Russes created a memorable *scandale* with their performance of Stravinsky's *Rite of Spring* in 1915.

Walk through the **gardens of the Champs-Elysées**, beyond the Rond-Point, down to place de la Concorde. First laid out in the 17th century by Louis XIV's landscape gardener, André Lenôtre, the gardens were considered an unsafe rural area until the second half of the 19th century, when the emperor's landscape gardener, Alphand, remodeled them into "a melody of forms and colors." Thereafter, they became the summer playground of pleasure-seeking Paris. Several Impressionist paintings testify to those times.

To your right is the **Grand Palais**, built for the 1900 Universal Exposition, now home to major retrospectives. In the northern section of the gardens you will notice an elegant peach-colored pavilion, home to one of the city's prestigious restaurants, Laurent, where you may be lunching later. For the time being, make your way past the **Marigny theater** and the **Pavillon de l'Elysée,** another well known restaurant. Built for the 1900 Fair, it was honored by all the crowned heads of Europe when they visited the fair, including Paris's favorite playboy, the Prince of Wales and future Edward VII. The restaurant was then known as the Pavillon Paillard (bawdy)... but no pun intended: Paillard just happened to be the proprietor's name.

North of the restaurant, behind the imposing wrought-iron gate across avenue Gabriel, you can glimpse the gardens of the **Palais de l'Elysée**, the residence of the French president and the one-time home of the Pompadour (see page 18). The British and American embassies are standing next door. Stroll along the **allée** (pathway) **Marcel Proust**, a reminder of the writer's childhood days when he played here with his red-headed sweetheart Gilberte. Even the garden toilets did not escape Proust's eye: he called them "a little rustic theater," run by a proud, fastidious woman, whom he nicknamed La Marquise, even though she depended on tips for a living. Times have changed. Today there is a fixed price for admission and her contemporary colleague altogether closes down at lunchtime.

Afternoon

By now it is 1 P.M. and you are ready for a great meal, in true French style. Make your way back to **Laurent**, at 41, avenue Gabriel (page 100). Once seated in your comfortable chairs, allow the members of staff to guide you through their list of wines and their recommendations of the day. Forget your watch. Savor. Sip. Relish. Enjoy! If you have too much wine, walk it off on your afternoon stroll. And if Laurent is beyond your budget, the surroundings of **Le Café Véry** in the Tuileries gardens, a short way beyond place de la Concorde, are just as pleasing. It is located beyond the central basin of the gardens, on the left hand side. The food is inexpensive and decent. If you only want a snack, walk a bit further, to **La Terrasse de Pomone**. In both cases avoid the lunchtime rush, which may involve long waits. Things calm down by 3 P.M.

The **Tuileries** deserve some time in their own right, and are even more romantic in winter, when the trees have lost their leaves, the benches have been deserted, and it's just the two of you, sharing the gardens with an impressive display of statuary beauties. Maillol's opulent nudes are a recent addition and are not the ones referred to by Henry Miller in the 1920s. Miller was so taken by the nudes that he claimed he had an erection every time he saw them.

Make your way back to the place Charles de Gaulle-Etoile (**Bus 73** from place de la Concorde would be my option, or **Métro 1** to gain time), and resume your visit of the city aboard the Paris OpenTour. Get off at the **Luxembourg Gardens** where you started out. Turn left

onto boulevard St-Michel, and head north. Catch Bus 96 at place St-Michel and get off at St-Paul. You have landed on rue St-Antoine, the gateway to the **Marais**.

Twenty-three palatial townhouses are still scattered about this one-time stronghold of the nobility. Most of them date from the 17th century, the golden age of the Marais, and are now mostly museums or other cultural institutions.

After a century and a half of decline, following the French Revolution and the demise of the old nobility, the Marais began to pick up again in the 1960s. Today it is excitingly eclectic, stylish, atmospheric, and suffused with history. It is top on my list after the Left Bank, though some would reverse my order of priorities. With so much gorgeous architecture around, so many exquisite courtyards and alleyways, and countless artsy boutiques and inviting eating places, you won't know which way to turn. The Marais is also the home of Paris's oldest Jewish enclave and a large segment of the city's gay community; their tiny geographical territories are

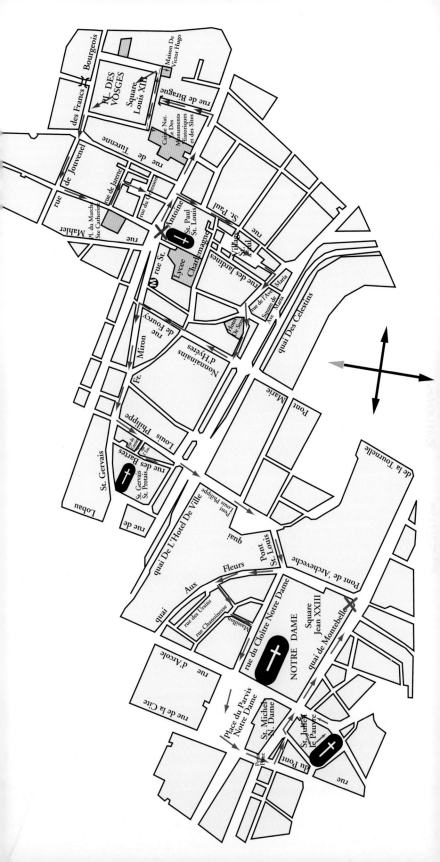

amazingly interwoven: to see a trendy young gay couple alongside a timeless Orthodox Jew is not uncommon.

The only drawback of the Marais is that it has become a victim of its own success and tends to be overcrowded. Probably better to enjoy it in the morning, before the crowds arrive. If you are after a secluded hideaway, avoid it at all costs on weekends and holidays.

Cross rue St-Antoine, walk east and turn left into rue Birague. Ahead is the **Pavillon du Roi** (the king's pavilion), a foretaste of the ravishing brick-and-stone **place des Vosges** (place Royale until the French Revolution): "The most beautiful quarter in the town of stylishness is the big square which can verily be said to be royal," wrote l'Abbé d'Aubignac in the 17th century.

Rue Birague offers the most spectacular approach to place des Vosges and was, in fact, its official entrance in aristocratic times. Imagine the court's most prestigious guests, the foreign ambassadors, making an appearance here on their way to the Louvre, to show off their magnificent attire to the no less glamorous nobility who played audience to them on the square's wrought-iron balconies. In 1612, the double wedding celebrations of Louis XIII and his sister Elisabeth, to the Infanta of Spain and her brother, took place here to coincide with the inauguration of the square. The celebration lasted three full days and nights and is still the most dazzling pageant on record here.

Turn left along place des Vosges and walk under the arcades to the **Hôtel de Sully** at no. 7, the one-time home of Henri IV's retired minister and treasurer, the Duc de Sully. As an old man, he strutted about under the arcades in the company of young wanton women, wearing preposterously outdated Renaissance garb. But he allowed his young wife her amusements, too: he not only tolerated her young companions, but even provided for their upkeep—as long as they kept out of his sight. In order to shield all parties from embarrassing encounters, he had a separate staircase installed, leading directly to his wife's apartments.

Cross the courtyard, visit the wonderful **French Heritage Bookshop**, and look at the second courtyard, behind the bookshop, leading to rue St-Antoine. Retrace your steps and continue beyond rue Birague to the southeastern corner of the square, where the **Victor Hugo Museum** is located (see page 200).

Cross the gardens of the square, or enjoy the art galleries and shops under the arcades. Better still—do both. Take the rue des Francs-Bourgeois, on the northwestern corner of the square, the neighborhood's busiest street. At the intersection with the rue de Sévigné stands the **Hôtel Carnavalet**, once the home of the famous letter-writer, the Marquise de Sévigné and now the **Museum of the History of Paris**. Follow the map south, past lovely, traffic-free place Ste-Catherine, which is exquisitely romantic by night and enlivened by affordable restaurant terraces in warm weather.

Continue on to rue St-Paul and the Village St-Paul, an enclave of

second-hand and antique dealers, scattered along a succession of
flowery cobbled courtyards that zigzag down to the river. Henri IV
himself used to take the rue St-Paul to the river, where he would bathe
in the nude on hot summer evenings, setting a new fashion among his
subjects. As many as 4,000 Parisians of both sexes emulated their
monarch, although the women did so behind a screen. It seems that it
was the women who showed the greatest interest in the anatomy of the
opposite sex. Or so the author of this verse suggests:

> On y accourt pour voir l'homme en son naturel
> Et tel qu'il est sorti des mains de l'Eternel.
> One rushes there to see man clad in Nature's garb
> And such as he came out of the Lord's hands.

Turn right into rue de l'Ave Maria. Ahead is the jewel-like **Hôtel
de Sens** (completed in 1520), a unique example of a late Gothic
mansion in Paris. It was from one of its windows that Henri IV's
repudiated wife, Marguerite de Valois, watched the execution (by
her order) of her 20-year-old ex-lover. Today the **Forney library** for
the decorative and fine arts is located here and is open to the public.
Walk into the courtyard, then circle the building. Notice on your
right the back of the 17th-century **Hôtel Aumont**, now the
Administrative Tribunal, a splendid example of the austere
harmony of French Classical architecture. Come back at night,
when the two floodlit monuments afford a magical sight.

Walk north along rue des Nonnains-d'Hyères, on to rue de
Fourcy, and turn left into rue François Miron. On your right is rue
Cloche-Perce—a flight of steps up and another one down, an old
street-lamp, a few scattered tables and chairs—an exquisite sight
graced with an indefinable touch of romance, and not a bad place for
an inexpensive bite! At 11–13, rue François Miron, to your right,
stand two medieval half-timbered houses, among the city's oldest.

The splendid **Hôtel de Beauvais** at no. 68 was once the home of
Cateau la Borgnesse (one-eyed Cateau), the chambermaid of Anne
of Austria. Although Cateau was hardly graced by nature, she had a
long stream of lovers and admirers and led a dynamic love life.
When Anne confided her concern to Cateau that her young son,
Louis XIV, might take after her frigid late husband, Louis XIII,
Cateau took matters in her own hands and set out to initiate the
young king to the facts of love. Her queen was delighted and
lavished on Cateau astounding gifts, including titles on both her and
her husband, a shopkeeper now appointed Councilor to the King.
The King's architect built this palace, of stones meant initially for
the extension of the Louvre. When Louis XIV got married, his
wedding procession, arriving from the east, stopped here, where the
most important members of the court had crowded to greet him.

Turn left into rue du Pont-Louis-Philippe and right into rue du
Grenier-sur-l'Eau, a picturesque old alley climbing up to the back
of the **church of St-Protalis-St-Gervais**. Stroll down the steps along

Hôtel de Sully

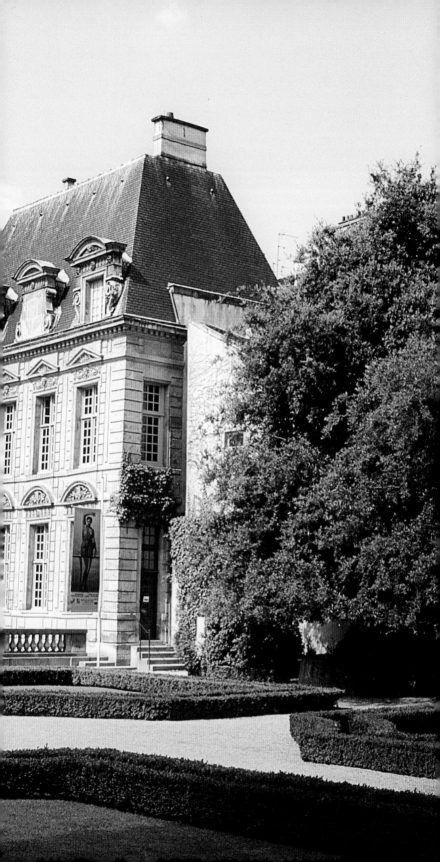

rue des Barres, which is lined with sunny terraces where light snacks are served. When you reach rue de l'Hôtel-de-Ville at the bottom of the steps, look to your left for another astonishing view of the Hôtel de Sens.

Cross the **Louis-Philippe bridge** and step into the **Ile St-Louis**, a self-contained architectural gem, much of which still dates from the 17th century. It is best seen along the quais. The island is essentially a miniature village, with a post office, school, church, little supermarket, even a tiny theater. But no other village in the world boasts such an array of appetizing food shops, restaurants, and tantalizing boutiques; not to mention, four lovely romantic hotels, and the city's most famous ice cream, Berthillon. The western tip of the island is reputedly Paris's most romantic spot: go down the steps, by the lapping waters, to discover the ultimate destination for a nocturnal kiss.

Cross the St-Louis footbridge to the **Ile de la Cité**, stroll through the gardens of **Notre Dame** and visit the cathedral. Meander also through the side streets lying north, and make sure to include **9, quai aux Fleurs**, where France's most famous lovers, Pierre Abélard and Héloïse (see pages 2–3), once lived.

Make your way to the Left Bank across the **Petit Pont bridge**, at the southwestern edge of the parvis de Notre-Dame (the cathedral square), and continue into rue St-Jacques. Turn left into rue de la Bûcherie, past a couple of café terraces. At no. 37 George Whitman's **Shakespeare and Company Bookshop** has been going strong since 1951, following in the footsteps of his friend Sylvia Beach, who had presided over the original at 12, rue de l'Odéon. The premises are an enchantment in their own right—a warren of nooks and crannies, packed with wonderful books all the way up to the ceiling. Many aspiring Hemingways have landed in this place; some have spent the night, some have stayed a week, even a year. Some have fallen in love here and now send over their offspring. George always opens his heart to those who come knocking on his door, as is clearly stated on the wall: "Be not inhospitable to strangers lest they be angels in disguise." In exchange for a bit of help in the shop, he offers them his hospitality, a bed, and a corner in which to write their own stories. Make sure to come here in April, when a blaze of cherry blossoms adorns the front of the shop.

Continue into square René Viviani, past the 4-century old rubina tree (the oldest tree in Paris). It huddles against the little 13th-century **church of St-Julien-le-Pauvre**, one of the city's three oldest churches. Visit the church, then make your way back to the river. Walk east along the quai de Montebello up to the Archevêché bridge. Settle for a leisurely drink on the deck of **Le Kiosque Flottant**, the barge moored opposite no. 2 of the quai. Across the water is Notre Dame, and all around, the blessed halo of a twilight sky.

Night

After freshening up at your hotel, catch a cab or make your way to the Sèvres-Babylone Métro station. Catch line 12 in the direction of Porte de la Chapelle. If you are looking for a lighter and/or less pricey meal, get off at St-Georges and head for **Le Tea Folies**, for an outdoor meal under the trees of the charming place Gustave-Toudouze (see page 119). If you want a substantial—and dearer—French dinner, get off at the Lamarck station and make your way east to **Le Beauvilliers** at 52, rue Lamarck, the most romantic restaurant on the hill of Montmartre (see page 86).

After dinner, make your way to the historical **Le Lapin Agile** cabaret, a picturesque rustic-looking cottage, standing charmingly at 4, rue des Saules, at the foot of Montmartre's sloping vineyard. In the early 20th century, Le Lapin was the haunt of Picasso, Modigliani, Utrillo, and all the other "children" of the hill. The *patron*, Frédé, was as prominent a figure in Montmartre as his painter clients. Frédé owned the donkey, Lolo, who was the author of one of the greatest hoaxes in the history of painting. The writer Dorgelès, who had few kind words for cubism or any of the painting of the day, daubed several brushes in bright paint and tied them to Lolo's tail. He then put under the donkey's tail a sizable canvas, on which the

four-legged artist was induced to give vent to his inspiration. Lolo needed little coaxing. In 1910, his work, *Soleil sur l'Adriatique*, was dispatched to the Salon des Indépendants.

Settle for a lively evening of a mix of old French songs and humor. Don't let the presence of your fellow tourists upset you: You are in for jovial entertainment in pure Gallic tradition.

Day Three

Spend your last morning in **Montmartre**. The mere mention of the name conjures up visions of the Moulin Rouge, French cancan, Toulouse-Lautrec, Pigalle, and our contemporary Amélie Poulain; visions too of true romance, sprouting against all odds in the heartland of lewd Paris, perhaps a bit further up the hill, closer to the **Sacré Coeur** and therefore that much closer to heaven.

Morning

Try to make it early, before assembly-line tourists take over, for the moment of grace when the hill is still imbued in pristine light. Take the Métro line 12 to Abbesses. You will emerge through **Hector Guimard's Art Nouveau canopy**, one of the city's emblematic

fixures. Place des Abbesses is named after the 43 abbesses of the glorious abbey of Montmartre, which was swept away during the Revo-lution after 650 years of history. One of them was seventeen-year-old Claude de Beauvilliers, who, you may recall, was seduced by the future Henri IV (see page 6). The last abbess, Louise de Montmorency, ended her life on the guillotine, a 71-year-old woman, decrepit and sickly, blind and hard of hearing.

Walk west, up rue des Abbesses, right into rue Ravignan, and head north to place Emile Goudeau, a lovely shady corner. On your left is **Le Bateau-Lavoir**, an artists' residence standing on the site of the historic Bateau-Lavoir (washhouse), where Picasso painted many of his Blue Period works, as well as *Les Demoiselles d'Avignon* in 1907, making this the birthplace of cubism.

Picasso's painter friends, such as Henri Matisse and Georges Braque, lived here too. But if you have any romantic illusions about their lives, this was more of a slum than a residence: There was no electricity, no heat, no running water, no sheets, and plenty of bugs. The furniture was no better than a jumble of junk. Picasso fled the Bateau-Lavoir, and Montmartre altogether, as soon as he could afford to.

Continue along rue Ravignan. On your left is the pretty **place Jean-Baptist Clément**, named after the mayor of Montmartre in 1871, during the Civil War of the Commune (the Paris proletariat). Three years earlier, he had written the celebrated love song, "*Le Temps des cerises*" (Cherry time), which became the hymn of the

Le Temps des cerises ❧ Cherry Time

Quand **nous chanterons le temps des cerises**
Les gais **rossignols et merles moqueurs**
Seront tous en fête
Les belles auront la folie aux têtes
Et les amoureux du soleil au coeur
Quand nous chanterons le temps des cerises
S'y plaira bien mieux le merle moqueur

Mais il est bien lourd le temps des cerises
Où l'on s'en va de cueillir en rêvant
Des pendants d'oreilles
Cerises d'amour aux robes pareilles
Tombant sous la feuille en gouttes de sang.
Mais il est bien lourd le temps des cerises
Pendants d'oreilles qu'on cueille en rêvant

J'aimerai toujours le temps des cerises
C'est de ce temps là que je garde au coeur
Une plaie ouverte
Et Dame Fortune en m'étant offerte
Ne pourra jamais fermer ma douleur.
J'aimerai toujours le temps des cerises
Et le souvenir que je garde au coeur.

When we shall sing out "cherry time,"
The merry nightingales and mocking blackbirds
Will all rejoice in mirth.
The maidens' heads will fill with fervor
And lovers' hearts with sun-drenched flames.
When we shall sing out "cherry time,"
The mocking blackbird will rejoice the more.

But cherry time hangs heavy in the air
When one goes in dreams of love
To pick red pendants for the ears.
Cherries of love, in passion wrapped,
Lying 'neath the leaves like fallen drops of blood.
But cherry time hangs heavy in the air.
Pendant earrings picked in dreams of love.

I shall cherish forever cherry time
And the remembrance of the open wound
Which lingers in my heart.
Even the gift of Fortune's favor
Will never be able to heal my grief.
I shall cherish forever the time of cherries
And the memory that lingers in my heart.

—Jean-Baptiste Clément

Commune after the government's slaughter of the Communards gave new meaning to the lyrics. The government troops had pushed the last forces of the Commune east, into the Père Lachaise cemetery at the end of May, during cherry time. The fighters' sweethearts picked cherries to hang behind their heroes' ears, cherries bright red like the color of the Commune, as red as the blood of the twenty or thirty thousand working-class Parisians who lay dead—men, women, and children.

Rue Gabrielle, to your right, is a countrified quiet street, at the end of which you can glimpse the Montmartre cable car gliding up and down the hill. Picasso lived briefly at no. 49. You may first wish to wander off into rue Berthe and rue Barsaque, quiet, atmospheric getaways. At the end of rue Barsaque you will cross the rue Chappe, with its steps climbing uphill and downhill on either side of the street as romantically as can be.

Back on rue Gabrielle, take the rue du Calvaire (on your left or right, depending on your approach), a steep flight of steps climbing uphill and named after the cross that once stood here. The climb may be tough, but it's well worth the effort—a breathtaking view awaits you at the top. Walk into **La Terrasse de Patachou** on your right and settle down for a drink. Forgive the waiters for their lax service and enjoy the flowers, the greenery, and the entire city spread at your feet.

Head for rue Poulbot, which runs out of the tiny place du Calvaire in front of you. At no. 11 is the **Salvador Dali Art Gallery**, where works by the Spanish surrealist are on permanent display. Continue to the junction of rues Norvins, St-Rustique, and Saules, a picture postcard of old Montmartre. **La Bonne Franquette**, on the corner of rue St-Rustique, was the haunt of the likes of Alfred Sisley, Paul Cézanne, and Emile Zola. It was the subject of van Gogh's *La Guinguette*, which now hangs at the Musée d'Orsay.

If you turn right into rue Norvins you will come to **place du Tertre**, the headquarters of the Montmartre tourist industry—be forewarned! According to the date and time of your visit you may or may not have to elbow your way through the square in order to reach the **Sacré Coeur**. Of course the view over Paris from the front of the Sacré Coeur is spectacular, but there is little feel of romance if you experience it at the wrong time. Once you've "seen" the place du Tertre, with its checkered tablecloths, Toulouse-Lautrec posters, and portrait painters, make your way back along rue Norvins and join me down rue des Saules, to the right. Turn right again, and find at 12, rue Cortot, the **Museum of Montmartre**, once the home or studio of many a famous painter, and a charming place to visit. Renoir lived down the hill but had his studio here, where he painted *Le Moulin de la Galette* and *La Balançoire* (The Swing). Utrillo lived here with his mother, the painter Suzanne Valadon, and her young lover Utter. The scenes of the turbulent threesome were famous throughout the hill, followed as they were by the occasional flying object. Suzanne Valadon had been the mistress of several of Montmartre's artists,

To Suzanne Valadon

*D*ear little Biqui
              It's impossible for me
not to think of your entire being; you are inside me in your entirety;
everywhere I see
              nothing but your
              exquisite eyes, your
              soft hands and
              little child's feet.
       You are happy; it's not my wretched thoughts that will
wrinkle your transparent forehead; nor any anxiety
about not seeing me.
       For me there is nothing but icy solitude which fills the
head with emptiness and the heart with sadness.
       Don't forget that your wretched friend hopes to see you at
least at one of the following rendezvous:
              1° Tonight at a quarter to nine at my place;
              2° Tomorrow morning again at my place
              3° Tomorrow night at Devé (Maison Olivier)
Let me add, Biqui darling, that I shall not be enraged if you can't
make it to these rendezvous;
       I have become terribly reasonable now;
       and despite
       the great happiness that fills me when I see you,
I am beginning to understand that you can't always do as you wish.
You see, little Biqui, there is always a beginning to everything.
       I am kissing you on your heart

                                        Erik Satie
                                        6, rue Cortot
                                        11 March 1893

including Toulouse-Lautrec and Degas. The musician Eric Satie
was desperately infatuated with her and rented a cupboard-size
room at no. 6, to be as close as possible to her. It also enabled the
impoverished musician to live high above the city and "above his
creditors," as he liked to put it.

Continue along rue Cortot and turn left into rue du Mont-Cenis,
once the ancient road that led north to the basilique St-Denis, the
burial place of the kings of France, and originally Saint Denis
himself, according to legend. The home of the composer Berlioz
stood at no. 24, a lovely house and garden where all the romantic set
used to gather—Chopin, Liszt, Sand, Delacroix. A disgraceful block
of flats now stands on the site.

Turn left into rue St-Vincent and walk along the vineyard. Notice **Le Lapin Agile** (see page 259) on your right as you reach the street corner of rue des Saules. Turn left into rue des Saules and right into rue de l'Abreuvoir. **La Maison Rose,** a picture postcard with its boxes of geraniums and bright green shutters, was frequented by Picasso in 1902—though it was more of a down-at-the-heels hovel at the time.

Stroll along rue de l'Abreuvoir across rue Girardon, where it narrows into the allée des Brouillards—the alley of mists, as romantic a name as this secluded spot deserves. At the end of the alley stands the sleepy **Château des Brouillards**, steeped in serene greenery, frequented and celebrated in the 19th century by the quintessentially romantic writer, Gérard de Nerval. It was just as appreciated by the painter Renoir, who moved with Aline and the children to this "paradise of roses and lilac," in 1892; it's the house on the left at the top of the stairs. Walk to the gardens of the Suzanne Buisson square on your left. A statue of the beheaded Saint Denis, carrying his head in his hands, can by seen by the fountain. The story goes that after his beheading, Saint Denis picked up his head and carried it to this fountain to wash off the blood. He then proceeded downhill to the north and finally collapsed and expired on the site where the basilique St-Denis was later built. The fountain was believed to have a purifying quality, as attested to by the following verse:

Jeune fille qui a bu à l'eau de Saint Denys
Sera fidèle à son mari.
A damsel who has drunk from the water of Saint Denys,
Will be faithful to her spouse.

The historical fountain, however, was situated south of the garden, now the site of the impasse Girardon. Step a little back from the fountain and raise your eyes south: the sails of the famous **Moulin de la Galette** can be seen peeping through the tree branches.

Exit on the southern side of the garden, across the impasse Girardon, and turn right into avenue Junot, Montmartre's showcase, which boasts some beautiful dwellings from the 1920s, notably no. 15 across the street, built by the famous Austrian architect Adolphe Loos for the dadaist, Tristan Tzara. Walk into the flowery alley, **villa Léandre**, at no. 25, an oasis of impeccably kept eclectic houses amidst little gardens and flowers and twittering birds.

Come back and walk into the neighboring no. 23, a dark, shady stretch of untidy vegetation, blissfully open to outsiders. Walk down the steps and through the gate. You have arrived at rue Lepic, Montmartre's winding "high street," once the home of Vincent and Theo van Gogh (no. 54). Turn left on rue Lepic and stop for lunch at **Chez Graziano**, at no. 83, where you have booked an outdoor table for today's lunch (see page 97). You are going to feast in a flowery environment under the sails of one of Montmartre's two surviving windmills—**le Moulin du Radet**. Enter, announce your name, and enjoy.

Afternoon

After lunch walk downhill along rue Lepic. **Le Moulin de la Galette** is on your right, a ravishing sight. At the bottom of the street a wonderfully lush street market awaits you with its colorful food stalls. Ahead is the boulevard de Clichy. On your right is the **Moulin Rouge**: You are standing on mythical soil, in the heartland of Toulouse-Lautrec and French cancan.

Cross the boulevard and walk into rue Blanche, where you will catch the no. 74 bus a little further down the street. But if you want to spoil each other with some great chocolate, first detour into rue Fontaine. At no. 30, Denise Akabo, the owner of **l'Etoile d'Or**, will walk you through all the different kinds of chocolate available in France. If you show the slightest interest, she will have all the time in the world to share her passion. She is inexhaustible and totally charming, and eternally youthful with her two bouncing pigtails.

Get off the bus at Louvre-Etienne Marcel on rue du Louvre and turn right (west) into rue des Petits-Champs. Ahead is **place des Victoires**, built in the 17th century in honor of the Sun King. Unfortunately, its glorious architecture has faded over the years, but it is a great place for trendy shopping, and a stronghold of designer clothes since the 1970s, when Kenzo first set up shop here.

Continue along rue des Petits-Champs west of place des Victoires and turn right into the **Galerie Vivienne**—a 19th-century arcade and a journey into another world, with its medley of wonderful old bookshops (alas, mainly in French), arty boutiques, and, above all, antiquated, indefinable atmosphere. Settle at **A Priori Thé**, one of the city's favorites, for your afternoon tea.

Stroll into the **Galerie Colbert**, the next arcade to your right, a stunning sample of French elegance, with its luminous peach-colored marble. Follow the map south to the gardens of the Palais Royal, "the countryside in the very heart of Paris," according to its one-time resident, Jean Cocteau. Cocteau lived at 36, rue de Montpensier, in the 1950s, while his much-admired writer-friend, Colette ("a fountain of ink," as he called her), lived at 9, rue de Beaujolais. She was a regular at **Le Grand Véfour**, which you may have noticed on your left under the archway, one of the city's gastronomic glories and top on my list (see page 96).

In the 18th century, the **Palais Royal** was the social hub of Paris, where culture rubbed shoulders with gambling and prostitution. Predominantly high-class prostitutes paraded here, "walked the Palace," the saying went, including no less than the Pompadour's mother. Low-class prostitution had to content itself with the bushes of the Tuileries gardens. The *soupers* held here were veritable bacchanalias. Not surprisingly, as soon as he alighted in Paris, Casanova headed here. The place belonged to Louis XVI's cousin, Philippe, the Duc d'Orléans and Duc de Chartres, who built the arcades and set them up as a profitable business. The King was horrified: "Cousin, you have turned shopkeeper and no doubt we shall see you only on Sundays." The Duke had his revenge during the Revolution, when under his new identity, Philippe-Egalité, he voted

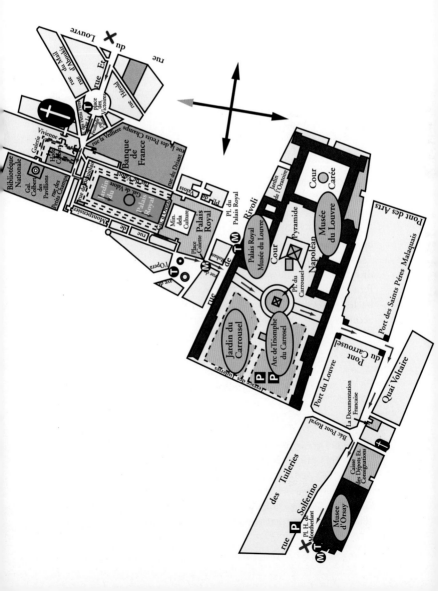

for the death of his royal cousin. But then, his cunning support of the revolutionary cause only delayed his own beheading by a few months.

More than a century before, Louis XIV had spent his childhood in the Palais Royal, where he once nearly drowned in the fountain. His favorite pastime was apparently playing "king and queen" with Marie, the little daughter of his mother's chambermaid. A violent revolt led by some of his subjects caused the family to flee to St-Germain-en-Laye, bringing to an untimely end a simple-hearted romance.

The gardens can get crowded in sunny weather, but never the arcades, which are lined with extraordinary boutiques. If you are out to splurge, **Shiseido**, at 142, galerie de Valois (the eastern arcade), is your ultimate address—a dim secret sanctuary of glowing rosewood paneling and beguiling lilac walls (see page 177).

Leave the Palais Royal through its southern exit. On your right is the celebrated **Comédie Française** and ahead is place Colette. Cross over. To your right is the avenue de l'Opéra, leading to the old opera house, the **Palais Garnier**. The avenue was laid out by Haussmann as an access to the Palais Garnier from the now-gone Tuileries Palace. Continue south on rue de Rohan and through the Louvre archway toward the Seine. To your left is the **Louvre**, with I.M. Pei's striking glass pyramid entrance. To your right is the **Arc de Triomphe du Carrousel**. Enjoy the spectacular vista of the Champs-Elysées beyond the obelisk at place de la Concorde.

Cross the **Carrousel bridge,** and enjoy some more of the city's breathtaking views—to the west, the Tuileries gardens on the Right Bank, the **Musée d'Orsay** facing them on the Left Bank; to the east the enchanting Pont des Arts and beyond it, the Ile de la Cité, resplendent at this time of day, splashed with golden light. Print it all in your hearts to take back home. Turn right on the **quai de Voltaire** and browse through the bookstalls, as Rudyard Kipling liked to do.

Catch the RER Métro line C at the Musée d'Orsay station in the direction of Versailles (west). Get off at Champ-de-Mars and head for the **Eiffel Tower**. I have saved it for the evening, hoping it would be less crowded. If this is the case, you may be in for a treat: according to the time of year, you may have arrived at the moment of grace, when twilight is about to unfold and set the city ablaze.

Night

You are dining on the water, and in slow motion—Paris at its ultimate.

Order a cab from your hotel to get you to your port of embarkation by 8:30 P.M., and another cab to collect you at 11 P.M., at the end of your ride.

It's going to be expensive, but well worth it, for the splendor is unique. For two full hours the illuminated monuments of Paris will flaunt their glamour as you navigate along the scintillating ribbon of the Seine. Several companies offer dinner cruises but most are noisy, flashy, and touristy. If you are young—go for them; why not? You may find them livelier and more fun. But for an extra €10 each, **Le Don Juan**, an intimate, oak-paneled yacht, offers a treat in quite a different league (see page 254).

As you disembark, your cab is waiting to take you on a Paris-by-night tour. Head west. Instruct the driver to stop at the corner of rues de l'Hôtel-de-Ville and Nonnains-d'Hyères, for a dazzling view of the **Hôtel de Sens** and the back of the **Hôtel Aumont** as you head west. Make sure to include the following landmarks on your route: the **Palais Royal, place Vendôme, place de la Concorde,** the **Champs-Elysées,** the **Arc de Triomphe,** the **Eiffel Tower** (from place du Trocadéro for a stunning view, and once more from close quarters, across the river), the **Alexandre III bridge,** the façade of the **Hôtel des Invalides,** and the **Invalides Church of the Dome,** seen to full effect from place Vauban. This to my mind, is the jewel in the city's crown, and a splendid parting gift for your romantic celebration.

Les Prénoms de Paris | Paris on and on

Le soleil qui se lève	The sun that rises
Et caresse les toîts	Caresses the roofs
Et c'est Paris le jour	And it's Paris by day
La Seine qui se promène	The Seine that strolls
Et me guide du doigt	And shows me the way
Et c'est Paris toujours	And it's Paris again
Et mon coeur qui s'arrête	And my heart that pauses
Sur ton coeur qui sourit	On your smiling heart
Et c'est Paris bonjour	And it's Paris hello
Et ta main dans ma main	And your hand in my hand
Qui me dit déjà oui	Already says yes
Et c'est Paris l'amour	And Paris is love
Le premier rendez-vous	The first rendezvous
A l'île st louis	On Ile St-Louis
C'est Paris qui commence	It's Paris beginning
Et le premier baiser	And the first ever kiss
Volé aux Tuileries	Stolen at the Tuileries,
Et c'est Paris la chance	And it's Paris good luck
Et le premier baiser	And the first ever kiss
Reçu sous un portail	Received under a doorway
Et c'est Paris romance	And it's Paris romance
Et deux têtes qui tournent	And two heads that turn
En regardant Versailles	And look to Versailles
Et c'est Paris la France.	And it's Paris, France
Des jours que l'on oublie	Days forgotten,
Qui oublient de nous voir	In turn don't see us
Et c'est Paris l'espoir	And Paris is hope
Des heures où nos regards	Moments when our eyes
Ne sont qu'un seul regard	Melt into one gaze
Et c'est Paris miroir	And it's Paris the mirror
Rien que des nuits encore	By now only nights
Qui séparent nos chansons	Separate our songs
Et c'est Paris bonsoir	And it's Paris good night
Et ce jour-là enfin	And at long last the day
Où tu ne dis plus non	When you no longer say no
Et c'est Paris ce soir	And it's Paris tonight
Une chambre un peu triste	A room a bit dreary
Où s'arrête la ronde	Puts an end to the round
Et c'est Paris nous deux	And it's Paris you and I
Un regard qui reçoit	Eyes that contain

La tendresse du monde	The tenderness of the world
Et c'est Paris tes yeux	And it's Paris your eyes
Ce serment que je pleure	The vow that I weep
Plutôt que ne le dis	Rather than speak
C'est Paris si tu veux	It's Paris if you will
Et savoir que demain	And to know that tomorrow
Sera comme aujourd'hui	Will be like today
C'est Paris merveilleux	It's Paris enchanting
Mais la fin du voyage	But the journey is closing,
La fin de la chanson	The end of the song
Et c'est Paris tout gris	And Paris is grim
Dernier jour, dernière heure	Last day, last hour
Première larme aussi	First tear too
Et c'est Paris la pluie	And it's raining on Paris
Ces jardins remontés	The gardens you cross
Qui n'ont plus leur parure	They've lost their leaves
Et c'est Paris l'ennui	And Paris is bleak
La gare où s'accomplit	The station where our final parting
La dernière dechirure	Plays itself out
Et c'est Paris fini	And Paris is over
Loin des yeux, loin du coeur	Unseen by the eyes, unfelt by the heart
Chassé du paradis	Chased out of paradise
Et c'est Paris chagrin	And Paris is woe
Mais une lettre de toi	But a letter from you
Une lettre qui dit oui	A letter that says yes
Et c'est Paris demain	And it's Paris tomorrow
Des villes et des villages	From towns and villages
Les routes tremblent de chance	The roads throb with luck
C'est Paris en chemin	And Paris is on its way
Et toi qui m'attends là	And you, who are waiting for me there
Et tout qui recommence	And it all starts again
Et c'est Paris je reviens	And it's Paris I'm back

—Jacques Brel

3

ROMANTIC HOTELS

Love is love, and that's a thing that

resembles nothing else.

—Jules Michelet

PARIS IS STUDDED WITH NUMEROUS EXCELLENT hotels, centrally located, spotlessly clean and providing all modern amenities. That being said, central Paris is a crowded, compact territory, where space is a rare commodity. Unless you are staying in a luxury hotel, don't expect vast closets and bathrooms, or much living space. Try to travel light, which will help keep your hotel room uncluttered and enhance your sense of freedom. Pack judiciously: Many basic outfits can be dressed up or down according to the occasion.

The hotels listed here have been picked out for their location and old-world charm. Most fall into the above- or just-above-average category, though a few are amazingly inexpensive, even bargains. For this special trip, where you stay can make a world of difference. Always specify whether you want a double or a twin bedroom and, whenever possible, opt for a room with a view.

For those who intend to go all out and splurge on this special occasion, I have included a few of the city's top-of-the-scale world-renowned luxury hotels at the top of the list. The rest of the listings follow by arrondissement.

Prices are for a room for two, unless otherwise stated.

Le Bristol
112, rue du Faubourg St-Honoré, 75008
Tel: 01 53 43 43 00
Fax: 01 53 43 43 01
Web: www.hotel-bristol.com
Price: €610 (Or €6,860 for the presidential suite!)

If at some point I decided to leave my Paris apartment for a splurge, a suite at the Bristol would be my destination (there are 48 of them, out of a total of 178 rooms).

I am not alone to rate the Bristol so high: It was voted best hotel in Paris and best hotel in France by *Condé Nast Traveller* magazine readers. If you haven't heard of it before, it's because it prides itself on its discretion. The truth is, many an international celebrity has stayed here—Ava Gardner, Marilyn Monroe, Rita Hayworth, Grace Kelly, Charlie Chaplin, Orson Welles... to name but a few.

Opened in 1925 on the much-altered premises of an 18th-century townhouse, the Bristol is located in the one-time aristocratic Faubourg St-Honoré, within minutes' walk from presidential Palais de l'Elysée and the Rond-Point-des-Champs-Elysées. The hotel features several magnificent art deco additions, notably an elevator and the swimming pool that is part of the 6th-floor fitness club. The pool resembles a yacht sailing toward a trompe-l'oeil of the French Riviera. It actually looks out on the roofs of Paris, so you can let your imagination fly between the two while you bask in the sun in one of the adjoining terrace's deck chairs.

The Bristol is owned by a family who has given it the feel of a private home. They have paid great attention to every detail—fabrics, color schemes, antique furniture and tapestries, paintings, cut flowers... both in the public areas and in the rooms, all of which feature vast, stunning marble bathrooms. It goes without saying that everything is gorgeous and stylish, enhanced by a magnificent garden where camellias alternate with geraniums, according to season, and where the air is filled with the balm of honeysuckle and with the song of birds. Under the shade of elegant Italian parasols, the garden is a heavenly oasis for any of your warm-weather meals. The 18th-century basin, dubbed Fontaine des Amours, adds a romantic touch. Or, if you want your own private garden, you can book Suites 954, 955, 964, or 965 with their amazing roof gardens, where you may sunbathe to your heart's fill after your own private breakfast, should you be too lazy to go downstairs. The breakfast buffet, though, is a cheerful sight, complete with Paris's best fresh orange juice. They squeeze nearly 300 pounds of oranges on an average day! Suite 729 provides another romantic pleasure: The Eiffel Tower in the center of the view from the king-sized bed.

I have never encountered such friendliness in any Parisian hotel of this category. None of the usual formal, off-putting stiffness of other first-rate hotels. I felt at home right away and was welcomed into every nook and cranny of the hotel, even behind-the-scenes. Ah!—the kitchens with their army of chefs presiding over the different sections for meat, fish, pastry, bread... The florists who gave me a bouquet of heavenly pansies... The cleaners, who iron everything by hand and wrap it delicately in silk paper before sending it back to your room.... And throughout all this, a happy, family mood pervades. At last a place where everyone seems proud of their work and committed to seeking perfection.

Le Crillon
10, place de la Concorde, 75008
Tel: 01 44 71 15 00
Fax: 01 44 71 15 02
Web: www.crillon.com
Price: low season €550–640 (rooms); €755–907 (suites)
high season €600–710 (rooms); €880–1,037 (suites)

A mythical address, overlooking place de la Concorde, "one of the predestined centers of the world," according to F. Scott Fitzgerald. It was built in the 18th century by Jacques-Ange Gabriel as part of a new royal square for King Louis XV. A room or a suite looking out on the square will afford you one of the world's most stunning cityscapes, especially after dark, in the glow of its dozens of street lights. Among the celebrity couples who have stayed at the Crillon,

President Kennedy and his First Lady, Jackie, rank top of the list. Of course, they stayed in the presidential suite, which overlooks place de la Concorde. You will have to pay €2,700 per night for such a luxury. But the sky is the limit at the Crillon: the Grand Bernstein suite may not give you the sky, but instead you can indulge in its 5 bathrooms, 2 saunas, 2 steam baths, and spectacular view of the place de la Concorde from its huge terrace. And its piano, of course.

Le Plaza Athénée
25, avenue Montaigne, 75008
Tel: 01 53 67 66 65
Fax: 01 53 67 66 66
Web: www.plaza-athenee-paris.com
Price: low season €587–640 (rooms); €755–5335 (suites)
high season €618–671 (rooms); €788–5641 (suites)
I love the Plaza on Paris's regal haute couture avenue Montaigne. I love its turn-of-the-century architecture and art deco design and I love the fact that it is almost like the extension of its contemporary neighbor, the historic Théâtre des Champs-Elysées, the one-time home of Diaghilev's Ballets Russes and Josephine Baker's Revue Nègre. I love its quintessentially Parisian brasserie and its geranium-filled patio, where you will be thrilled to have a leisurely lunch or a starlit dinner in summer. Last but not least, the celebrated chef, Alain Ducasse, now reigns supreme over the destiny of the Plaza's cuisine.

If you are among the lucky ones who can stay at the Plaza, note that the Presidential Suite will cost you less than the Royal one, from €3,810 to 3,964 depending on the season, but it's definitely the one most conducive to love: a split-level gem, it boasts 2 bathrooms, a sauna, work-out equipment, and a fabulous roof terrace. Needless to say it comes with a magnificent view of Paris, with the Sacré Coeur and the Eiffel Tower as a special bonus.

Le Ritz
15, place Vendôme, 75001
Tel: 01 43 16 30 30
Fax: 01 43 16 36 68
Web: www.ritzparis.com
Price: low season €580–680 (rooms); €800–5100 (suites)
high season €630–730 (rooms); €850–7700 (suites)
The Ritz hides its splendor inside one of the palatial townhouses of the royal place Vendôme, which Jules-Hardouin Mansart built in honor of the Sun King, Louis XIV (the Invalides Church of the Dome is his other Parisian masterpiece). Standing in the heartland of the world's greatest jewelers, it is itself an architectural gem, and come night, it sparkles with magic splendor.

The sumptuous staircase inside the hotel was Charles Ritz's addition, intended as a gallant homage to the fair sex, a pedestal down which they would glide in their evening gowns and enchant the world below. The Ritz was also the first Parisian hotel to install private bathtubs—quite a revolution in 1898.

And of course, Fitzgerald and Hemingway hung out in its bar (now named after the latter), Proust had his own suite here, and Coco Chanel actually made it her permanent home. More to the point, in *Love in the Afternoon*, Gary Cooper and Audrey Hepburn made it the stage of their tender romance

Today's Ritz is in the hands of Al Fayed, who has updated the fabulous kitchens, which house a famous cooking school. It also has a great patio garden, which serves meals in fine weather, and a first-class restaurant. But it is the ravishing marble spa and its voluptuous pool that delight me the most, a world of serene silence where you will be pampered like a Cleopatra.

La Vie en Rose
Bateau Jolia, 11 quai St-Bernard, 75005
Tel: 01 43 54 03 46
Fax: 01 43 29 79 15
E-mail: BargeInn@aol.com
Price: €650 with breakfast (3-day minimum)
Imagine spending several days in the privacy of a luxury barge located in the city's most romantic spot. Just the two of you, no other guests. Imagine having your breakfast in the flowery roof patio with the Ile St-Louis and Notre Dame as a backdrop, painted gold by a rising sun. Imagine being rocked gently by the Seine as you luxuriate in a bubble bath before being lulled to sleep wrapped in down comforters. Add to this an exquisite breakfast, with delicious croissants straight out of the oven, wearing the soft bathrobes you'll take home at the end of your visit. The champagne flows, the collection of CDs is vast… Laura Ann Kamm and David Novick, the

proprietors, have thought of every detail to make you utterly content on board this tiny and bountiful island of bliss. And when you want to mix with the crowds, the romantic narrow streets of the Latin Quarter and the Marais are basically around the corner. No wonder Laura and David had a love-at-first-sight affair with the barge and bought it on a whim!

1ST ARRONDISSEMENT

Hôtel Henri IV
25, place Dauphine, 75001
Tel: 01 43 54 44 53
Price: €28–68

The fact that a hotel on the lovely place Dauphine, halfway between the Louvre and St-Germain, and just behind the Ste-Chapelle, can offer rooms at €28 defeats my imagination. The fact that among them are the hotel's three most romantic rooms (complete with balconies overlooking the 17th-century place Dauphine), is simply miraculous. At this price you cannot expect private bathrooms or frills, but if you are willing to experience the more modest Paris of the 1950s, don't dither and make your reservation this instant, because the place gets filled up in no time, as you may have already guessed.

Place Dauphine was laid out by the initiative of Henri IV, whose equestrian statue stands on the nearby Pont Neuf. And by the way, it was because Yves Montand's musician stayed in this hotel (in Room 18) back in 1949, that Montand discovered the place Dauphine and made it his lifelong home, as did his companion, actress Simone Signoret. The hotel has also made it into the pages of literature: in *Nadja*, the eponymous heroine tells the surrealist André Breton of an underground passage leading to the Palais de Justice and bypassing the Hotel Henri IV.

3RD ARRONDISSEMENT

Le Pavillon de la Reine
28, place des Vosges, 75003
Tel: 01 40 29 19 19
Fax: 01 40 29 19 20
E-mail: pavillon@club-internet.fr
Web: www.pavillon-de-la-reine.com
Price: €350–585 (suite) with private parking

You are paying for the location. It is beautiful, especially the public areas. Walking up the stairs from the breakfast room is simply regal. The rooms have the same open beams as in many of the Marais and Left Bank hotels, the same stripped stone, the same vaulted basement for breakfast... an ancient feel for sure. In winter you will enjoy the open fire in the lobby.

My favorite rooms: Suite 8 has low ceilings and beams, and a pleasing view over an inner courtyard; Suite 9 is similar, but a bit smaller; Suites 12, 14, and 18 are split-level and look out on the garden; Suite 15 is also split-level, but more spacious, with a balcony overlooking the garden; Suite 77 is under the roof and looks out on other old roofs. It is cozy and full of charm. Book Suite 47 if you want a four-poster bed.

4TH ARRONDISSEMENT

Hôtel de La Bretonnerie
22, rue Ste-Croix-de-la-Bretonnerie, 75004
Tel: 01 48 87 77 63
Fax: 01 42 77 26 78
Price: €104–170
Closed in August

A gorgeous wood and wrought-iron period staircase and a profusion of open oak beams greet you as you enter this 17th-century townhouse in the Marais, a few steps away from Notre Dame, Centre Pompidou and place des Vosges. All 27 rooms are individually redecorated periodically. Period furniture and warm carpets enhance the welcoming atomosphere. On my last visit I loved the blue Room 33, the yellow 34 (both of which had charming bathrooms), and the sunny, spacious 21.

Hôtel des Deux-Iles
59, rue St-Louis-en-l'Ile, 75004
Tel: 01 43 26 13 35
Fax: 01 43 29 60 25
Price: €142

Under the same ownership as the Hôtel de Lutèce (see below), with the same level of comfort. I praise them both, with a slight preference for the Hôtel de Lutèce.

Hôtel de Lutèce
65, rue St-Louis-en-l'Ile, 75004
Tel: 01 43 26 23 52
Fax: 01 43 29 60 25
Price: €142

Staying on the bejeweled Ile St-Louis is unquestionably one of the most romantic experiences when visiting Paris. The downside of the experience is that you are not going to get the space you will in a more modern building. But if you are after warm wood paneling, beautiful French floor tiles, cheerful fabrics in your rooms, the old silver-gray roofs of Paris framed in your windows, and the pleasure of being in the heart of the Ile St-Louis, then make your booking several months in advance.

I was struck by the fact that the chambermaid who showed me around had been working here for nearly 25 years and loved her work. She spoke of the hotel, its staff, and clients with the pride and loyalty of a mother for her child. She and her colleagues make sure that everything is spotlessly clean and fresh, and above all, that you will be totally happy.

Le St–Merry
78, rue de la Verrerie, 75004
Tel: 01 42 78 14 15
Fax: 01 40 29 06 82
Price: €128–186; €272 (suite)

A plunge into Romanticism with a capital R, the way Victor Hugo would have done it, deep into medieval Paris, at its most enchanting and most spectacular. And in a great location, on the less touristy, eastern edge of the Marais, within a few steps from the Centre Pompidou and Notre Dame. The "plunge" actually includes a climb up a gorgeous, spiral staircase (not enough space for an elevator to be installed here), and if you want the best room, you will have to climb it up to the fourth floor. If you are willing to put up with this, and with small bathrooms, you are in for something very special and unique. All the rooms are decorated with genuine medieval furnishings, lovingly collected over the years by the previous owner. A magnificent stain glass window stands as an unwitting reminder that rue de la Verrerie was once the stronghold of the stained-glass guild, suppliers of the churches of old Paris.

The hotel is located in the one-time presbytery of the neighboring 15th-century church of St–Merry. Room 12 has two flying buttresses that run from the church through its ceiling—a stunning sight! Room 17 has a double view, overlooking rues St-Martin and St-Jacques (across the river), once the ancient Roman road, and the splendid church of St–Merry. From 9 A.M. on you will also be graced with the quarterly chiming of the church bells. Room 20, the hotel's very large top-floor suite, is simply magnificent. You are just under the roof, with beautiful beams overhead and old Paris roofs outside the windows. It is definitely worth the splurge.

Youth Hostel/MIJE
11, rue du Fauconnier, 75004
Also at Hôtel Charpentier, 6, rue de Fourcy
Also at Maubuisson, 12, rue des Barres
Tel: 01 42 74 23 45
Web: www.mije.com
E-mail: MIJE@wanadoo.fr
Price: €27 per person with breakfast; shower and basin in each room; shared toilets in the corridors; sheets provided, but not towels. Lunch and dinner at €8–9, in the vaulted dining room
Closes between noon and 3 p.m. for cleaning.
If you are young and traveling on a shoestring, these three hostels are a great way to stay in the romantic Marais. Each has a few rooms for two (usually bunk beds), but they are hard to come by. Book well in advance.

All three hostels have the feel of a medieval abbey, with their Spartan simplicity, immaculate cleanliness, and beautiful wood furniture. The hostels on rues du Fauconnier and Fourcy even have charming courtyards. Some journalist described the MIJE as "the most beautiful youth hostel in the world." This is not surprising since the Hôtel Charpentier on rue de Fourcy was once the home of Louis XIV's future chancellor, Gilles Charpentier. (Though by the turn of the 20th century, it had becom a brothel called Grosse Margot. And next door was one of the city's most famous brothels, the Moulin Galant, also known as Le Fourcaga. It was closed, like all the others, in 1946.)

The Hôtel de Maubisson was the one-time Paris foothold of the women's abbey of Maubisson—and it is believed that Pierre Abélard and Héloïse may have stayed here.

5TH ARRONDISSEMENT
Hôtel des Grandes Ecoles
75, rue du Cardinal-Lemoine, 75005
Tel: 01 43 26 79 23
Fax: 01 43 25 28 15
Price: €100–244
As soon as you turn into the driveway, you leave Paris behind. You have come to a corner of provincial France, made up of a spacious garden and three village houses. Old shady trees, sun-drenched

flowerbeds, songs of birds—nothing is missing. The dining room, next to the reception in the main building, has lots of lace and an old piano, and feels like the old home of someone's great aunt. If it weren't for the key to your room, you might forget to pay upon departure. Indeed, many of the clients are regulars who have become like family, as you can see from the correspondence and pictures stuck up behind the reception desk. On my last visit, on the lookout for signs of romance, I noticed among them a drawing of a red heart. It was offered to Marie, at the reception desk, by a little Swiss girl who had stayed here once and with whom she had since been corresponding. The old German couple standing next to me gave Marie a book of poetry. They were leaving the next day and, in return for their gift asked her to read to them one of the poems. What a touching farewell.

So staying at the Hôtel des Grandes Ecoles is definitely a love affair, and Madame Flock and her right-hand woman, Marie, are so generous that they serve breakfast until noon.

Hôtel du Parc St-Séverin
22, rue de la Parcheminerie, 75005
Tel: 01 43 54 32 17
Fax: 01 43 54 70 71
Price: €100–244 (Room 70)
Besides its great location in the oldest part of the Latin Quarter, the main attraction of this hotel for the pair of you, is Room 70. Its immense roof terrace offers a head-spinning, nearly 360-degree view

of Paris to be enjoyed by you alone. Breakfast here at sunrise, have a drink at sunset, or a moonlit glass of champagne. As the expression goes, *L'amour c'est l'égoïsme à deux* (Love is selfishness shared by two).

6TH ARRONDISSEMENT

L'Hôtel
13, rue des Beaux Arts, 75006
Tel: 01 44 41 99 00
Fax: 01 43 25 64 81
Price: low season €236–260; high season €595–686

On the night of November 29, 1900, Oscar Wilde died almost anonymously in this hotel, at the age of 46. It was a tragic ending, after the two-year ordeal in jail that destroyed his health. His wit, however, remained unimpaired to the end, as reflected by his last comment: "I am dying beyond my means." This note, along with an unpaid bill for 2643.40 francs, now hangs on the wall in his room, no. 23. Only Robin Ross, his devoted old friend, and "Bosie" Douglas, his demon, attended his funeral and followed his hearse to the Père Lachaise, alongside a handful of the hotel staff who left the note "To our tenant" on the wax bead wreath.

In 1984, another famous guest at the Hôtel, the Argentinean Jorges Luis Borges, left the following written homage: "This hotel... where one can't find two identical rooms. It seems to have been sculpted by a cabinet-maker." Jean-Paul Besnard, the present owner of the Hôtel, took the "sculpture" one step further. For many years, he had dreamed of owning a hotel in his beloved St-Germain-des-Prés neighborhood. Thanks to serendipitous timing, this one was put on sale by Monsieur Dubucheron when Besnard was ready to buy it and lavish on it his boundless passion and imagination. As far as romance goes, it has few rivals. It starts at the reception with the Venus/Cupid emblem. Or rather it starts way back four centuries ago when, legend has it, Queen Margot had a love nest on this site. Today each of the twenty rooms feels like a love nest, whatever its style, whatever its size. They are so eclectic that you'll have to come back many times and try them all out. Nothing could be further apart than the voluptuous, opulent 19th-century boudoir that is Room 54 and the fresh Art Deco Room 36. The sunny, soft orange hue of the walls and the mirror-covered furniture that once belonged to the celebrated singer Mistinguett make this room a stunning period-piece.

If you want a spectacular view and a fantastic terrace all for yourselves, book Room 62, la Cardinale. The old roofs of Paris and the belltower of St-Germain will be your backdrop.

The public areas are just as eclectic and include a lobby filled with Jean Cocteau paintings, a cozy library, and a wonderful restaurant, Le Bélier. Downstairs, under a romantic vault, you may relax in the smoking room or luxuriate in the jacuzzi or sauna in the fitness club. The well, it is rumored, was once used as a fridge by Queen Margot and her companions when they repaired to this hideaway.

With so much going for the Hôtel, you will not be surprised to find out that it has been favored by the grand and the mighty. Ava Gardner, Marcello Mastroianni, Roman Polanski, Roberto de Niro, and Claudia Cardinale are among those who stayed here.

Hôtel de l'Abbaye
10, rue de Cassette, 75006
Tel: 01 45 44 38 11
Fax: 01 45 48 07 86
Price: €180–360

You will be made to feel at home right away as you cross the cobbled courtyard and step into this cozy, cheerful hotel where clients keep coming back year in, year out. Everything is tasteful and of the finest quality—the oak paneling, the fabrics, the furnishings (including some gorgeous antiques scattered here and there), the bathrooms... There is a lovely garden, where you will breakfast amid flowers and greenery, bird song and the fountain's trickling water. Part of the garden has recently been converted into a conservatory so that the treat can be

prolonged in winter. In winter too, you will enjoy your champagne seated by a happy fire. Add to this a great location on a very quiet street, in the heart of the shopping area of the Left Bank, barely five minutes' walk from the Luxembourg Gardens.

Room 3, on ground level, has its own tiny patch of garden for a private *tête-à-tête* breakfast, and a separate shower that Americans seem to appreciate. It was also Marcello Mastroianni's home away from home. Room 4 is much the same, but even more spacious, with a prettier view of the garden.

Four wonderfully romantic split-level suites (301, 302, 303, 304) come complete with

terraces brimming with bushes and flowers—space ideal for a heavenly breakfast among the romantic roofs of Paris.

Hôtel d'Angleterre
44, rue Jacob, 75006
Tel: 01 42 60 34 72
Fax: 01 42 60 16 93
Price: €122–259 (top-floor apartment)

Besides its characteristic Left Bank charm—open oak beams, breakfast in a lovely flowery patio garden, beautiful furnishings— the hotel also has history. This is where the newly wed and impoverished Hemingway and Hadley stayed back in 1921. Today, they wouldn't recognize the upgraded place, under Japanese management. They used to dine across the street at the Pré aux Clercs (still standing) for 6F, wine included. The best kept secret of the place, though, is the stunning, huge, top-floor apartment, with its magnificent beams and extraordinary array of eclectic antiques.

Hôtel Le Clos Médicis
56, rue Monsieur-le-Prince, 75006
Tel: 01 43 29 10 80
Fax: 01 43 54 26 90
E-mail: clos_medicis@compuserve.com
Price: €150–180

In this 18th-century townhouse, you are but a few steps away from the Luxembourg Gardens and right in the heart of the Latin Quarter. All 38 rooms are bright and decorated with beautiful fabrics. In winter you will love the open fire in the cozy lobby; in warm weather, you will enjoy breakfast in the leafy courtyard.

Hôtel des Marronniers
21, rue Jacob, 75006
Tel: 01 43 25 30 60
Fax: 01 40 46 83 56
Price: €132–148

A wonderfully chintzy hotel in the heart of St-Germain-des-Près. The pleasure begins with a great courtyard that craves the hoofs of a horse-drawn carriage

Make sure you book a room overlooking the garden filled with shady chestnut trees. My favorites are Rooms 11 and 12, level with the trees, but I also recommend Rooms 41 and 43 on the 4th floor, and Rooms 51, 52, and 53 on the 5th floor, all of which pleasantly overlook the church tower of St-Germain.

Hôtel de Nesle
7, rue de Nesle, 75006
Tel: 01 43 54 62 41
Web: hoteldenesle.com
Price: €69–99

If I had to classify the hotels of Paris irrespective of their category, this hotel would top my list. The young manager of this ravishing, yet astonishingly inexpensive, hotel refers to it humbly as a luxury youth hostel. In terms of price, he is right, but that is as far as the comparison holds. I, who am long past the age of backpacking, would be delighted to spend time here. Each room is sheer enchantment, decorated with thematic murals associated with French history and art—Molière, Delacroix, scenes from the French Colonies, to mention but some.... The artist is the manager's stepfather, because this is a family business. You may have to forego a private bathroom (only ten rooms have private showers and toilets), but everything is shining clean and you may even ask for the key to enjoy the wonderful and totally unexpected garden at the back, which would make a charming setting for a wedding and a perfectly romantic nest for a marriage proposal.

La Louisiane
60, rue de Seine, 75006
Tel: 01 44 32 17 17
Fax: 01 44 32 17 18
E-mail: hotel@lalouisiane.net
Price: €67 (Room 80); €100–124 (Room 10)

This historic landmark drips with romantic associations from the heyday of post-war St-Germain when the likes of Simone de Beauvoir, Jean-Paul Sartre, and Juliette Gréco could be seen filing in and out of here. Furthermore, resisting the swell of the tide, it still holds on to the very reasonable prices of yore. Add to this a great location in the midst of the bustling market stalls of rue de Seine, and the shops along rue de Buci, and you are in for a real treat. You will get a smashing view of this colorful street scene from several of

the rooms, among them oval-shaped Room 10, once occupied by
Miles Davis. And if you are a lover of Paris here on your own, try the
tiny Room 80, barely an arm's stretch from the city's old rooftops.
Who says singles are not entitled to a romantic stay in Paris?

Millésime
15, rue Jacob, 75006
Tel: 01 44 07 97 97
Fax: 01 46 34 55 97
Price: €170–185; €210 (Millésime "special")

Even from the street, you will notice the warm ochre colorings and
bright Provençal air of this charming hotel. If you want to play
Romeo (or Juliet) to your sweetheart, try the room nestling atop the
picturesque flight of steps, overlooking the inner courtyard.

Relais Christine
3, rue Christine, 75006
Tel: 01 40 51 60 80
Fax: 01 40 51 60 81
Price: €315–700

As you walk under the elegant archway of this early 17th-century
townhouse, you will sample the gracious living of the French
nobility, whose dwellings were always set off the street, behind a
courtyard. You will love the cobbled courtyard, with its green bushes
and patches of flowers. At night, when lit up discreetly, it is simply
divine. In summer it is set ablaze by red geraniums overflowing
from all the windows.

Inside the building, the marble flooring, oak paneling, open fire,
period staircase, and very helpful concierge at the reception desk,
will all make you feel comfortable right away.

If you tell the hotel that this is your wedding or anniversary (or
just a birthday), a bottle of champagne and a bouquet of flowers will
welcome you to your room.

Behind the hotel's main building lies a lovely garden, in keeping
with the traditional canon of a Classical townhouse, "between
courtyard and garden," as the saying went. It has a lawn, fragrant
honeysuckle and jasmine creepers, rose bushes, rambling ivy in
plenty and an outburst of joyous birds. Rooms 11 and 12 and Suite
14/15 have private access to the garden, with a little terrace where
you can breakfast or have room service at any time of day or night.

The rooms come in all shapes, colors, and sizes, and their prices
vary accordingly. My recommendation is Suite 72. Tucked away at
the end of the staircase on the top floor, it looks out on the hotel
gardens amid a jumble of old, crooked roofs, the towers of the
church of St-Sulpice, and the bells of Notre Dame. Make sure to
book it at least six months prior to your arrival.

The gorgeous breakfast room is located in the basement, in the medieval vault of the one-time Augustine convent. You will love the thick ancient walls, and the ancient well that is still there.... Relais Christine offers leisurely living, a sense of history, grace and beauty, and a great location close to the river and its two most romantic bridges.

Relais Médicis
23, rue Racine, 75006
Tel: 01 43 26 00 60
Fax: 01 40 46 83 39
Price: €168–258

A delightful small hotel (only sixteen rooms), close to the Luxembourg Gardens and next to the elegant 18th-century place de L'Odéon, lush with flowers and greenery, luminous with a lingering touch of sun-bathed Provence, the kind of place that easily sustains happiness.

Relais St-Germain
6, carrefour de l'Odéon, 75006
Tel: 01 44 27 07 97
Fax: 01 46 33 45 30
Price: €266–358 (Molière)

A beautiful 17th-century townhouse in the heart of the Latin Quarter, complete with genuine antiques, spacious, tasteful rooms, and open oak beams. The jewel in the crown is the room at the top, known as Molière, complete with a tiny balcony, big enough for just you two and your champagne. Meanwhile Paris goes about its bustling business on the colorful Odéon junction at your feet.

Below: Relais St-Germain

Hôtel St-Paul
43, rue Monsieur-le-Prince, 75006
Tel: 01 43 26 98 64
Fax: 01 46 34 58 60
Price: €128–144

Located in a 17th-century townhouse, this establishment is under British management and combines the best of French and British tastes. Beautiful oak beams and Haute Epoque furniture create an old-world elegant atmosphere of well-being. My favorite rooms are 21, 31, 41, and 51, which all overlook a profusion of tree branches, and 26, overlooking the courtyard. I also love the delightfully decorated vaulted breakfast room.

Hôtel des Sts-Pères
65, rue des Sts- Pères, 75006
Tel: 01 45 44 50 00
Fax: 01 45 44 90 83
E-mail: espfran@micronet.fr
Price: €106–274

A Left Bank old-timer, the hotel is located in one of the early townhouses of the Faubourg St-Germain, built by Louis XIV's architect, Daniel Gittard. This being the heartland of publishing houses, the hotel is a draw to literati and also, occasionally, to well-known people from the world of the arts and music. All rooms are furnished with antiques and many overlook the flowery patio where breakfast is served in warm weather. The Fresco Room, with its genuine 17th-century painted ceiling, is the hotel's highlight, but is rarely available, alas. Try at least to catch a glimpse of it during your stay.

7TH ARRONDISSEMENT

Hôtel Duc de St-Simon
14, rue de St-Simon, 75007
Tel: 01 44 39 20 20
Fax: 01 45 48 68 25
Price: €194–313

If I had to pick out one hotel at gunpoint, this would probably be the one. Welcome to the once-upon-a-time world of the Faubourg St-Germain. As you cross the porch and step into the cobbled, wisteria-filled courtyard (in heavenly bloom in late April into May), you can almost hear the sound of hoofs, as imaginary guests alight for dinner, straight out of the pages of Proust or Henry James. Inside feels much the same, as the layout of a private home has been preserved, with its cozy corners and lovely antiques. The rooms, which come in different shapes and sizes, and the bathrooms, with their beautiful Salerno tiles, are all beautiful. Truly a smashing place. Perfection of impeccable refinement and old-world charm.

Hôtel La Serre
24bis, rue Cler, 75007
Tel: 01 47 05 52 33
Fax: 01 40 62 95 66
Price: low season €54–70; high season €59–90

This is a cheerful, very friendly hotel with a family feel, on the inexpensive side. It stands right in the heart of the colorful and mouthwatering market street, rue Cler, and is very conveniently located on the Left Bank, half way between the Invalides and the Eiffel Tower. If the sight of the Eiffel Tower kindles your romantic flame, make sure to book Room 505, where you can see it from your bed! It's even better after dark.

Hôtel de la Tulipe
33, rue Mallar, 75007
Tel: 01 45 51 67 21
Fax: 01 47 53 96 37
Price: €110–115; €215 (apartment)

A great bargain, and a great location, half way between the Invalides and the Eiffel Tower, with the Champs-Elysées within walking distance across the river. Standing on the site of an old convent, the hotel is full of rustic charm and has a lovely paved courtyard where breakfast is served in sunny weather. Yellow tablecloths and earthenware tiles, open beams and stripped stone, iron chair frames—all contribute to create a cozy countrified feel throughout the dining room.

Hôtel Verneuil
8, rue de Verneuil, 75007
Tel: 01 42 60 82 14
Fax: 01 42 61 40 38
E-mail: verneuil@cybercable.fr
Web: www.france-hotel-guide.com
Price: €137–177

Rue de Verneuil is a quiet, discreet side street in the one-time aristocratic Faubourg St-Germain, a stone's throw away from the Musée d'Orsay, and across the river from the Louvre. The hotel is located in a 17th-century townhouse whose elegant but somewhat formal façade made me anticipate a stand-offish welcome. But I have nothing but praise for the enthusiastic welcome I received at the reception desk, as I walked in incognito. I almost forgot to look around and take in the wonderful lounge and the abundantly filled bookshelves that give it a feel of a private home. The interior design is stylishly understated with a skillful blend of the old French spirit of the Faubourg and the conveniences of modern times. All rooms and bathrooms are tastefully decorated, but vary in size (and price, accordingly). Breakfast can be taken in your room or in the stunning vaulted stone cellar.

13TH ARRONDISSEMENT

Le Vert Galant
41, rue Croulebarbe, 75013
Tel: 01 44 08 83 50
Fax: 01 44 08 83 69
Price: €76–84

This is a truly Parisian neighborhood, off the tourist beaten track (yet within a short ride from the famous rue Mouffetard and the Latin Quarter), across the street from the lovely gardens of René le Gall. The hotel is a pleasant two-story countrified-looking building with fifteen rooms that all overlook its own quiet gardens. See also the Etchegorry in the restaurant listings—it belongs to the same family.

16TH ARRONDISSEMENT

Le Raphaël
17, avenue Kléber, 75016
Tel: 01 53 64 32 00
Fax: 01 53 64 32 01
Price: €382–992

Despite its location just off the Arc de Triomphe and only a few steps away from the Champs-Elysées, the Raphaël is one of the lesser-known gems among the luxury hotels of Paris, discretion being its keyword. It opened the year of the 1925 Art Deco Exhibition, as an annex to the Majestic next door (since sold and now a government conference center). Paris was then the unquestionable cultural and artistic center of the world, and the Raphaël became the discreet *pied-à-terre* of the arts and the political world. The memory of the romance of such legendary couples as Roberto Rossellini and Ingrid Bergman, and Katharine Hepburn and Spencer Tracy still haunts the cozy Bar Anglais. The glamorous Kennedys, Ava Gardner, Cary Grant, Clark Gable, and Marlon Brando are among the many others who have stayed at the Raphaël. And famous writers too, as varied as John Steinbeck and Barbara Cartland.

In his autobiography, pianist Arthur Rubinstein refers to "the delicious Monsieur Tauber," then the hotel's owner. Another famous pianist, Vladimir Horovitz, had his grand piano carried all the way up to Room 601 on the 6th floor—no small feat—when he gave a rare Paris concert. He was accompanied by his wife, the daughter of Arturo Toscanini. Others may remember Stéphane Grapelli's concert here in 1997, accompanied by pianist Petrucciani, in what turned out to be a very moving farewell to the public, as Grapelli died six months later and Petruccini the following year.

But it was Gershwin's stay in the above-mentioned Majestic that is most important for those interested in Paris romance. He settled there on March 25, 1928. A few months later he left as his legacy the mythical "An American in Paris." For those of you who think that Paris was blissfully traffic-free back then, let me set things straight. The opening scene of *An American in Paris* evokes the car horns at place de la Concorde during rush hour, as Gershwin had already heard them back in the late Twenties and worked them into his composition: he bought a collection of taxi horns on the avenue de la Grande Armée and tried them out in the hotel room with the help of two young pianists whom he instructed to go "quack, quack, quack." *An American in Paris* premiered at Carnegie Hall on December 13, 1928.

If you are considering splurging, the Raphaël offers a discreet alternative to the other palatial hotels mentioned earlier. It's probably more conducive to secluded romance. You will feel at home right away, and will have the benefit of the same level of luxury without the ostentatiousness. If you are head-over-heels in love and can afford a splurge at something like €3,000 a night, you can have a stunning three-floor apartment with the entire city at your feet, including the use and the pleasure of an amazing roof garden, filled with rosebushes, geraniums, and lavender (complete with inebriating scents and the song of birds), not to mention its spectacular view of the Arc de Triomphe and the Eiffel Tower. The roof restaurant offers a 360-degree panorama of all the monuments of Paris. Imagine a July 14th dinner there, with a display of fireworks above the Eiffel Tower just for the two of you. What a regal treat!

Courtesy of Le Raphaël

4

LOVERS' RESTAURANTS AND SALONS DE THÉ

*When Paris sits down to eat, the
whole world is stirred.*

—*Briffault*

ONI, THE PROPRIETOR OF LA ROSE DE FRANCE, once displayed the following announcement on his restaurant window:

Le Midi succès assuré en affaire,
Le Soir Triomphe certain en Amour.
At midday, guaranteed success in business;
At night, sure Triumph in love.

As a general rule, follow Toni's statement. Night is definitely when you should be dining out, and that means not before 8 P.M. Of course, many of the outdoor restaurants on this list are just as pleasing at lunchtime. Remember, too, that some of the top restaurants have special lunch menus at more affordable prices. You won't get the same choice, but the quality will be superb just the same and your outing will remain an unforgettable gastronomic experience.

Unless otherwise stated, prices are for an average meal exclusive of wine, since the sky may be the limit as far as wines go, alas. Prices of set menus are included whenever applicable.

Asian
30, avenue George V, 75008
Tel: 01 56 89 11 00
Web: www.asian.fr
Price: €55
Open daily

The song of birds welcomes you into an imaginary tropical forest. Slender, black-clad Asian beauties serve you throughout your meal. The red wooden boards throughout reflect the Vietnamese belief that red is the emblem of happiness—it is the color donned by every bride. Book a table in the bamboo garden—it's definitely the most romantic corner of the establishment. The food is a contemporary and refined mix of Vietnamese, Thai, Chinese, and Japanese.

Atelier Maître Albert
1, rue Maître Albert, 75005
Tel: 01 46 33 13 78
Price: à la carte €38; set menus €34, €45 (with wine and cheese)
Open Monday — Saturday

Tonight you are dining in the midst of history. Just to your south, at the end of rue du Maître Albert, is place Maubert, an open-air section of the University of Paris in the Middle Ages, where Maître Albert used to teach standing on a trestle table. Maître Albert, one of the great learned men of the Middle Ages, was also known as Albert le Grand.

Maubert may be a contraction of Maître Albert—unless it comes from Mauvais Albert (Bad Albert), whose favorite occupation was alchemy, which was forbidden by the church. Despite the name, I cannot guarantee that his *atelier* (workshop) stood on the site of tonight's restaurant, but you are certainly not far off, and definitely in the heart of the medieval university that grew out of Notre Dame. Take time to stroll the side streets after your meal—they are utterly romantic and blissfully uncrowded.

Stepping into the restaurant, you will be struck by the smell of fire and wood, and by the pleasing layout of the vast yet intimate premises. There are plenty of old beams in the ceiling, a great wall of stripped stones, lots of cushions, soft light, soft music, and, above all, a late 15th- or early 16th-century fireplace, perhaps the oldest in Paris. It is believed to have come from the castle of Guillaume Gouffier de Bonnivet, Francis I's admiral and closest friend.

Before you settle down, you may want to enjoy a drink at the bar, seated on the swings—the *patron* will be happy to tell you the story behind them.

I highly recommend the menu for its vast selection and excellent cooking. The *parmesane d'aubergines tomatées au basilic* (parmesan gratin of eggplant, tomato, and basil) and the *ravioles de champignons, velouté aux quatre épices* (mushroom ravioli with four-spice cream sauce) are exquisite appetizers. Follow with *filet de canette aux poires* (spit-roasted duck with pears) and a *poêlée de St-Jacques au jus de truffes* (scallops sautéed in truffle juice)—both were delicious. A red Sancerre from the Domaine de St–Pierre accompanied our meal pleasantly.

The desserts were hard to choose from: The *moelleux au chocolat, glace vanille* (hot chocolate cake with vanilla ice cream) melted harmoniously in my mouth, and the *soupe d'agrumes, sorbet citron* (orange and grapefruit soup with lemon sorbet), was the lightest and most pleasant way to finish off. Monsieur Guyard, the restaurant manager, modestly protested it to be "such a simple dessert to put together." It may be so, but we all know that the simplest things are often the hardest to come by.

Le Beauvilliers
52, rue Lamarck, 75018
Tel: 01 42 54 54 42
Price: €100
Open Monday evening—
Saturday; closed second
half of August

I've got news for you—the best of Montmartre is NOT around the Sacré Coeur and the place du Tertre. Take to your heels and make your way to the quiet rue Lamarck, where only locals and foreign connoisseurs convene. Le Beauvilliers is certainly one of the most romantic addresses on the hill, even more so if you reach it heading east on rue Caulaincourt, then up rue de l'Abbé Patureau to your right, a steep, leafy flight of steps, which is to Montmartre what a canal is to Venice, and equally romantic.

Once inside, you will find yourself in a medley of the Second Empire and the Belle Epoque. It's so well done, exquisitely patinaed and dripping with the finest of period china, silverware, and crystal, and an exuberance of tall bouquets of flowers, that you would never guess it all dates only from 1974. The lights in the three salons have been dimmed and evoke a boudoir: at any moment, you seem likely to cross paths with Cora Pearl, Caroline Otero, or another notorious courtesan, on the arm of some titled fool. Or, if you have been fortunate to come here on a warm night, you could settle on the terrace, a heavenly nest of foliage, lush ivy, and blooms of rhododendron and hydrangea in spring.

The cuisine is on par with the setting, as only befits a restaurant that honors Antoine Beauvilliers, the chef of Marie Antoinette and Louis XVI's brother, the Comte de Provence and future Louis XVIII. After the dismantling of the aristocracy during the French Revolution, Beauvilliers became the first restaurateur in Paris. Edouard Carlier, the proprietor and founder of Le Beauvilliers, perpetuates the tradition of high gastronomy and offers his guests a culinary experience worthy of those lavish days.

We started our meal with a *cul d'artichaut, rempli de tourteau*, artichoke stuffed with crab and tied together with an emulsion of mustard and herbs. It was exquisite, light and perfect for summer weather. This was followed by *ravioles de fromage pochées dans un consommé de volaille*, a gratin of cheese ravioli, poached in chicken consommé, with mushrooms and chives. We shared our two main courses, so as to have a taste of each: first we were served a poached monk fish, stuffed with mushrooms and accompanied by a delicious cream of *mousserons* (meadow mushroom) and a bit of zucchini, then *foie gras* fried in the pan, which came with figs cooked in a sunny Banyuls wine, and a compote of celery. This astonishing combination, if somewhat on the rich side, worked divinely. Though I must confess that I chose it partly because of its poetic name: Who can resist *foie gras* when it comes with figs *ivres de vin* (drunken from wine)? Afterwards, a refreshing assortment of berries was the most pleasing end to an exquisite meal.

Le Bristol (Hôtel Le Bristol)
112, rue du Faubourg St-Honoré, 75008
Tel: 01 53 43 43 00
Price: à la carte €120–140; set menus €57, €110
Open daily from October 1 to April 30
(Summer garden restaurant from May 1 to September 30)

After sitting in the hotel bar, looking out at the gardens and listening to the standards drifting over from the grand piano, we headed for what promised to be a gastronomic event, for Eric Frechon, the Bristol's renowned chef, had just been awarded a second Michelin star. (At the age of 37, this is quite an achievement.) Monsieur Jean-Paul Montellier, the restaurant director, stood smiling at the door, waiting to let us into what was once the private theater of Jules de Castellane's palatial mansion, perfectly oval in shape and entirely covered with warm red oak paneling. The restaurant sparkled with the glow of eight spectacular Baccarat chandeliers, echoed by crystal sconces dripping delicately down the walls. An exquisite ceiling, crisscrossed by ribs of gold leaves and enhanced by charming paintings, looked like the lid of a larger-than-life jewel box. I loved the perfect proportions and harmony of volume, just the right size to accommodate 130 guests at ideally spaced tables—no one can beat the French in the art of handling space. A gorgeous piece of 18th-century French tapestry hangs on one section of the wall, pointing subtly to the one-time stage.

Actually, the entire restaurant is a stage, animated by a precise ballet of waiters, some in tails, some in long white aprons, carrying to each table a succession of dishes in shining Limoges china and glittering Christofle silverware. And how satisfying to discover the wine being handled by expert female *sommelières*! This is quite a revolution in a male-dominated profession. And with its 1,000 vintages and 30,000 bottles, the Bristol's cellar is one of the largest in France.

After a splendid glass of Mumm de Cramant champagne, we ordered a golden Limoux Blanc, a pure Chardonnay from the "High Valleys," to accompany our heavenly appetizers—*oeuf en coque de pain brûlé, mouillettes d'aspèrge au beurre truffé, gros macaronis* (macaroni stuffed with truffles, artichokes and duck foie gras, gratinéed with parmesan cheese). I then opted for the sheer simplicity of a Breton lobster casserole—the aroma of the sea and of fennel that rose when the lid was lifted nearly made me swoon. It was all prepared in grand style before our eyes, and served with yet another of Frechon's concoctions: endive braised in orange with cilantro. My companion delighted in a *sole au jus de palourde*, cooked in peppered olive oil. A splendid white Bourgogne, a Guillot-Broux from the area of Macon, accompanied us. To finish: a *gratin d'agrumes au beurre d'amandes* (citrus gratin in almond butter), accompanied by a delicious grapefruit sorbet. Note, too, the *soufflé au Grand Marnier* with orange slices—one of the house classics. (Allow for twenty minutes' preparation.)

By the time we were ready to leave, all was quiet and we could hear once again the languorous notes of the grand piano.

La Closerie des Lilas
171, boulevard du Montparnasse, 75006
Tel: 01 40 51 34 50
Price: €77
Open daily

Although most people go to La Closerie des Lilas for its brasserie and its bar, its restaurant boasts, without any doubt, one of the most exquisite terraces in Paris. During the day, combine lunch with a stroll in the Luxembourg gardens. At night, when its bowers are dotted with shimmering lights, it looks utterly romantic. Nevertheless, there are no lilac trees here, and there never have been. The lilac was across the boulevard du Montparnasse, where the Bullier café now stands, but that's how myths go. On the other hand, the fact that La Closerie is the birthplace of the myth of Montparnasse is irrefutable. In 1905 André Salmon and Paul Fort sent out thousands (or hundreds... more plausibly) of invitations to the artist community, urging them to convene here and turn Montparnasse into the world's center of art. Before they knew it,

"everyone" showed up—Picasso, Modigliani, Fernand Léger, Alfred Jarry... Huge gatherings took place here every Friday, presided over by Paul Fort, the "Prince of Poets." On one occasion Alfred Jarry, trying his luck with a young lady, took out a pistol, pointed it at the mirror and pressed... Thereupon the playwright turned to the horrified lady and exclaimed, "Now that the mirror (pun on *glace*, which means both "mirror" and "ice") is broken, let us talk." Fashions have a brief life span in Paris, and by the time Hemingway made La Closerie his home in the 1920s, the fun had shifted to the Rotonde and the Dôme, one block further west.

Nostalgia is perpetuated nightly at the brasserie and bar with the help of its jazz pianist, but on this special night the above-mentioned terrace is your destination. I hope the weather is with you, but if not—there's a glass roof. Meals are only à la carte, but who can resist splurging in such delightful leafy surroundings and among fashionable Left Bank locals? Whether you opt for meat or fish, seafood or *foie gras*, everything is wonderfully fresh, perfectly cooked and beautifully presented. I highly recommend their *filet de boeuf au poivre* (steak in pepper sauce) or *quenelles de brochet* (pike dumpling). Chocolate *profiteroles* or a delicious *millefeuille* (puff pastry) will be a perfect end to your meal. After dinner, stroll to Carpeaux's stunning fountain depicting the four corners of the world. Head north toward the avenue de l'Observatoire; it's just a few steps away.

Coconnas
2bis, place des Vosges, 75004
Tel: 01 42 78 58 16
Price: à la carte €38; set menu €23

Open Tuesday—Sunday

Here, on Paris's oldest square, is one of the city's most beautiful outdoor-eating spots, especially after dark, when the deserted square is dotted with the soft magic of old streetlights. In spring or early summer, when the days extend into the evenings, the sunsets and the surrounding brick-and-stone houses take on a golden glow just as dinner begins. Last time we arrived at twilight and lingered into dusk over the house cocktail, a mix of *pousse rapière* wine from southwest France, champagne, and orange juice. The restaurant's nice for lunch, too, especially on a hot day when the shady arcade is a cool blessing. Note that the restaurant is open on Sunday, which is rarely the case. But avoid weekend lunchtime, when place des Vosges, and the Marais in general, overflow with day-trippers.

Book a table away from the street, preferably close to the restaurant windows. You will be sheltered from drafts and car fumes and also enjoy a pleasing view of the restaurant. In cold weather it is just as pleasant to sit indoors, and maybe even more romantic, especially at night, when the stripped brick and stone and rich, red curtains glow with the mellow lights of wrought-iron chandeliers. An engraving depicting the wedding of Louis XIII in 1612, on the occasion of the opening of the square, then place Royale, hangs on one of the walls (see page 40). The square was actually built under his father, Henri IV, who was assassinated in 1610 and never saw his masterpiece completed.

Henri IV is nonetheless celebrated here by way of one of Coconnas's specialties (à la carte only)—*la vraie poule au pot du bon roy Henri*—boiled stuffed chicken with stock and vegetables from Henri IV's native Béarn, in southwestern France. Apparently, the dish owes its name to the king's decree that all the famished subjects of his war-ridden kingdom be given chicken every Sunday. On my last visit here, however, I went for a wonderfully fresh cod, wedded to a subtle sauce with a touch of honey. It was delicious. It was a warm summer night, so I had started off with their *salade maraîchère*, which brought to the table wonderful garden freshness. My companion enjoyed his delicate asparagus soup just as much.

Queen Margot, Henri IV's priceless first wife, is also celebrated here—*les douceurs de la Reine Margot* heads the listings of the restaurant's sweets. We feasted on strawberry soup and a *moelleux au chocolat*, which we shared between us. It was hard to decide which to save for the last mouthful. The berries tasted and smelled as if they had just been hand picked outside the back door. They were superb with their accompanying mint sorbet, and with the chocolate cake too, for that matter. A good Chiroubles Beaujolais accompanied our meal. Service can be slow at times, but with a very satisfactory menu for as little as €23, one can't complain. Besides, you are here to relax and enjoy being surrounded by 400 years of history.

Le Coupe Chou
9, rue de Lanneau, 75005
Tel: 01 46 33 68 69
Price: à la carte €38; set menus €23, €31
Open daily

An ancient crooked house covered in greenery, leaning against a cobbled crooked street corner, makes for an exquisite picture of old Paris, as you approach it from place M. Berthelot. You are in the heart of the Latin Quarter. The Sorbonne is just behind you; on your right is the Collège de France, founded by King Francis I in order to break the monopoly of Latin and promote the French language and the humanities. The medieval city walls are a few steps away; beneath your feet lie remnants of the Roman city; all around you is a maze of narrow old streets that were home to shops and thriving colleges back in the Middle Ages.

They say that one of the shops belonged to a sinister barber, who mistook his clients' throats for their beards and then made off with their purses. The bodies were then carted to the butcher's across the street, where they were concocted into succulent meat pies. The scene of the crime was where you are dining tonight, and the weapon was a barber's blade razor, known as *coupe chou*.

Have no fear! No trace of this gory past remains on these quintessentially romantic premises, made up of dark, eclectic warrens of old stones and beams and occasionally some picturesque flights of steps. Mind your heads as you penetrate the dim nooks lit by candles and crackling open fires, each a different dining area: the barber's hall, the library, the winter garden. In summer you can also have your meal on the sidewalk, but what's the point? Le Coupe Chou calls for indoor dining. That's where you will find the magic

—and the 18th-century baroque music. Have your drinks in the cozy drawing room, where you may also retire for coffee after your meal. You can linger in these comfortable armchairs into the early hours of the morning.

The menu is rich in variety. On our last visit, my companion and I opted for their lightest dishes, starting with a *tartare aux legumes frais*, a prettily served fresh vegetable mix, heightened by a sprinkling of olive oil, followed by excellent haddock and salmon. We finished off with their traditional *millefeuille* (puff pastry), an excellent conclusion to an atmospheric evening.

Etchegorry
41, rue Croulebarbe 75013
Tel: 01 44 08 83 51
Price: à la carte €46; set menus €29, €36 (with a half bottle of wine)
Open Tuesday—Saturday

This delightful inn, which feels as if it's hidden blissfully somewhere beyond the confines of Paris, is in fact a mere few minutes' ride from the Latin Quarter, just behind the Gobelin workshops. The picturesque name of the street ("crumbling beard"), commemorates the Croulebarbe family, who owned extensive lands and a windmill here, at least as far back as 1214. In the 19th century, when this was Madame Grégoire's cabaret, the likes of Victor Hugo and Chateaubriand made it their Sunday destination. It was a place of merry making and songs washed down by wine, as confirmed by the famous *chansonnier*, Béranger.

The rustic two-story house still looks exactly as it did then, though it no longer looks out on the river Bièvre, but on a lovely garden, the square René-le-Gall, worthy of a stroll in its own right.

Today the place gets filled with a genuine French word-of-mouth clientele who know a good place for food and atmosphere. Monsieur Laborde's jovial southwestern lilt is another reassuring ingredient, not to mention the wonderful display of desserts, which will whet your appetite as soon as you step in. The downstairs is more bustling and atmospheric for a cozy winter dinner. In summer I would go for a table by one of the flowery windows upstairs, looking out on the garden. Make sure to reserve your table well in advance.

The establishment specializes in southwestern cuisine, among the best on the gastronomic map of France. It is traditional, rich, and served in lavish quantities, so don't order too much. Celebrate first with a *pousse rapière*, a divine combination of Armagnac liqueur and Blanc de Blanc, to be followed by an exquisite, mellow white Jurançon to go with your appetizers. The Etchegorry salad, with its subtle *foie gras* and succulent melon, is a light way to start, as this is going to be a big meal. A *piperade* is a typical Basque specialty of tomatoes, peppers, and eggs beaten into an omelette, but I would go for their *escalope de foie gras aux raisins*, served warm, which is simply divine. In winter, the *cassoulet aux haricots blancs tarbais* is a great heartwarming dish, prepared the way they do it in the Pyrénées town of Tarbes. The desserts are mouthwatering—great chocolate concoctions such as *l'assiette du chocolatier*, the *palets en chocolat à la nougatine glacée*, which come with fabulous Italian meringue, or *les truffes glacées au chocolat et le fondant au chocolat* (ice chocolate truffles with chocolate sauce). A traditional *pruneaux et poires braisés au Madiran*, prunes and pears braised in a heady Madeiran wine from the area of Pau, goes down very well in winter. If you wish for something lighter, I recommend the day's assortment of sorbets, a gentler conclusion to a copious meal.

La Fontaine de Mars
129, rue St-Dominique, 75007
Tel: 01 47 05 46 44
Price: €40–60
Open daily

An old neighborhood standard, located discreetly off the tourists' route, quite close to the Eiffel Tower, and very close to the celebrated market street of rue Cler. Dine downstairs on commendable fare in the cozy atmosphere of a genuine *bistrot*. In summer, enjoy a romantic dinner under the street's arcades, facing the picturesque Fontaine de Mars. Specialties from southwest France are included on the menu, and always worth a try. But what won me over on my last visit was their *pâté sur un lit de cresson* (pâté on a bed of cress), as beautiful as a flower and as subtle as the best of gourmet concoctions. It made my day.

Le Grand Véfour
17, rue de Beaujolais, 75001
Tel: 01 42 96 56 27
Price: à la carte €130; lunch menu €69
Open Monday — Friday lunch

I am at a loss to describe what's ahead of you. Le Grand Véfour is located in the resplendent Palais Royal, one of Paris's most romantic addresses, and the city's center of both culture and debauchery in the late 18th century (see page 53) when it opened. At the time it was known as Café de Chartres, after the landlord of the Palais Royal, Philippe d'Orléans, Duke of Chartres and cousin of Louis XVI (the name is still carved on the wall facing the gardens). Many famous Parisians have honored the restaurant since—Balzac, Colette, Jean Cocteau, as well as performers from the Callas to Madonna, and famous couples, including Josephine and Bonaparte, and more recently, Woody Allen and Soon-Yi—and now the privileged pair of you (make sure to reserve your table two to three months in advance).

The French go down on their knees when they are enthusiastic about a dish—*se mettent à genoux*, as the saying goes—a godly posture expressing both fervor and reverence. Sometimes the hands are brought together as if in prayer, to stress the point. There's no more fitting a spot for culinary worship than this intimate sanctuary. Fifty lucky diners eat amid the splendor of the painted ceiling, friezes, and wall panels, as they multiply infinitely in the glowing mirrors around. I love the voluptuous maidens on the wall panels, the enticing allegories of pastry and sorbets, wine and fowl, of forbidden fruit and beguiling music. For the best optical mirage ask to be seated at Madame Tallien's table in the mirror-filled, cozy Balzac suite. On winter nights, when each table is graced with its own glowing candlestick, the place becomes a magical forest of lights.

The service is about to commence. The officiating priests glide toward your table with two glasses of Tattinger champagne (Le Grand Véfour belongs to the Tattinger company, as do the Crillon Hotel and the Baccarat crystals). Allow your waiters to guide you through the bounties of France and the astounding talent of chef Guy Martin.

Every time I come here, Martin seems to have carried his art to new heights. His boundless imagination pours into his pots and pans before being turned out onto your plates as astonishing culinary paintings. His summer menu on our last visit was a celebration of the sunny season, basted in nature's palette of olive oil, wild thyme, coriander, and berries and accompanied by wonderful wines—a 1996 Pessac-Léognon château Olivier white wine to go with the fish, a 1997 Châteauneuf du Pape (château le Nerthe), accompanied our meat and a divine 1999 Muscat Beaumes de Venise, Domaine des Bernardins, watered our sweets. The turbot could not have been fresher, and was exquisitely enhanced by argan oil from Morocco and served with a heavenly slice of country bread loaded with fresh tomatoes and black olives. The tenderest lamb, basted in grape juice and mustard, was served with a ravishing concoction that turned out to be a combination of mashed garlic and chocolate-coffee truffle. This was truly the working of a wizard. After a round of the best of Savoie's cheeses we finished off with a delicious *millefeuille* of berries with a sorbet of wild thyme. Even more unexpected was the rhubarb that came with a sorbet of strawberries and olives and a touch of balsamic vinegar. How does Guy Martin come up with such mindboggling inventions?

Graziano
83, rue Lepic, 75018
Tel: 01 46 06 84 77
Price: à la carte €47;
set menu €21, €28;
lunch menu €12
Open daily

I recommend Graziano especially for lunch and for outdoor eating. This Italian restaurant is located in one of Montmartre's two surviving windmills—the Moulin du Radet (the more famous Moulin de la Galette is around the corner). Reserve your table in advance in the flowery back garden, where pressure-cooker Paris fades away. The best way to enjoy this outing is to treat it as a conclusion to your leisurely exploration of lesser-known Montmartre (see page 229). If you're blessed with good weather, resting your feet in this bucolic oasis, while washing down your meal with wine, might turn out to be one of the highlights of your trip.

Lapérouse
51, quai des Grands-Augustins, 75006
Tel: 01 43 26 68 04
Price: à la carte €95; set menu €85
Open Monday—Friday & Saturday evening

If there is one restaurant in Paris where Venus has set up her shrine, Lapérouse is unquestionably the one. It started in the 18th-century when the ground floor of this lovely townhouse, which overlooks the Seine and the Louvre, was converted into a jolly wine tavern catering to merchants from the nearby market. Before long they found the private rooms upstairs conducive to discreet transactions, away from the public eye. In the latter part of the 19th century, when a new breed of Parisiennes—courtesans, *demi-mondaines*, and *horizontales* of all sorts—blossomed in the new neighborhood around Parc Monceau, the private rooms of this remote restaurant proved even more conducive to rendezvous. (In fact, they say that a secret underground gallery linked the restaurant with the Senat, the French higher chamber, located in the Luxembourg Palace.) The restaurant's private rooms were turned into boudoir-lounges decorated with gorgeously carved wood paneling, dainty paintings, rich drapings, and glowing gilt-framed mirrors. When offered a diamond, the savvy courtesan would scratch her name on the mirror with it to ensure it wasn't fake. You can still see a sample of this venal love in the smallest of the lounges, now renamed La Belle Otero after the celebrated fiery courtesan who dined here many a time.

The intimate beauty of the place did not escape the literary set either—Victor Hugo, Guy de Maupassant, Alexandre Dumas, Emile Zola, George Sand, and Alfred de Musset enjoyed here the best gourmet cuisine, prepared by a string of renowned chefs, such as Auguste Escoffiers, "the king of cooks and the cook of kings," and Edouard Mignon, who also lavished his talent on the Tsar of Russia and the American President Wood-row Wilson. No wonder "Maison Lapérouse" was praised to the sky by "the prince of gastronomes," Curnonsky, the greatest food critic of his time. In 1933 the discerning, hedonistic, sensuous Colette spent many an hour in one of the ornate recesses of Lapérouse, writing her novel *The Cat*.

Today the chef of this celebrated house is the wonderful Alain Hacquard, who trained in some of the best establishments in Paris and will delight you with his quality, creative dishes and their beautiful presentation. The *saumon maziré au café et crème de pivèche*, an astonishing blend of salmon and coffee, will please your palate and set your appetite going. Imagine then a dish of mullet served with zucchini, accompanied by cardamom orange butter, or game in a sauce of green mango, or prawns fried in a vinaigrette made of mandarin oranges and radicchio. The desserts are just as inventive, such as *fondant au chocolat coeur d'orange coulis de persil*, the marriage of chocolate, orange, and parsley, or *bavarois à la poire, crème fouettée à l'églantine, fraises de bois de Malaga*, a combination of pear, Malaga wild strawberries, and whipped cream spiced in wild rose. This is the craftsmanship of a magician, enhanced by a choice list of wines that the wine waiter will be delighted to guide you through.

You will have but one dilemma: the choice of your table. The main dining room offers a magnificent nocturnal view of the Seine, the Louvre, the Pont Neuf, and the Pont des Arts. Make sure to reserve a table with a view. If you prefer absolute privacy—say, for a proposal—the Belle Otero lounge is the one for you. It has no windows, no "ears", no "eyes," just one table laid splendidly for a festive *tête-à-tête*, and a secret door, which came in handy in those licentious days gone by.

Note: Despite the display of a model of the 18th-century navigator's ship and the world map mural, the restaurant's connection to that Jules Lapérouse is pure fabrication. The Jules Lapérouse who took over the establishment back in 1840 was no relation whatsoever to the explorer.

Lasserre
17, avenue Franklin D. Roosevelt, 75008
Tel: 01 43 59 53 43 and 01 43 59 67 45
Price: à la carte €153; lunch menu €55; dinner menu €130
Open Tuesday—Saturday

> *On vient ici pour être heureux*
> You come here to be happy
> —Courtine (food critic)

I often walk past this elegant townhouse, which is discreetly set back from the tree-lined avenue and somehow conveys an air of self-confident refinement. But to cross its threshold—ah! From the palatial lobby, you are shown to a bejeweled little elevator, and then you ascend to a heavenly gastronomic experience under the Parisian sky. One of the highlights of Lasserre is its celebrated sliding roof that, weather permitting, opens to the heavens. When closed, the restaurant ceiling, covered with Touchague's beautiful paintings, remains an enchantment, and even then, the roof slides open every so often, so as to let out the smoke, adding a theatrical touch to this sumptuous stage, entirely crafted according to René Lasserre's instruction. Here the art of high gastronomy is acted out amid slender balustrades, rich drapings, and sparkling chandeliers. You will love the split-level floor and the low partitions, brimming with flowers, that break up the vast restaurant and make each table intimate. And what a table! Resplendent with shining silverware, including some authentic period pieces lovingly collected by Lasserre over the years, glittering crystal and lovely fresh flowers, it is a setting for a royal feast! So make sure to reserve your table upstairs.

After a glass of champagne to whet our appetites, we had an exquisite salad of fresh truffles, followed for my companion by a *pigeon André Malraux*, deliciously stuffed with mushrooms and dried fruit, a favorite of President de Gaulle's minister of culture, who dined here almost every day. I savored the *rosettes d'agneau aux senteurs d'hiver, mitonnée de petits oignons, figues et légumes oubliés*, an astonishing marriage of lamb and prickly pear, accompanied by baby onions. We finished off with exquisite chocolate *profiteroles* and a superb tangerine soufflé. Or try Lasserre's traditional *timbale elysée Lasserre*, vanilla ice cream with seasonal fruit, topped by whipped cream and caramelized sugar, served in a tulip-shaped biscuit.

Or the *crêpes au grand marnier*, a famous classic preceded by a ballet of flames as they are prepared before your very eyes.

A gentle piano, and an extraordinary red Château Canon, a 1976 St–Emilion accompanied us throughout the evening.

As we were about to leave, the charming Monsieur Louis, the stage director and master of ceremonies, handed me a miniature porcelain casserole with the bonus of a friendly smile, the parting gift offered to every woman who dines here. The tradition is so old that more than half a million of them have been scattered throughout the world by now, be it in the homes of anonymous one-timers, or those of Audrey Hepburn, Romy Schneider, or Paulette Godard.

The curtain fell. The little upholstered elevator dropped us to earth. We were helped into our coats and stepped out into the real world. Paris was deserted, the night was cold, but the glow of our evening kept us warm as we wandered the streets, utterly happy. Which is what Monsieur Lasserre, once a thirteen-year-old orphan from the Basque town of Bayonne, had always wanted for his patrons.

Laurent
41, avenue Gabriel, 75008
Tel: 01 42 25 00 39
Price: à la carte €150; lunch menu €65
Open Monday — Friday & Saturday evenings; closed holidays

This seductive peach-and-ivory pavilion that nestles among shady chestnut trees is one of the city's understated landmarks, the kind of place that shuns the limelight and instead prides itself on a clientele of faithful regulars. But with the French president and the British and American ambassadors residing across the street, the city boasts few more prestigious addresses. The Laurent is also a historical building, once part of the development plan of the Champs-Elysées as Paris's summer playground, initiated by Louis-Philippe and carried out by the celebrated Jacques-Ignace Hittorff, Paris's pet architect. Hittorf's impressive legacy also includes the palatial townhouses that girdle the Arc de Triomphe and the fountains of the place de la Concorde, and the charming fountain of the four seasons, which now stands outside the restaurant. The Laurent was first known as the Café du Cirque, after the Summer Circus, which no longer exists (now the site of the children's sandbox). It was later renamed after one of the establishment's proprietors. Besides the circus, there were once other glamorous establishments here—the Ambassadeurs, the Alcazar, gone with the glitter and music of the Belle Epoque—but the gardens are still lovely, especially in early summer, when the rhododendron is ablaze.

The pleasing peach-and-ivory color scheme prevails indoors, where everything feels airy, spacious, and reassuringly comfortable. The main dining area is delightfully round, with a charming hint of a garden rotunda, thanks to the slender pillars that frame each of its vast windows.

During the day they open up to the air and the garden's flowers. At night, a ribbon of lights encircles the restaurant, as the garden's lamps glow through the windows. A gorgeous flower arrangement cascades in the center of the room, and tiny bouquets of fresh flowers and lit candles stand on each table. It all looks utterly romantic and promises to be a great meal. But if you can save Laurent for warm weather, all the better. Eating outdoors, under the old leafy chestnut trees, beside the rushing water of Hittorf's fountain, is simply divine.

We came here for lunch recently, on a perfect early summer day, and were greeted to a glass of house champagne, a superb 1993 blanc de blanc. The Laurent takes pride in its 30,000 bottles, all personally chosen by the tireless Philippe Bourguignon, who runs the show in the restaurant impeccably, but is also, first and foremost, a wine expert. Frankly, I don't see how he finds the time for his perpetual treasure hunt throughout France. He has written a couple of books and gives talks on wine. Needless to say, you can trust him and his head wine waiter to help you along. They spoiled us with a 1999 Savigny Lapières, a young, fresh, fruity Bourgogne Pinot Noir that went well both with the warm weather and the wide variety of exquisite dishes, lovingly concocted by Philippe Braun, a disciple of the celebrated Joël Robuchon.

We started with what we believed was a pretty avocado mousse. When we dug into it, we were as incredulous as children to see a gorgeous red layer of sunny gazpacho mousse underneath. It was simply divine. My companion had a delicious tomato soup with basil. For our main dish we had *ravioli de veau mitonne aux artichauts croquants*, ravioli stuffed with veal and small onions in their caramelized juice, which gave the dish a subtle sweet touch. Brittany artichokes accompanied the dish beautifully. And I was altogether bowled over by the *pommes soufflées*, which were as light as feathers and looked like delicate paper lanterns. I was told they have a full-time cook just for them—talk of religious devotion!

I heroically resisted the assortment of chocolate treats and only had a taste from my companion's dish, but my dessert was more original and certainly more suited for the weather anyway: *fraises compotées, sorbet de fromage blanc acidulé*. Besides the fact that a sorbet made of white cheese was something totally new to me, and was honestly fantastic, the unexpected warmth of the slightly cooked strawberries turned the combination into a marriage made in heaven. Need I say more? Yes: the place remains happy and relaxed, despite its high rank; the staff is adorable; the set menu is served even at night. For such food and such a setting, this is an incredible deal.

Lena et Mimile
32, rue Tournefort, 75005
Tel: 01 47 07 72 47
Price: set menu €30 (with wine)
Open Monday evening—Friday

There are plenty of cheap good places in Paris for a hearty French meal, if you know where to look, but ones with romantic atmosphere are harder to come by. The outdoor terrace of Lena et Mimile is a delightful exception. On a warm summer night, few locations in Paris correspond better to my nostalgic, postcard vision of old Paris. And you can eat for as little as €30, including wine.

I like to come here by way of rue Mouffetard and then left under the archway of rue Jean Calvin. The sight of the restaurant terrace perched at the top of a flight of steps, above the streaming water of a street fountain, always makes me happily anticipate my meal. Order a table on the terrace's edge so you can watch the village scene unfolding in the tiny square below—the odd stroller stopping to rest on one of the green benches, the inevitable pair of interlaced lovers on another bench, two neighbors engaged in a chat while out dog-walking, a skipping little girl followed by her mother. It's as though you've walked into the opening scene of Erik Satie's *Parade*.

The food is just as pleasing. In keeping with the warm night, we shared between us a terrine of eggplant and a terrine of *chèvre* (goat cheese), both of which were exquisitely refreshing. The *petits ravioles au Pistou* brought all the aroma of Provence to my plate, while my partner's *mousse de brochet* (pike) was just as evocative of the south. Everything was in perfect harmony: the food, the wine, the temperature of the night. After agonizing over the desserts, I yielded to an exquisite *charlotte aux framboises*, but I am definitely going for the *poire au vin glacé à la cannelle* (pear with iced tea and cinnamon) next time around. If you want something more aphrodisiac, order their homemade chocolate mousse. I had it on another occasion and it was delicious.

Al Mounia
16, rue du Magdebourg, 75016
Tel: 01 47 27 57 28
Price: €31
Open daily (but check Sundays—it may not be open)

The door is discreet and dimly lit, on a quiet street between the Champs-Elysées and the Trocadéro. An elegant private club? No: The door opens and you are transported across the Mediterranean to some Moroccan palace. Magnificent wood carvings by Moroccan craftsmen surround you, as you settle into soft cushions at a low round copper table. Arabic music drifts by.

Monsieur and Madame Cherif, the owners of Al Mounia, are from Tunisia and Morocco respectively, and offer you dishes from both countries.

As an appetizer, try their delicious pastilla, a Moroccan pastry stuffed with chicken, crushed almonds, and cinnamon, and spiced with saffron. Or perhaps their *brique à l'oeuf*, a Tunisian pastry mixed with an egg. A refreshing Moroccan salad would be a good idea before a heaping pile of couscous, the backbone of North African fare that has deservedly gained the status of a French national dish. Or go for their celebrated tajine of choice lamb simmering in an earthenware dish, accompanied by an exquisite blend of prunes and almonds, olives and lemons, onions and grapes....sheer delight. If at the end, you don't have room for their delicious pastries, try the refreshing orange salad with its touch of orange blossoms (*fleur d'orangers*).

Le Paprika
28, avenue de Turenne, 75009
Tel: 01 44 63 02 91
Price: à la carte €38–46, (with wine); set menus €20, €23, €27, €38
Open Monday lunch, Tuesday—Saturday; closed August

The address in itself attracted my attention, for this is one of my favorite arrondissements. Somehow it has managed to travel through the modern age unspoiled, carrying with it more artistic memories and cultural heritage than any other. This is 19th-century Paris par excellence, blessedly overlooked by tourists, and, more surprisingly, even by most Parisians.

It was pouring when we arrived, and we wondered if we should have stayed home. But as soon as the door opened, and we heard the passionate glissandos of the violin, we knew we were in for a cozy treat. Here timeless Budapest meets timeless Paris. Madame Rollet is in the kitchen, concocting savory Hungarian dishes—stuffed cabbage, *hortobágyi palacsinta*, crêpes stuffed with chopped paprika veal and cream sauce, a delicious goulash, or a heavenly *píritott libamáj*, a *foie gras* steak served with noodles.

Monsieur Rollet is in the dining area, taking care of all the details, which, naturally, include the wine. Ours was an excellent Hungarian Tokaji, amazingly reasonably priced, as was the food. And all the while, the superb violinist held his audience captive. Ask to be seated in the back room, where you get a full view of him and his two fellow musicians at the cybalum and the bass.

This was one of the happiest nights I have enjoyed in a Parisian restaurant. Forget about being uptight here. Just loosen up and allow your Central European soul to overflow as you finish the evening with a copious helping of apple strudel and a glass of *barack pálinka* (apricot brandy).

Le Pavillon Puebla
Parc des Buttes Chaumont, 75019
(At the corner of rue de Botzaris/avenue Simon Bolivar)
Tel: 01 42 08 92 62
Price: à la carte €50–65; set menus €29, €39

Open Tuesday—Saturday; closed 3 weeks in August and 1 in winter
Tucked in an oasis of greenery inside Paris's most romantic park, Le Pavillon Puebla is among my favorites for outdoor eating. True, it is far from the center of the city, but leaving the hustle and bustle is worth the Métro ride, which is surprisingly shorter than it may seem. Besides, the Buttes Chaumont and the countrified network of streets next to it are so enchanting, that I have recommended them for one of the walks in Chapter 7 (see page 225).

Chef Christian Vergès is a big, charismatic guy with the sunny disposition and the lilting accent of his native southern France. We were out under the trees of the garden terrace, lazily sipping kir before our appetizers, when he came up to our table in his white cooking gear and greeted us with a warm handshake. He had great suggestions for our lunch, which he interspersed with spicy and culinary anecdotes from his childhood in the Roussillon, where Spain is just around the corner. His grandmother was actually Spanish—hence the name of the restaurant and the predominance of Catalan dishes on the menu.

Following Vergès's advice, we tasted several of these specialties, which he has recreated with great flair. The *anchoide*, a blend of candied pepper, green sauce, and olives, was followed by *boutifand*, grilled black pudding served on a chestnut pancake. For our main course we tried two specialties—a duck with figs and spices, which came in a heavenly sauce that made you want to wipe your plate clean, and a rabbit accompanied by a *gratin à l'ailloli*, a delicious garlic-based mayonnaise. Christian still recalls his grandmother's *ailloli*, which she used to spread on a slice of bread for his afternoon snack. This she alternated with olive oil, and every third day with red wine and sugar, which left him somewhat tipsy.

To finish off we had poached apricots with caramel, accompanied by a pistachio ice cream, an earthy dessert that beautifully tied the meal together. So did the 1999 Côte du Roussillon that saw us through the entire adventure, a happy, unfussy red wine, suitably light for lunch. On our way out, we peeped into the indoor restaurant. It was totally deserted, as everyone was sitting outside, enjoying the nice weather. But the recorded jazz music was on, and I pictured it on a winter night, with its old-fashioned cozy interior of gray-blue velvet upholstery and draperies and cut-glass chandeliers. It must be a wonderful place for a candlelit dinner.

Le Pré Catelan
Bois de Boulogne, Route de Suresnes, 75016
Tel: 01 44 14 41 14
Price: à la carte €120–150; set menus €75, €105
Open Tuesday—Saturday, Sunday brunch; closed February school holidays

Ideally you would come here in dashing horse and carriage, like Maurice Chevalier or Louis Jourdan in their white morning gear in Vincente Minnelli's *Gigi*. The golden age of gracious living is gone, for sure, and the shadow of Marcel Proust has long forsaken the place, but even though you might have to content yourself with an ordinary cab ride to get here, the Pré Catelan remains a splendid spot in the Bois de Boulogne, and also one of the city's finest restaurants.

I can think of few more pleasing outings than coming here for lunch on a beautiful summer day. I was lucky the last time I came here, for it was one of those spectacular days when everything seems just perfect, the crystal clear light, the pleasant temperature, a happy mood of anticipation to match my growing appetite. I had to hold my breath as the cab drove deeper and deeper into the woods. As we pulled up to the opulent turn-of-the-century pavilion that houses the restaurant, the sun poured on the emerald lawn, the roses, and the lavender.

Nobody was sitting indoors, but I made a mental note of it for a future winter night. I can imagine dining there, close to the crackling fire, surrounded by designer Caran d'Ache's cherubs carved in the walls. An outdated chandelier hangs from the ceiling, the tables are candlelit, and Beethoven and Schubert play in the background.

After a glass of exquisite Chardonnay Cramant champagne sipped in the almond green conservatory, we retired to a shaded nook in the garden, where our table was laid with gorgeous Bernardaud porcelain, specially designed for the restaurant. The tables are well spaced to ensure privacy; inevitably, your neighbors' conversation will be drowned out by the birds.

Relaxed and happy, we gave ourselves over to the stupendous talent of chef Frédéric Anton, as one by one his delicacies alighted on our table, sweeping us into a head-spinning round of gourmet pleasures with the help of Marsannay 1998 red wine from the domain of Charlopin. With each dish came a new surprise, astonishing to both palate and eye. Everything was subtle and dainty, made with the craftsmanship of a goldsmith. Every so often the breadbasket, with one of the most festive assortments I'd ever seen, was brought over. If you yield to the walnut bread, you'll be done for... let this be a warning!

Our feast began with a dish of *étrille*, a small crab that came with an exquisite crab mousse, followed by a *carotte confite*, magnificently wedded to gingerbread caramel. Our next treat was an astonishing dish of clams, gratinéd in Sarrasin butter and green peas that had been stewed with black truffles. This was followed by simply miraculous frog legs fried in a blend of crushed nuts, stewed shallots, and cider juice. Our main fish dish was monk fish, served with a subtle anchovy marmalade and asparagus grilled in thyme and lemon juice. Finally we tackled some prawn ravioli in olive oil before enjoying a much-needed pause.

The last act consisted of two overwhelming sweets. First came a rhubarb marmalade covered by a magically ethereal vanilla concoction called Zéphyr, which says it all. Then, in keeping with the sylvan surroundings, we concluded with a dish of wild strawberries dipped in delectably chilled yogurt, enhanced by an aroma of mint. It came in a shell made of Lenôtre's famous chocolate.

Perhaps the most praiseworthy aspect of the meal is the fact that when we drove back to Paris through the Bois de Boulogne, we felt as light as a feather.

Relais Louis XIII
8, rue des Grands Augustins, 75006
Tel: 01 43 26 75 96
Price: à la carte €110; lunch menu €37; set menu €58;
Saturday night menu €89
Open Tuesday—Saturday; closed August
What can be more pleasurable than a gourmet meal in a beautiful place with an interested history? Manuel Martinez, one of the city's up-and-coming chefs, was awarded a second Michelin star in 2001. He arrived here in 1996 from the celebrated Tour d'Argent, which is itself no small feat.

The morning we were to move, Pablo was in a bad mood. "I don't know why I should go through with this," he said. "If I had had to move every time women started fighting over me, I wouldn't have had time for much else in my life." I told him I had no interest in fighting with anybody over him. "Maybe you should have," he said. "I generally find that amusing. I remember one day while I was painting Guernica in the big studio in the rue des Grands-Augustins, Dora Maar was with me. Marie-Thérèse dropped in and when she found Dora there, she grew angry and said to her, 'I have a child by this man. It's my place to be here with him. You can leave right now.' Dora said, 'I have as much reason as you have to be here. I haven't borne him a child but I don't see what difference that makes.' I kept on painting and they kept on arguing. Finally Marie-Thérèse turned to me and said, 'Make up your mind. Which one of us goes?' It was a hard decision to make. I liked them both, for different reasons: Marie-Thérèse because she was sweet and gentle and did whatever I wanted her to, and Dora because she was intelligent. I decided I had no interest in making a decision. I was satisfied with things as they were. I told them they'd have to fight it out themselves. So they began to wrestle. It's one of my choicest memories."

—Françoise Gilot, from *Life with Picasso*

The establishment commemorates Louis XIII, the son of Henri IV, who was proclaimed king on this site, which was then the famous Augustine monastery, on the night of his father's assassination, May 10, 1610. Not that the Augustines had any reason to feel good about Henri IV, who had confiscated some of their land in order to open the parallel rue Dauphine, to the west. The poor monks' protestations were spurned energetically, with the king arguing that a much greater profit would be generated by urban development than by the growing of cabbage. The monastery disappeared with the Revolution, and nothing much of interest occurred here until the 1930s, when a basic restaurant, Le Catalan, stood on this site and nourished the artistic community of Paris, notably Picasso, whose studio was located across the street.

Much of the original monastery has survived—the stonework, the vaulted cellars, the gorgeous oak beams. We loved the downstairs best—it is spacious and elegant, yet nonetheless atmospheric and warm, glowing with flickering candle flames on each table. You can entrust yourself entirely to the recommendations of the staff, but we surrendered to the pleasure of their lobster ravioli, one of the chef's prize dishes. So is their Challandais duckling, roasted in honey and Indonesian pepper. For dessert, their vanilla *millefeuille* (puff pastry) is as good as it gets, while their chocolate *gourmandise* will altogether send you to higher spheres.

La Rose de France
24, place Dauphine, 75001
Tel: 01 43 54 10 12
Price: à la carte €30–38; set menu €24; lunch menu €21
Open daily; closed 3 weeks in August
Nestling in the tree-filled, bejeweled place Dauphine (see page 210), this is one of Paris's best-kept secrets, even though it is right at its heart, on the western tip of Ile de la Cité. Here silence prevails, traffic is restricted to the odd stroller, while cars are altogether out of bounds, thanks to Toni, the old proprietor of La Rose de France, who chaired the association of the place Dauphine and got rid of the clutter after twenty years of fierce battle.

The triangular place is all yours tonight, as you are dining outdoors, although I always loved coming here in winter, when Toni would greet me in his cozy, cheerful little nest and spice the evening with his colorful, humorous comments and good-natured personality.

Toni is a man of all trades—chef, host, *sommelier*, and entertainer all in one—and he lavished on his customers his good-humored and genuinely French disposition. He always served exemplary seafood from his native Brittany and succulent desserts. The place has just been taken over by Gilles Lecros, who has promised me nothing will change. I am keeping my fingers crossed...

Le Toupary
2, quai du Louvre, 75002
Tel: 01 40 41 29 29
Price: à la carte €70; set menu €35; lunch menu €12, €18, €25
Open Monday—Saturday

It feels unreal to walk through a department store after closing hours and be welcomed by a smiling hostess who seems to have been waiting there all evening for you and no one else. An equally welcoming staff waits for you at the top floor as the elevator opens. Quiet jazz plays as you are shown to a table across the dim, carpeted restaurant. You are now seated at the front window, which you have carefully booked well ahead of time, and before your astounded eyes is the most glorious, panoramic view of Paris imaginable, glowing like an open scroll against the darkening sky.

We dined on their set menu, which is reasonably priced, and quite good. It was scallop season and their scallops were very good. The soup, *langoustines creme de cresson des fontaines* (cream soup of prawns and watercress) was fantastic, as was the chocolate soufflé. A great white Sancerre wine accompanied our meal. To have the most sparkling view of Paris as a setting for your dinner, at this price, is the best value for money I can think of in the City of Light.

La Tour d'Argent
15-17, quai de la Tournelle, 75005
Tel: 01 43 54 23 31
Price: à la carte €167; lunch menu €60
Open Tuesday—Saturday

> You come to La Tour d'Argent to dine.
> Having arrived, you gaze.
> —Sacha Guitry

Even the threshold of La Tour d'Argent is a feast for the eyes. There's the gorgeous 17th-century wrought-iron gate that originally belonged to the Duchess of Uzès. The six splendid lanterns that illumine the façade. The silver lettering of the legendary restaurant. The true vocation of Claude Terrail, the landlord of the place, has always been the theater, and his mentor and source of inspiration is the actor, director, and writer Sacha Guitry. Inside, gilded angels, warm wood paneling, an old French Savonnerie tapestry, paintings of old Paris, old mirrors and silk draperies welcome you to the grand salon, where an atmosphere at once theatrical and intimate prevails. Alas, you won't have much time to linger here before you are ushered to the elevator and whisked to the sixth floor—seventh heaven.

The first time I walked into the restaurant, I couldn't help but gasp at the view—the back of Notre Dame hugged by the two arms of the Seine. (Note that tables with river views are difficult to come by—make your reservation very early). We raised a toast of sparkling house champagne. With the islands of Paris at our feet, this was a perfect prologue to a theatrical, gastronomic experience, which is as the theatrical Terrail wishes it.

There was no such view in 1582, when the first restaurant opened here, an inn on ground floor. Henri III came here one day and was amazed by the strange utensils some diners were using rather than their fingers—forks, recently introduced from Venice. The fascinated king kept coming back, and the inn became fashionable. Later Henri IV, the Duc de Richelieu, and many others would call it home. The celebrated *épistolère* Madame de Sévigné would come here to savor her beloved hot chocolate.

The house was demolished during the Revolution, but a new era of glory began during the Second Empire, when Musset, Sand, Dumas, Balzac, and Offenbach flocked to the new Haussmannian building. The illustrious chef Frédéric became the landlord of the place, introducing in 1890 the celebrated *canard au sang*, which the famous Brillat-Savarin described as "a new dish that does more for man's happiness than the discovery of a new star." Duck became La Tour d'Argent's specialty, and every duck served here has been numbered ever since. When Frédéric died in 1916, La Tour d'Argent was taken over by André Terrail, Claude's father, who came here from the celebrated Café Anglais, the city's gastronomic glory in the 19th century that was swept away in the wake of post-Haussmann demolitions. In his early years, André had served there, among others, the future Edward VII. Later he married the proprietor's daughter, Augusta, which explains why a little museum containing cherished memorabilia from the Café Anglais has been set up by Claude Terrail here.

Claude Terrail took over in 1947. The war was over and the world's celebrities streamed in once more—showbiz personalities, politicians, crowned heads and lovers, not the least on the list, the newly wed Princess Elizabeth and Prince Philip of England, who enjoyed the restaurant's 185,937th duck, on May 16, 1948. The chair in which Edward VII had sat at the Café Anglais and the bowl of George V were brought up from the "museum" for the occasion. By the time Humphrey Bogart and Lauren Bacall dined here, the number of ducks had risen to 280,101.

Our own duck on our recent visit was number 944,740. It was *à l'orange*, a classic that has always been my favorite. It was preceded by an astonishing appetizer, a puff pastry with an egg preparation tucked under a mantle of *foie gras* and truffle. To finish, the refreshing strawberry *millefeuille* was an obvious choice on that warm summer night. Of course, La Tour d'Argent's wine cellar is as legendary as the restaurant. We chose a 1991 Morey-St-Denis, "Premier Cru Les Sorbets," a red Bourgogne worthy of the occasion.

Right: Au Vieux Paris

Le Train Bleu
La Gare de Lyon
12, place Louis-Armand, 75012
Tel: 01 43 43 09 06
Price: à la carte €50; set menu €40
Open daily

This place is an homage to the railway's golden age, when the Blue Train chugged you down to the French Riviera. Inaugurated on December 8, 1922, it was all luxury and mahogany paneling and carried among its passengers the Windsor couple, Brigitte Bardot, Walt Disney and all the stars of the silver screen until the 1960s. There were other tantalizing destinations down south—the Alps, Italy, and further still lay exotic North Africa, beyond the Mediterranean shores. These are displayed in spectacular murals on the walls and ceilings of this gigantic dining hall, framed by dazzling period gildings, in particular in the Golden Hall, where I recommend you dine. This is a bustling, busy place, known to both locals and tourists, but your privacy is entirely preserved by the spacing of the tables. There are many good dishes and drinks and your waiter will be delighted to help. A superb *crème brûlée* and an unrivalled *crêpe suzette* were the happy conclusion to our last meal.

Au Vieux Paris
24, rue Chanoinesse, 75004
Tel: 01 40 46 06 81
Price: dinner menu (with house wine) €50; special menu saveurs d'Odette €50; lunch menu (with house wine) €30; average price of wine €20; excellent regional house wine €10
Closed Sundays in August

Tonight you are headed for Ile de la Cité, where it all began. The ghosts of Héloïse and Abélard linger around the corner and the ringing bells of Notre Dame conjure up visions of a pining Quasimodo and a wild Esmeralda. This is Paris at its most romantic, the one Victor Hugo flamboyantly embroidered. Be thankful that historical events put an end to Baron Haussmann's career before he had time to wipe out the last remaining old streets north of Notre Dame, a deserted haven where silence prevails. Au Vieux Paris is located in one of the island's two oldest houses, dated the early 16th century. The millions of tourists who cram into the cathedral square and gardens every year rarely venture here; those who do, have heard of it by word of mouth.

The enchantment starts outside, at the sight of the venerable, rustic house, framed by flowers and drowning in greenery. If you visit in the spring, the purple blossoms of the blooming wisteria drape down the wall. But you may find it even more special in winter, when after dark the old, silent stones shimmer in soft light.

Inside it feels deliciously snug, with all those glowing lights and the gleaming dark wood of the bare tables. The upstairs, all draped in crimson, feels like the private dining hall of a manor house. Book Table 106 to have the belltowers of Notre Dame perfectly centered in your window.

And now, *passons aux choses sérieuses*—let us proceed to serious matters, as the French say when referring to the business of food.

Your hosts are a charming couple from the Aveyron, a glorious, unspoiled area in the southwest of the Massif Central, an area still dotted with medieval castles and bathing in sunshine and hospitality. The lord of the manor, Georges de la Rochebrochart, is in the dining area, where he and the other staff will make you feel at home right away, inviting you to climb down to the "family" cellar and pick your own wine, the way it's done at home. Don't feel intimidated, as they will help if you are at a loss.

Odette is in the kitchen, which means—alas!—you will be deprived of her smile and delightful accent. Her lovingly prepared savories will make up for it, though. She uses the best produce, picked directly from friends' farms back home. If you are adventurous and want to discover new regional specialties, go for her *saveurs d'Odette*, which will enable you to sample a bit of everything in smaller quantities.

We first had a kir of champagne and wild berries, which came with a wonderful pancake, made of seven different green vegetables and as light as a feather. Only severe self-discipline made me hold back, in view of what was yet to come. Next, I had a lamb-lettuce salad, layered with *carpaccio de foie gras*, and prettily decorated with red pepper. My partner started with a tomato soup with basil and claimed enthusiastically it was the best imaginable. A *coufidou* followed, an Aveyronnaise version of *boeuf bourguignon*, which gets macerated in Marcillarc red wine for eight days before being cooked on a low flame for an entire day. The cow comes directly from a farm in Aubrac and the meat melted in our mouths. If you prefer fish, their scallops (not available in summer) are stuffed in all simplicity with parsley and garlic and are deliciously fresh. They also serve two different fish daily, in white Chablis. The sweets were on a par with the rest—Odette's *crème brûlée* delights as soon as your spoon slides into it for your first mouthful. The warm chocolate cake is just as tantalizingly good: It is doused in a Brillet Poire William, a blend of pear and cognac that dates back to the 17th century.

But if you can't make up your mind, which is always my dilemma, go for the *farandole*, an assortment of four different desserts. Mine consisted of fresh fruit salad, cream cheese with berry jam, an apple tart, and a warm chocolate dessert, nothing fancy but all homemade by the expert Odette. She couldn't have made me happier.

As soon as I got home I phoned several of my friends to tell them to rush to Au Vieux Paris and within a week I was back with a new set of visitors.

TEA FOR TWO, OR SALONS DE THÉ

The Paris institution of the *salon de thé* goes back to the 19th century, when it focused on tea and dainty pastry and catered mostly to genteel women. Today men come here in greater numbers (though usually with their women companions), to escape the more noisy and smoky atmosphere of Parisian bistros and cafés. Besides the traditional pot of tea and pastry, you may enjoy light meals and wine, usually of good quality and at reasonable prices. Most close at 7 P.M. See also Chapter 6 on museums for mention of lovely museum gardens where you can have afternoon tea as well, such as the Jacquemart-André Museum, the Rodin Museum, and the Musée de la Vie Romantique.

Dalloyau
2, place Edmond-Rostand, 75006
Tel: 01 43 29 31 10
Open Monday — Friday 8:30 a.m. to 7 p.m.; Saturday & Sunday brunch from 8:30 a.m. to 1 p.m.
The pastry and ice cream of Dalloyau are top of the scale, and the location of their *salon de thé* opposite the Luxembourg Gardens is among my favorites. In cold weather it is just as pleasing to sit upstairs by the window looking out on the gardens and the lovely fountain of place Edmond Rostand. (See also page 146.)

Les Deux Abeilles
189, rue de l'Université, 75007
Tel: 01 45 55 64 04

Open Monday—Saturday 9 a.m. to 7 p.m.; closed 3 weeks in August

If you happen to be passing through this part of the city, a short walk from the Eiffel Tower, this neighborhood place is worth your attention. It is run by two charming hostesses, mother and daughter, who hover busily as bees (hence *abeilles*) around the kitchen and three-room restaurant. The place has a lovely patina, with old-fashioned rose wallpaper, art deco lights, and a 16th-century dresser that combine to create the feel of a provincial French home.

I very much enjoyed the southern touch of the menu, notably the tomato and thyme tart, the chive flan with tomato *coulis*, and various eggplant dishes. The chestnut and chocolate pudding was to die for, but my favorite dessert was the red fruit crumble, made jointly by mother and daughter. It was slightly tart, as it should be, and the dough just crumbled at the touch. A nourishing meal with wine (red Chinon or Bordeaux, or white Chardonnay) and coffee at the price of €17.50 is unquestionably a good deal and accounts for all the regulars—who are always the best guarantee of a place's worth.

If you come for breakfast, you will get English scones (mother's specialty), soft-boiled eggs or omelettes, and delicious cinnamon toast. Try also the house special, stewed apples and pears, sprinkled with orange-flower water and cinnamon, either as a dessert or as part of your breakfast. Forget about your diet for once and have it with white cream cheese. Truly divine.

In the afternoon you might try the geisha tea, heightened by a flavor of orange flower, or the *douchka*, which in spite of its Russian name is a blend of Chinese and Indian leaves. La vie en rose commemorates Edith Piaf's most famous love song and is therefore suitable for the occasion too. On a cold winter day indulge in their hot chocolate with whipped cream; in summer settle outside and order their apple and blackcurrant juice.

A small selection of regional honey, jam, and tea can be bought on your way out. They come from the Cevennes, the wild, awesome mountains north of Provence, where the Protestant Huguenots once found refuge and where you might consider traveling on your next trip to France.

Fauchon
26, place de la Madeleine, 75008
Tel: 01 47 42 90 10

Open Monday—Saturday 8:30 a.m. to 7 p.m.

Although Fauchon was one of the first to set up a *salon de thé* in Paris, over a hundred years ago, the recently opened premises have kept none of the old dust. They are elegant, discreet, fresh, peaceful, and unassuming, traditional yet modern in spirit and taste. Here is an ideal place to rest if you've been on your feet all day long, scouring this exhausting shopping area.

You can come here for breakfast, coffee break, a light three-course lunch, or tea. At all times of day, the staff is very friendly and efficient. And whatever you order, you are sure to enjoy—this is, after all, France's "temple" of gastronomy. (See also page 146.)

If you are having tea, try their teacakes. They are astonishing.

Le Franc Pinot
1, quai de Bourbon, 75001
Tel: 01 46 33 60 64
Open only for Sunday brunch 11:30 a.m. to 4 p.m.

This is in fact is not a *salon de thé* at all but a small jazz club (see page 000), on the wonderful Ile St-Louis. But on Sundays, the jazz accompanies a gargantuan brunch for as little as €17. There are only 20 seats, so a reservation is recommended.

L'Heure Gourmande
Passage Dauphine, 27, rue Mazarine, 75006
Also at 22, rue Dauphine, 75006
Tel: 01 46 34 00 40
Open Monday—Saturday 12 to 7 p.m. (9 p.m. in summer),
Sunday 1 to 7 p.m.; French songs on first Sunday of every month,
from 5 to 7 p.m.

A charming, cobbled nook hidden between the Latin Quarter and St-Germain—cozy indoors in winter; delightfully cool on the cobbled alleyway in summer. On the first Sunday afternoon of each month, you can enjoy French songs accompanied by a guitar. On all other occasions, you will enjoy substantial portions of great food at very reasonable prices.

Ladurée
16, rue Royale, 750008
Tel: 01 42 60 21 79
Open Monday—Saturday 8:30 a.m. to 7 p.m., Sunday 10 a.m. to 7 p.m.
Also at 75, avenue des Champs-Elysées, 75008
Tel: 01 40 75 08 75
Open daily 7:30 a.m. to 1 a.m.

The oldest teahouse in Paris started out as a *boulangerie*, opened by Louis Ernest Ladurée in 1862. After a ravaging fire in 1871, he turned it into a *patisserie*. It was his wife, Jeanne Suchard, who had the idea of adding a *salon de thé*, a more suitable establishment for decent women than the disreputable cafés. This was back in the glorious days of the Belle Epoque, when the surrounding area was becoming the ultimate chic. Ladurée chose no less an artist than the celebrated Chéret to decorate the premises with a stream of rosy, chubby angels,

including the Angel of Pastry, who floats in an azure sky above your head. Today the place is a victim of its own popularity. Avoid the crowds by coming off peak, because their savories are definitely worth the trip, if the place is reasonably quiet. Taste their dainty cucumber sandwiches, their caramel macaroons, or their frosted cream puffs.

The recently opened place on the Champs-Elysées is among Paris's "in" places. It is huge, plush, overly done up, and crowded. Not exactly my idea of romance, except perhaps for an early breakfast, the best time of day to enjoy the Champs-Elysées.

Le Loir dans la Théière
3, rue des Rosiers, 75004
Tel: 01 42 72 90 61
Open daily 11 a.m. to 7 p.m.

Although I love all the teahouses on this list, this one is where I always end up—this major landmark of the Marais is simply the place where I feel best. The name means "the dormouse and the teapot," which, as you will see painted on one of the walls, is an *Alice in Wonderland* reference. The jumble of heartwarmingly quaint, even rickety, furniture—old chairs and leather armchairs, tables of various sizes, shapes, and heights—seems to have been bought over the years at different secondhand sales. The walls are covered with old posters from exhibitions and theater performances, which bring alive the city's cultural past. Those events must have been attended once by the same breed of Parisians as those who now come to this place: cultured Parisians, but the pleasant, unaffected type. The waiters are charming, although they tend to forget about you toward the end of the meal. But if you are busy enjoying yourselves, you can forget that they have forgotten you. You may be asked to share your table with others, but it really doesn't matter—everyone is so relaxed and informal. The food is excellent and the prices very reasonable. On our last visit I had a copious dish of Mediterranean vegetables, nice wine, a delicious pastry, and coffee for just €15.

No reservations are accepted, so avoid peak hours (before noon or after 2:30 P.M.) Sunday lunch can be packed, except when the weather is nice and Parisians migrate to the sun.

Mariage Frères
30, rue du Bourg-Tibourg, 75004
Tel: 01 42 72 28 11
Open daily 12 to 7 p.m.
Located on the premises of the famous and oldest teashop in Paris (see page 149), you can enjoy here an elegant light meal of excellent quality. You will have to put up with long queues, though—the place is very popular at most times of day.

La Pagode
57, rue de Babylone, 75007
Open daily 2 to 9 p.m.
Imagine being head-over-heels in love with your wife. Imagine she is Asian and homesick for her homeland and you wish to dazzle her and bring her some comfort. This true love story happened in Paris in 1896, when Monsieur Morin, one of the owners of the Bon Marché department store, gave his wife a full-size pastiche pagoda as a birthday gift and had it set up at here, a few steps from his department store. This was during the festive and decadent times of the Belle Epoque and the exotic pagoda had no other use than as a stage for the lady's balls and entertainments.

In 1931 it was turned into a cinema, to which a second hall was added in 1973, as well as the Japanese garden and the tearoom, whose profusion of greenery and bamboo bushes are particularly delightful on hot summer afternoons. You can come here even if you don't intend to see a film—though you very well may. One of the two halls has kept its spectacular Japanese decorations, and both halls screen quality films, some of which are in English.

Paris Mosque
39, rue Geoffroy-St-Hilaire, 75005
Tel: 01 45 35 97 33
Open daily 11 a.m. to 11 p.m.

If you have romantic notions of Arabia, head for the patio garden of the Paris mosque. It has shady fig trees, a fountain, and lots of decorative ceramics, which are most welcome in the heat of summer. The sound of the fountain's water and the song of birds will pleasantly accompany your mint tea, provided you come here on a weekday morning, before it gets overcrowded, or on a warm night if you happen to be in the neighborhood

A Priori Thé
35–37, galerie Vivienne, 75002
Tel: 01 42 97 48 75
Open daily 9 a.m. to 6 p.m.

Located in perhaps the city's most atmospheric arcade, this establishment was opened by American Parisians donkey years ago. Only the delightful Peggy is still around. She has the knack for blending English silverware, Wedgwood china, Asian tea, and American salads and desserts: cobblers, frozen yogurt with honey, and above all, divine chocolate walnut brownies. I also loved her cheese and raspberry cake and her green tea with orange peel. The place is so popular that booking is essential at lunchtime. Make sure you reserve your table outside, where all the fun is to be seen and had.

Tea Folies
6, place Gustave-Toudouze, 75009
Tel: 01 42 80 08 44
Open Monday—Saturday 10 a.m. to midnight, Sunday brunch 11 a.m. to 7 p.m.

This tree-shaded corner in the heart of 19th-century Paris is pleasantly over-looked by locals and tourists alike. Despite the presence of two Indian restaurants, the atmosphere remains quint-essentially Parisian, with a touch of the old days. The Tea Folies was started by a Franco-British couple (and now run by France Newton only, the French half of the couple). This is probably why the French media find it exquisitely English, and I find it exquisitely Parisian. It probably has a touch of both, and certainly no trace of the historical enmity between the two nations. Everything is blissfully harmonious in this picturesque, quiet little spot, just below Montmartre. The food is very good and is served at all times of day. Their caramel meringue with almonds draws people from all over Paris.

CRÊPERIES

Crêpes are wonderful—they are inexpensive, fun to eat, have a huge variety of ingredients to satisfy all tastes, and can be a substitute for a meal.

As crêpes come from Britanny, you should have them in the Montparnasse area, the headquarters of the Breton community since the middle of the 19th century, when the Montparnasse railway station became their gateway to the city. I find it difficult to recommend a specific *crêperie* because their quality can fluctuate even between two close visits. I therefore recommend you walk up and down rue du Montparnasse, south of boulevard du Montparnasse (in the 14th arrondissement) and sniff around. The street is literally lined with *crêperies*. Besides, it's very picturesque, with a pleasant mix of foreigners and locals.

CAFÉS

Like most Parisians I have my cafés, those where I feel most at home and sometimes even like part of the furniture. Following is a list of some of my favorites—choose their terraces. Be prepared, though, to have your territory invaded by cigarette smoke; Parisians have no use for the constraints of laws and regulations, and the ban on smoking in public places is often perceived as an assault on the citizen's freedom.

Most of the cafés on this list have been going for decades, and are part of the cultural heritage of Paris. I have, though, left out some of the hyped places that are the talk of the town, because I find them pretentious and not particularly friendly.

Le Bonaparte, 42 rue Bonaparte, 75006
Le Café de la Mairie, 8 place de la Mairie, 75006
Le Café de la Musique, place de la Fontaine aux Lions
   (La Villette), 75019
La Chope, place de la Contrescarpe, 75005
Le Contrescarpe, place de la Contrescarpe, 75005
Les Deux Magots, 6 place St-Germain-des-Prés, 75006
Le Flore, 172 boulevard St-Germain, 75006
Le Flore en l'Ile, 42 quai d'Orléans, 75004
Le Fouquet's, 99 ave des Champs-Elysées, 75008
Ma Bourgogne, 19 place des Vosges, 75004
La Palette, 43 rue de Seine, 75006
Le Rostand, 6 rue de Médicis, 75006

5

SHOPPING FOR THE
HEART & SENSES

*The only way to get rid of temptation
is to yield to it.*
— Oscar Wilde

CAN THINK OF FEW PLACES WHERE TEMPTATION flaunts itself as shamelessly as in Paris. I am the last person to push consumerism and in fact believe you can skip shopping altogether and enjoy strolling hand-in-hand elsewhere instead. If, though, you can appreciate beauty without acquiring it (what you do in museums, after all), or if you can afford to spend at least a little, then this chapter is definitely for you. If you are among the privileged few who can actually splurge, then this chapter is a must.

I have been ruthlessly selective in drawing up my list of shops, reducing it to those alone, among my very favorites, that reflect Paris's spirit of romance. Some are veritable treasure troves or unusual places, born from a love affair between owner and shop.

Don't shy away from the expensive ones: those are where I often unearth affordable gems, tucked discreetly among more costly goods. All it requires is a stroke of luck and patience. Take your time to look around and strike up a conversation with the shop owner or assistant. Unless they are busy, they will be delighted to talk and will become increasingly helpful as friendship develops. Remember, this is not a hurried shopping expedition, but a pleasure.

For your convenience, the shops appear within the alphabetically-listed categories below, and in alphabetical order within each category. Also, I provide an outline of the main shopping streets in central Paris, if you just wish to wander.

GREAT SHOPPING STREETS

Right Bank, western section

Upmarket and usually expensive, or very expensive. Mainly mainstream fashion & jewelry.

rue Cambon, 1st arr.
rue Castiglione, 1st arr.
rue du Fg St-Honoré, 1st arr.
rue François I, 8th arr.
avenue George V, 8th arr.
place de la Madeleine, 8th arr.
avenue Montaigne, 8th arr.
rue de la Paix, 1st arr.
rue Royale, 8th arr.
rue Tronchet, 8th and 9th arr.
place Vendôme, 1st arr.

Right Bank, central section

Sophisticated with an antiquated and exotic touch.

galerie du Grand-Cerf, 2nd arr.
galerie Montpensier (at the Palais Royal gardens), 1st arr.
galerie de Valois (at the Palais Royal gardens), 1st arr.
galerie Véro-Dodat, 1st arr.
galerie Vivienne, 2nd arr.

Right Bank, eastern section (the Marais)

Artsy, with a wide range of prices.

rue des Francs Bourgeois, 3rd and 4th arrs.
place des Vosges, 3rd and 4th arrs.
rue du Pont-Louis-Philippe, 4th arr.

Left Bank

A cross section of western Paris and the Marais; the best of both worlds and the most sophisticated.

rue du Bac, 7th arr.
rue du Cherche-Midi, 6th arr.
rue du Dragon, 6th arr.
rue de l'Echaudé
rue de Grenelle (up to Raspail), 6th, 7th arrs.
rue Jacob, 6th arr.
rue du Pré-aux-Clercs, 7th arr.
rue des Quatre-Vents, 6th arr.
rue St-Sulpice, 6th arr.
rue des Sts-Pères, 6th, 7th arrs.
rue de Seine, 6th arr.
rue de Tournon 6th arr.

The Islands

Artsy & creative, like the Marais. More affordable than you would expect.

rue St-Louis-en-l'Isle

ACCESSORIES

Le Grain de Sable
79, rue St-Louis-en-l'Ile, 75004
Tel: 01 46 33 67 27

Open daily 11 a.m. to 7 p.m.

You wouldn't expect to find such terrific, inexpensive buys on the Ile St-Louis, and yet this is a veritable treasure trove, especially in winter. Some of my best buys in town come from this shop—gloves, scarves, hats, and the occasional piece of jewelry. They also carry nice scents. In summer they have a fabulous collection of hats for weddings, each stunningly imaginative and tasteful. This is where I bought my hat for my son's wedding!

Passion d'Avril
26, rue de Bièvre, 75005
Tel: 01 46 33 70 72

Open Sunday 2 to 7 p.m, Tuesday—Saturday 11 a.m. to 8 p.m.; closed second half of August

With such a promising name, I couldn't forego this charming boutique, hidden on one of the city's side streets. It's full of tasteful, inexpensive finds, including lovely scarves, handbags, and jewelry— and also interesting decorative items for your home.

BEAUTY

Crabtree and Evelyn
177, bd St-Germain, 75006
Tel: 01 45 44 68 76
Open Monday—Saturday 10 a.m. to 7 p.m.
The Paris offshoot of the famous British company. All the fragrances
of an English garden and an endless variety of wonderful soaps.

Occitane en Provence
55, rue St-Louis-en-l'Ile, 75004
Tel: 01 40 46 81 71
Open daily 10:30 a.m. to 7:30 p.m.
Also at 18, place des Vosges, 75004
Tel: 01 42 72 60 36
Open daily 10:30 a.m. to 7:30 p.m.
Franchised companies and chains don't usually thrill me, but
Occitane is one of the rare exceptions. Paradoxically, I first
discovered Occitane on the King's Road in Chelsea, London, across
the street from their British rival Crabtree and Evelyn (which,
incidentally, I had first discovered on the boulevard St-Germain in
Paris). They had a wheelbarrow brimful of lavender outside, and it
looked so pretty on that sunny spring afternoon that I simply had to
cross the street and follow Oscar Wilde's advice. I found myself
shopping feverishly, buying armfuls of gifts for the Francophiles I
was about to visit in California.

It all began in 1976, when Olivier Baussan, a native from the
south of France, started making his own beauty products and selling
them in local markets. By 1979, Occitane was a proper company
with a turnover of 4 million francs. By 1986 it had risen to 36
million! In 1995 Occitane started spilling over the international
borders and three years later had 120 shops in 24 countries. This
success story is hardly a surprise—who would not succumb to such
astonishing combinations of scents as their amber and lavender, rose
and pepper, tomato and blackcurrant, cinnamon and orange... and at
such reasonable prices?! Not to mention the ecological philosophy
behind their products: everything is natural and reflects the
company's respect and love for nature.

So why not indulge in an aromatic escape to Provence via the Ile
St-Louis or place des Vosges, their two most romantic locations in
Paris, and treat both yourselves and your home to fragrant soaps,
oils, candles, incense sticks and cones, or incense rings to be fitted to
your light bulbs... They even carry scents that go into your vacuum
cleaner! As a final touch, your purchases will be handed to you
exquisitely wrapped, in the most ravishing colors.

BEAUTY PARLORS

Guerlain (see also page 176)
68, avenue des Champs-Elysées, 75008
Tel: 01 45 62 11 21
Open Monday — Saturday 9:30 a.m. to 6:30 p.m.

Paris is studded with excellent beauty parlors. I have tried many and have been disappointed by none. Guerlain, though, has a long history; the treatments they offer are among the best in town. What a pleasure to be pampered by expert, gentle hands on these luxurious, high-ceilinged premises, decorated back in 1939 by the famous Christian Bérard, Jean-Michel Franck, and Alberto Giacometti. Although each room has been updated to ensure the best contemporary treatment, each retains its old-world charm. Past and present are also brought together by way of the Imperial cream, an offshoot of Guerlain's historical Imperial scent, which will be rubbed into your skin after an initial scrub. Anointed in a blanket of lemon and orange blossom fragrance, you will be left to drowse off in the still hush of this historic establishment.

CHOCOLATE

Wine was favored by the ancient gods of Greece, but chocolate was revered by the gods of ancient Mexico, or at least by Quetzalcoatl, the plumed serpent-god of the Aztecs, who, legend has it, relished it above all else. The early Spanish settlers, in the wake of Christopher Columbus, were quick to discover the aphrodisiac qualities of these enchanting beans and, fortunately for us, spread them all over.

A l'Etoile d'Or
30, rue Fontaine, 75009
Tel: 01 48 74 59 55
Open Monday 2:30 to 8 p.m., Tuesday—Sunday 11 a.m. to 8 p.m.;
closed July, August, & early September

If you are walking north toward this shop, your eyes will be so busy with the sight of the Moulin Rouge straight ahead that you may overlook this unassuming address on your right. Unless, of course, the door is open, with its heavenly aroma spilling onto the street. Denise Acabo, the charming queen of the place, is as youthful as her two bouncing braids, yet as knowledgeable as they come. She knows where to unearth the best of the best chocolates from all over France and she gathers them under her roof. She guarantees that nothing she sells is over eight days old. And because she is so committed to quality and knows that heat is chocolate's worst enemy, she is closed during the summer months.

Debauve & Galais
30, rue des Sts-Pères, 75007
Tel: 01 45 48 54 67
Open Monday — Saturday 9 a.m. to 7 p.m.

This is Paris's oldest chocolate shop. In fact, Napoleon's official architects, Percier and Fontaine, the designers of the rue de Rivoli, the Carrousel Arch, and the Malmaison, also designed this place. With its slender pillars set in a semi-circle, the shop truly looks like a temple, or, as Anatole France put it in his *Little Pierre*, "a palace of fairies." As for Messieurs Debauve and Gallais, their pedigree was no less impressive than their architects. After serving as pharmacists to Louis XVI, they started selling chocolate as a "cure" (or was it a commercial gimmick?), which, not surprisingly, made them quite popular. They were acknowledged by the illustrious gastronome, Brillat Savarin, to be the greatest chocolate-makers of their time.

Today their beans come from all corners of the world, a head-spinning variety from the best of dark chocolate, to orange blossoms, to truffles spiced with tea, to their boxes of "Incroyables," where the marriage of bitter and sweet is, in fact, incredible.

Michel Chaudun
149, rue de l'Université, 75007
Tel: 01 47 53 74 40

Open 9:45 a.m. to noon, 1 to 7:15 p.m. Tuesday—Saturday;
closed August

One Sunday afternoon, when the shop was closed, I was astonished by its window display of true-to-life African sculptures—made of chocolate.

I lost no time in contacting Michel Chaudun, for his was the most interesting and original chocolate shop I had ever seen. He sounded so jovial on the phone, I couldn't wait to meet him. I was rather surprised to find a thin man—not one with the plump face and generous belly I'd been expecting. When I expressed my surprise at his slight dimensions, Monsieur Chaudun put me right and informed me that chocolate is not fattening. (Though further investigation somewhat diminished my euphoria: It depends *how much* you eat. Alas.)

Michel Chaudun's first ambition was to become a cabinet-maker; hence his fabulous carvings into this aphrodisiac substance, which in his hands becomes as enticing to see as to taste. A committed craftsman, Chaudun believes that the artisan is an indispensable keeper of traditions, who nevertheless has a responsibility to be creative and innovative. His own talent and imagination are such that he breathes life into his chocolate creations, whether they be lambs, violins, Egyptian sphinxes, or Fabergé eggs. "Good chocolate must shock," he said, and I *was* thunderstruck by each sample this smiling wizard offered me, especially by the Sarawa, which is spiced with five kinds of pepper, as treacherous as the most magical of fairy-tale potions.

He began to train as a pastry cook in his native Loire Valley in 1961, at just fourteen. Three years later, he apprenticed at Paris's celebrated Lenôtre, and then with Witmer in Switzerland, where he perfected his art and was rewarded by several prizes, such as the Tutankhamen gold medal. He opened his own shop here in 1986 and soon came up with a new chocolate filled with cocoa beans, which he called Colomb as a tribute to Christopher Columbus, who had revealed them to the Western World. This remains the specialty of the house, and is definitely to die for. So are the tiny cubical truffles known as *pavés*, a nod to the Latin Quarter's cobblestones, which were dug up and hurled at the riot police during the 1968 student insurrection. If you are traveling on a shoestring, at least indulge in a tiny box for a few euros. You can also buy your lover a chocolate-made heart, or a chocolate-made horseshoe as a lucky charm. There are also astonishing *bonbonnières*, either surmounted by a Cupid or carved with intricate romantic roses. If your lover happens to be a dentist, you can buy him or her a chocolate dentist's kit, complete with a mirror, a drill, and false teeth. For lawyers, Chaudun has a scale of justice; for musicians, plenty of melodious notes, as well as strings and winds. You can even have your initials carved in chocolate. Or, you can just buy the most gorgeous selection of any kind of chocolate you crave, and it will be handed to you, in an equally beautiful box of understated elegance.

Puyricard
27, avenue Rapp, 75007
Tel: 01 47 05 59 47
Open 10 a.m. to 1 p.m., 2 to 7 p.m. Tuesday—Saturday; closed August
Also at 106, rue du Cherche-Midi, 75006
Tel: 01 42 84 20 25
Open 10 a.m. to 7 p.m. Tuesday—Saturday

Belgium may have been put on the map internationally when Brussels was chosen as the seat of the European Community's major institutions. For gourmets, though, Belgium had always been important—for its unrivalled chocolate.

The founding mother of Puyricard was a Belgian, Madame Roelantsd, who left the Congo 35 years ago, after that country's political upheaval. She herself never ventured north of Aix for fear of missing the sun. But what began as a hobby developed into a full-scale family industry with outlets throughout sunny Provence, and these two in Paris.

They carry 92 varieties, with a predilection for dark chocolate. They offer gorgeous wrapping for special occasions such as Christmas and Valentine's Day, when they use crimson velvet and heart-shaped boxes.

CLOTHING (FOR WOMEN)

Anamcha
11, rue du Pré-aux-Clercs, 75007
Tel: 01 42 84 25 46 66
Open Monday—Saturday 1:30 to 7 p.m.; closed August

Romi Loch-Davis is a beautiful, young South African who studied film before moving on to design. Her designs have drawn the attention of the most prestigious, cultural television channels in France and of clients from all over the world. Although her garments are not within everyone's means, if you can afford to splurge for a special occasion, don't miss her little shop located on one of the quiet streets of St-Germain-des-Prés. Go, even if only for the pleasure of looking.

Romi uses the most fabulous Italian fabrics to create sensual visions largely inspired by the turn of the 20th century. You could imagine a Sarah Bernhardt, or perhaps a Klimt model wearing her gowns.

Catherine Vernoux
26, galerie Vivienne, 75002
Tel: 01 42 61 31 60

Open Monday—Saturday 10:30 a.m. to 7 p.m.; closed first two
Mondays of August

As I strolled through this most romantic arcade, I walked past a
shop window bathed in enchanting soft light and stopped at once to
look. The magic continued inside, where, among the ravishing
display of fluid garments, floating scarves, and snug cushions, I
noticed a beautiful face, framed by silver hair and lit up by two
sparkling eyes and a gentle smile. This was the warmhearted
Catherine Vernoux, a fairy godmother in whose hands any pumpkin
may become a splendid carriage. She selects her merchandise from
far and wide and then puts everything together with the talent of a
maestro, creating a symphony of subtle hues and textures, at
astonishingly reasonable prices. Did her earlier career in the cinema
rub off? She once worked for Louis Malle, among others.

La Cour des Francs-Bourgeois
8, rue des Francs-Bourgeois, 75003
Tel: 01 48 87 14 76
Open Tuesday—Saturday 10:30 a.m. to 7 p.m.; Sunday &
Monday 2:30 to 7 p.m.; closed late July for 1 month

Located in the back of a charming courtyard in the Marais, this inexpensive outlet carries a wide selection of stylish, inventive, feminine clothes.

Etienne Brunel
37, rue de Grenelle, 75007
Tel: 01 45 48 26 13
Open Tuesday—Saturday 11 a.m. to 8 p.m.; closed August

You have entered the land of the ephemeral. Yards and yards of a magical translucent paper as light as chiffon and dyed in an infinite kaleidoscope of shades—from a delicate silvery pearl to almond green or an aquatic turquoise, from lilac or rose to deep gold, crimson or fire—ready to adorn you as a one-time Cinderella, Titania, or other Sleeping Beauty. You will have to pay well over €1,000, but you will definitely look the part of a fairy tale princess, for these gowns are truly fabulous, feminine, and flattering. A wedding gown requires two separate scheduled appointments for the fittings.

Gaggio
18, rue Jacob, 75006
Tel: 01 56 24 90 50
Open Tuesday—Saturday 10 a.m. to 1 p.m., 3 to 7 p.m. & by
appointment 2 to 3 p.m.; closed 2–3 weeks in August

With a bit of imagination you will glide into this Venetian palace aboard a gondola. Or perhaps into the Fenice opera draped in a fluid velvet cape that shimmers gold, black, and deep purple. (Gaggio actually did work for the Fenice during its restoration in the 1950s.)

This is Gaggio's Paris showcase, a living museum more than a shop, where you are welcomed by an exceptionally friendly host who will make you feel at home. Everything here—capes, jackets, coats, dresses, trousers, skirts, cushions, curtains, wall hangings, drapery, shawls, handbags, hats—is designed by the young Emma Gaggio, a beautiful Venetian blonde who, on our last visit, even had the time to play shop assistant, with her melodious Italian accent and graceful simplicity. She is the fourth generation in this family business, which made its name draping the glamour of the Serinissima in velvet and silk. Emma doesn't design only the clothes, but also the traditionally-inspired fabrics, with patterns that draw from the Renaissance, Byzantium, and the Orient. These are printed into sensuous materials, mirroring the waters of Venice. No wonder Gaggio's fabrics are sought after by the most prestigious fashion houses, among them Christian Dior, Givenchy, Yves St-Laurent, Ungaro, and Valentino.

Despite the glamour, you can find affordable gifts here, such as photo albums, guest books, and diaries. Scarves start from €154 and jackets range between €655 and €1,145. These are hand-dyed, hand painted, gorgeous and timeless, so the prices are far from outrageous.

Marie Mercié
23, rue St Sulpice, 75006
Tel: 01 43 26 45 83
Open Monday—Saturday 11 a.m. to 7 p.m.

Marie Mercié is a poem in herself. She welcomed me all dressed in flamboyant red, her shining dark eyes and dark hair looking terrific under an equally flamboyant red hat.

Her love for hats and all things theatrical goes back to childhood, when she designed clothes for her dolls. She still loves stories and fairy tales, and there is always one behind her hats and her fashion shows. Before designing new hats, she first writes their story. One season saw a trail of cubist hats; another, a celebration of the circus. Another collection was inspired by a poem by the great 14th-century poet, Charles d'Orléans. She graduated from the Sorbonne with a degree in art history and archeology and had an earlier career as a journalist.

You will simply be amazed by what you discover in this shop, and don't worry about being eccentric. Once you dare brave the street for the first time with a hat on your head, you will never want to be without one again. There is a right hat and a right color for every face. Let the shop assistant help you along; you can even have them made to order. Perhaps your lover is as impassioned as that American tourist who once walked into the shop and bought ten different hats for his girlfriend. At an average price of 1,200 Fr per hat, this was a gallant act. Today you should allow for an average of €244.

FLOWERS

There is no shortage of flower shops in Paris, from the modest neighborhood ones to the most sumptuous, from the flower stands in every street market to the city's famous flower markets on place des Ternes and place de la Madeleine. (Paradoxically, you will not find cut flowers at the Marché aux Fleurs, the flower market on Ile de la Cité, which specializes in potted flowers and plants, as does the market along the quai de la Mégisserie, west of place du Châtelet.)

Céline Dussaulte
10, rue St-Sabin, 75011
Tel: 01 49 23 09 32
Open Monday — Friday 10:30 a.m. to 8:30 p.m.; Saturday 10:30 — 7:30 p.m.; closed end of July for about 4 weeks
If your romantic meanderings take you to the Bastille area, this is a wonderful florist to stop by. Painted panels of graceful flowers blend beautifully with the cut flowers in the vases, and the panels are actually for sale themselves.

Celine's passion for flowers goes back to her early childhood. She sets herself no rules when she makes up a bouquet or a flower arrangement, but just lets her instinct guide her. She has a soft spot for flamboyant bouquets and loves to use impassioned crimson or fuchsia coronations, the likes of which I have never seen—they are simply stunning. She is versatile, though, and will make up a romantic pastel bouquet just as happily, to suit your taste. It won't be cheap; but, in view of the quality of her flowers and her talent, this is hardly surprising. Since 1999, she has been supplier to the Bastille Opera House, making up the bouquets for opening nights.

Christian Tortu
6, carrefour de l'Odéon, 75006
Tel: 01 43 26 02 56
Open Monday—Saturday 10 a.m. to 7 p.m.; closed 2 weeks mid-August
Paris's most famous and celebrated florist, Christian Tortu is first and foremost a revolutionary who turned the French approach to flower arrangement topsy turvy. If the French Revolution was about human equality, Tortu's revolution is about the equality of all flowers and plants.

His family had been market gardeners in Anjou down the generations for as long as they can remember. Christian had his own patch of garden by the age of six. Rambling through bucolic Anjou with his nature-loving grandfather, he stumbled upon nature's little miracles at every step—a neat patch of lettuce, a bough of a fruit tree, a fallen leaf lying on a roadside, a humble wild flower huddling against the garden wall or peeping out between two flagstones... and always in the background, the eternal circle of the seasons.

Nature is his guide in creating each of his bouquets. He bestows the same attention and affection on all plants, following his mood, his whim, or a chance encounter. The end result can be totally unexpected: he may even make a bouquet of green plants, and—why not?—add a thistle or a fruit. After all, in nature's cycle, a flower is no more than the brief moment of youth, seduction, desire, and reproduction—Why should nature's other moments be neglected?

In 1983 Christian carried his ideal to the heart of the Latin Quarter. Before he knew it, he became Paris's pet florist, working for the most prestigious houses. His bouquets accompany the fashion shows of Dior, Valentino, and Chanel, as well as the Cannes Film Festival and many other scintillating events. He has even set up shop on New York's 5th Avenue, selling scented candles, oils, and other flower-based products. Even more important, he has been the teacher and inspiration to a new generation of florists, who have spread the message throughout the city, the best of whom are listed here.

Whatever your budget, Christian's team will come up with a fragrant surprise that will be sure to delight your sweetheart.

Aux Fleurs du Bac
69, rue du Bac, 75007
Tel: 01 45 48 01 01
Open Tuesday—Saturday 9 a.m. to 8:30 a.m., Sunday 10 a.m. to 3 p.m.
This is an exquisite outdoor florist's, tucked under an arcade, amid the gourmet shops and tasteful boutiques of the lovely rue du Bac. It has a heart-warming street-market feel and is run by a young and cheerful staff, who are likely to present you with a gift of a rose, accompanied by a smile. It's just a nice gesture, but it's the kind of gesture that makes my day and makes me want to come back.

Lachaume
10, rue Royale, 75008
Tel: 01 42 60 57 26
Open Monday—Saturday 8 a.m. to 7 p.m., Saturday to 5 p.m.;
closed for a few weeks at the end of July

The fact that Lachaume has been standing at this address for over 150 years is a recommendation in itself. Lachaume is the oldest florist in town—Marcel Proust used to come daily to buy a camellia to stick in his buttonhole on his way to Maxim's. Countless other celebrities were supplied by this shop, including Ari Onassis, who ordered flowers for the funeral of Maria Callas.

Money is no object to those who shop here. There was the enamored lover who had his entire car covered with Lachaume's flowers as a token of love for his sweetheart. Another ordered 37 different bouquets to celebrate his beloved's 37th birthday.

What I enjoy most about Lachaume is that it seems unshakably timeless. Ever since I first passed it decades ago, I've been enchanted by the freshness, the scent, and the beauty of its endlessly long roses.

Lhuillier
9, rue du Marché-St-Honoré, 75001
Tel: 01 42 60 52 15
Open Monday—Saturday 9 a.m. to 8 p.m.

This place was a landmark when it was located on place Vendôme. But somehow its move didn't matter. The narrow pavement here looks so pretty with its lush seasonal bushes, climbing and spreading all over the place. Besides, rue du Marché-St-Honoré is full of character and wonderful shops, definitely an address worth discovering.

Lieu-Dit
21, impasse du Maine, 75015
Tel: 01 42 22 25 94
Open Monday—Friday 10 a.m. to 7 p.m.; Saturday 10 a.m. to 1 p.m.; closed August

Alain grew up in the heart of Paris, just off the Pont Neuf. The romantic place Dauphine and the Vert-Galant little garden on the western tip of the Ile de la Cité were his childhood playgrounds. Simone Signoret's daughter was among his playmates and the house he lived in went back to the time of Henri IV. Quite an impressive beginning for a little Parisian. Yet, since early childhood, it was the first buds of spring that moved this young city dweller, the miracle of life as it first peeps out of the soil, the row of potted flowers blooming on his sister-in-law's windowsill.

Lieu-dit means a tiny locality, so insignificant in size that few maps grant it a mention. Alain definitely took great risks when he left his very prosperous flower shop off the rue Mouffetard, by the Latin Quarter, for this secret, countrified, cobbled alleyway on the quiet side of Montparnasse. It turned out to be a visionary idea, as this place is more of an artist's studio than a flower shop, and most of Alain's clients are not passersby. He works with such luxury hotels as the Plaza Athénée and with such fashion designers as Giorgio Armani, Versace, Cerruti, and Ferragamo. But have no fear, you will be treated just as splendidly if you walk into this heavenly and historical oasis, one of the last vestiges of old Montparnasse, which all but gave way to concrete high rises several years back. And you needn't buy more than a bunch of pansies or violets if that is all you can afford. Alain will put them together for you with the same friendly attention. Even if you don't intend to buy any flowers, I would visit Lieu-Dit come what may, for it enjoys the most romantic location I can think of, with the further asset of having the little known Musée du Montparnasse as a neighbor. Come spring, Alain's flowers illuminate the alleyway with their palette of ravishing hues; come autumn, the Virginia ivy steals the show, when it sets the alleyway ablaze in glowing shades of crimson and gold.

Marianne Robic
41, rue de Bourgogne, 75007
Tel: 01 44 18 03 47
Open Monday — Friday 8 a.m. to 8 p.m.; Saturday 8 a.m. to 7 p.m.; closed August

After your visit to Musée Rodin, you may want to wander into rue de Bourgogne, a neighborhood street lined with exciting shops. Marianne Robic is one of the city's best-known florists and fills her shop with the freshest and the most ravishing cut flowers. Almost all her customers are regulars for whom she loves to put together tailor-made bouquets in keeping with their personalities and with the occasion. In your case, she may suggest a romantic bouquet of roses or sweet peas, or even a tiny charming one of violets. Best to come here on a Tuesday or Thursday, when the new supplies arrive and the shop bursts with fragrant hues.

Moulié
8, place du Palais-Bourbon, 75007
Tel: 01 45 51 78 43
Open Monday — Saturday 8:30 a.m. to 8 p.m.

Located behind the National Assembly, in an exquisitely understated square of the old Faubourg St-Germain, blissfully overlooked by passersby, this shop explodes with some of the city's most beautiful flowers.

Au Nom de la Rose
4, rue de Tournon, 75006
Tel: 01 46 34 10 64
Open Monday — Saturday 8:30 a.m. to 9 p.m.; Sunday 9 a.m. to 2 p.m. & 3 to 6 p.m.

> *Roses, roses,*
> *Living gems of infinity.*
> —F. G. Lorca

Gentle carpets of rose petals strewn on the shop's windowsill and front pavement are an irresistible invitation. This is one of the top florists in the city, and the only one that sells nothing but roses—in all colors, for all occasions. They are all fresh garden roses, which accounts for the wonderful fragrance when you step in. Au Nom de la Rose does flower arrangements for the city's most prestigious functions, including the debutant ball at the Crillon. This should not deter you from buying your sweetheart a single rose, if that is all you can afford. You will be greeted with the same friendliness. And if for some reason, your bouquet does not last the week, it will be replaced, graciously.

Olivier Pitou
23, rue des Sts-Pères, 75006
Tel: 01 49 27 97 49
Open Sunday 10:30 a.m. to 7 p.m. ; Monday—Saturday 9 a.m. to 9 p.m.; closed August

Olivier Pitou has carried his love of flowers onto the narrow pavement of this old street of Faubourg St-Germain. Whether you step in to buy a bouquet or just walk by, his shop is the highlight of this section of the street, an ever-changing pleasing sight—a feast of daffodils and hyacinths in early spring, an outburst of lilac as spring progresses, a profusion of rambling pale roses when summer takes over, and happiness throughout the year.

Au Pot de Fer Fleuri
78, rue de Monge, 75005
Tel: 01 45 35 17 42
Open daily 9 a.m. to midnight

For the last forty-odd years Violette has been presiding over these theatrical premises come rain come shine. Born on May Day, when lilies of the valley are given to loved ones as lucky charms, and baptized Violette, she truly believes that she was destined to become the messenger of flowery bliss. Many a bouquet, put together by her hands, has accompanied Parisian romances.

If you happen to be in this area, try the "World of Violette," as she calls her shop, where neighbors drop in for a chat like old-time villagers. And don't forget: Violette is with her flowers "every day until midnight."

Vertumne
12, rue de la Sourdière, 75001
Tel: 01 42 86 06 76
Open Monday—Saturday 9 a.m. to 7 p.m.; closed August

How romantic to be wandering off the exciting rue du Marché-St-Honoré with its mouth-watering food shops and stumble unexpectedly on this charming flower shop, tucked away on one of the quiet side streets. The young and beautiful Clarisse Béraud is as sunny as the flowers she arranges for her clients, and full of talent and imagination. Greenery is never spurned by Clarisse, nor are fruits (after all, she has named her shop after the god and protector of fruit trees). She also has a passion for aromatic herbs—thyme, jasmine, lavender, sweet marjoram—which she weaves into her bouquets in happy harmony. Definitely an address worth your detour.

FOOD

Dalloyau
101, rue du Faubourg-St-Honoré, 75008
Tel: 01 42 99 90 00
Also at 2, place Edmond-Rostand, 75006
Open 8:30 a.m. to 7 p.m.; Saturday & Sunday brunch 10 a.m. to 1 p.m.
This venerable house goes all the way back to 1802. During the Second Empire, their chocolate macaroons brought them to the limelight. Somehow, from just a Dalloyau-made almond paste and egg whites (plus those inimitable and inexplicable tricks of the trade), these chefs create miracles.

Every month celebrates a new combination of flavors—chestnut and blackcurrant, fennel mint and chocolate. Their *Arlettes*, *Opéras*, *Faubourg*, and *Croquante aux Agrumes* are all heavenly. If you love bread, try the lemon bread or the fig bread.

Although Dalloyau's main address is at rue du Faubourg-St-Honoré, recently redesigned tastefully in chocolate, caramel, and vanilla hues, I personally have a soft spot for their tea room on rue de Médicis, facing the Luxembourg gardens. I often go there for ice cream, which can also be bought in a cone and enjoyed in the gardens.

Fauchon
26 & 30, place de la Madeleine, 75008
Tel: 01 47 42 60 11
Open Monday—Saturday 9:30 a.m. to 7 p.m.
The ultimate temple of gastronomy. Of course the place de la Madeleine is named after its celebrated church, but I doubt that the latter draws as vast a crowd of worshippers as Fauchon and Hediard (see next entry). I doubt, too, Auguste Fauchon could have predicted the head-spinning success of his venture, when he first came up to Paris from Normandy in the 1880s and set up his fruit-laden wheelbarrow on this square. By 1886 he opened his first shop, which expanded little by little to the impressive pink-and-pearly gray shop that today occupies a substantial chunk of the place de la Madeleine.

In 1899 Auguste Fauchon added a tea house, the Grand Salon de Thé, which was quite a novelty in those days. (The façade said "5 o'clock tea" in English). A new salon de thé opened in 1999, to celebrate the first centennial of the venture. Its two floors blend elegantly French classic style and contemporary features, with their dark wood parquet floors, blond wood furniture, soft carpeting, comfortable armchairs, and luminous shades of pink, straw yellow, and deep maroon. Everything is so peaceful and quiet that you can forget you are in one of the busiest, traffic-ridden spots in the capital. It's a lovely, discreet spot for a coffee break, lunch, or tea. You can even have your breakfast here beginning at 8 A.M. If the weather is with you, settle on the outdoor terrace and choose among Fauchon's 23 kinds of coffee. Outdoor Paris is at its best in early morning. Or, if you come later, you will choose from an overwhelming assortment of teas and 70 different kinds of pastry, including some astonishing house specialties, such as Darjeeling tarts, Earl Grey macaroons, and Darjeeling crackers. At my last visit, I had an ideal light lunch that began with a lovely chilled zucchini soup, with pinenuts and pesto, followed by a very light turbot with gamba and basmati rice.

There are also endless gifts to choose from, ranging from a bottle of champagne for as little as €29, to a basket or case bursting with a profusion of Fauchon's mouth-watering bounty for as much as €1,450. With their newly expanded wine cellars containing 2,500 vintages, their 40 varieties of chocolate, their astounding array of fresh fruit, not to mention their *foie gras*, truffles, and such gourmet standards as *canard à l'orange* and *coq au vin*, you are in for a gastronomic feast.

Hédiard
21, place de la Madeleine, 75008
Tel: 01 43 12 88 88
Open Monday—Saturday 9 a.m. to 10 p.m.
Also at 126, rue du Bac, 75007
Tel: 01 45 44 01 98
Open Monday—Saturday 9:30 a.m. to 9:30 p.m.
Restaurant at 21, place de la Madeleine, 75008
Tel: 01 43 12 88 99
Open for breakfast 8:30 a.m. to 10 a.m.; lunch noon to 2:30 p.m.; tea from 3 p.m. to 6 p.m.; dinner 7:30 to 10 p.m.

Hédiard is the other gourmet landmark of place de la Madeleine. Although, like everyone else today, they have branched off to new specialties, spices, oils, mustards, and condiments still remain their main activity. This tradition goes back to the early 1800s when Ferdinand Hédiard, an apprentice joiner from a village near Chartres, happened to be visiting the port of Le Havre and was fascinated by the bundles and crates of goods from all over the world piled up on the dockside. In 1854, he opened a Parisian shop, the "Comptoir d'Epices et des Colonies" on rue Notre-Dame-de-Lorette, just north of the boulevards, then the social heart of Paris. Rewarded with enthusiastic recognition during the 1867 Universal Exposition, he moved to the more prestigious address on place de la Madeleine in 1880, soon to be followed by Fauchon. With its piles of crates, baskets, and old hangings, his shop recalled an oriental market and was filled with the unique fragrance of coffee, vanilla, and spices, to customers' delight. The final touch was provided by slender shop assistants from Martinique who served buyers exotic fruits and vegetables, among them Alexander Dumas, a renowned gourmet who tasted here his first pineapple. Colette, Jean Cocteau, Jean Gabin, Marlene Dietrich, and Charlie Chaplin also shopped here in later years. Yet Ferdinand Hédiard himself never left France!

Today you will enjoy their great gift shop, with its imaginative combinations of Turkish delights and preserved chestnuts, or superb

Nîmes jams, which are cooked slowly in their traditional copper cauldrons, using a wooden ladle to fill the jars so that the fruits remain intact. Honey, syrups, fruit jellies, marzipans, vinaigrettes, tomato sauces, ratatouilles, chutneys, terrines—all are part of your feast, not to mention over 90 different spices. And of course great coffees and teas. They also have an excellent collection of 1,500 wines, champagnes, and liqueurs and an attractive, very comfortable restaurant on the first floor, where you can have a peaceful break from your shopping spree.

Lenôtre
44, rue d'Auteuil, 75016
Tel: 01 45 24 52 52
Also at 48, place Victor Hugo, 75016
Tel: 01 45 02 21 21
Also at 61, rue Lecourbe, 75015
Tel: 01 42 73 20 97
Also at 121, avenue de Wagram (pastry only), 75017
Tel: 01 47 63 70 30
All locations open daily 9 a.m. to 9 p.m.
Unquestionably top of the scale and internationally renowned, Lenôtre is a versatile sorcerer who blends in his cauldron the flavors and aromas of all four corners of the world.

Lenôtre's initial specialty was and remains their unrivalled pastry. Seventy years ago, as a farm child in Normandy, Gaston Lenôtre made cakes and pastry for his family. He eventually became France's greatest pastry chef, whose succulent and mouthwatering dainties are dispatched the world over. All the above addresses offer

irresistible gourmet gifts, which can also be sent anywhere in the world. They are very big on chocolate, with such specialties as the *caprice noisette* (made of chocolate, hazelnut praline, and caramelized hazelnuts) and an intense, mouthwatering ganache flavored with four head-spinning spices. If you want to go all out and indulge properly, try their *mirroir des iles*, a concoction of milk chocolate, caramel, banana, mango, and passion-fruit. I doubt it will make you lose weight, but a sin confessed is half forgiven, they say.

But chocolate is not all. Lenôtre carries fruit jellies, *marrons glacés* (candied chestnuts), marzipan, and everything comes in beautiful wrappings, even in silver plated boxes or crystal bowls and glasses. Definitely a place where you can make each other happy. To be sure, try *l'entremets au chocolat Baileys*, which may send you directly to aphrodisiac spheres.

Mariage Frères
30, rue du Bourg-Tibourg, 75004
Tel: 01 42 72 28 11
Open daily 10:30 a.m. to 7:30 p.m.

I once walked into this aromatic haven during the week of Valentine's Day; the shop was as crowded as usual, but I managed to glimpse on the counter a large tea container that said Elixir d'Amour. For yes, tea can be an aphrodisiac. You could also try their Eros, which is flavored with hibiscus and mallow flowers.

Certainly not-to-be-missed for any tea lover, Mariage Frères takes pride in its more than 450 blends. The oldest tea importer in the capital, it goes back to June 1854, when the two brothers, Henri and Edouard Mariage, opened their business at this address, which was then their parents' home. The family had been trading with the east since the 17th century, when their ancestor, Nicolas Mariage, traveled to Asia and even signed a trade agreement with the Shah of Persia on behalf of Louis XIV.

Now Mariage Frères has other outlets, but this is the one to visit, with its old-world charm and display of Old China tea chests, scales, sieves, and colonial countertops that make the place a living museum. It's one of those unique places that, despite incredible popularity, has remained an authentic gem. (See also page 118).

GIFTS FROM AROUND THE WORLD
Alchimie Lointaine
40, rue de Verneuil, 75007
Tel: 01 42 61 33 60
Open Tuesday—Saturday 11 a.m. to 8 p.m.

This is an Ali Baba's cavern of treasures of teak, batik, Ikats, wicker, bamboo, ebony, mango tree, earthenware, and wrought iron. The shop is sprinkled with the scent of the Orient and prices are just as dreamlike, starting at just a few euros.

Esther Gossart is the alchemist who has gathered these treasures from the ends of the world and brought them to the heart of Paris. Whether as large as furniture or as small as a pretty bowl, everything is meant to embellish your home and give pleasure, a good enough reason to walk into this charming street.

Annam Heritage
objets d'art et artisanat d'Asie
3bis, rue Cler, 75007
Tel: 01 53 85 91 99
E-mail: abt@worldonline.fr
Open Monday—Saturday 11 a.m. to 7 p.m, plus Sunday mornings & Monday afternoons in December; closed August

Did you know that in Vietnam brides wear red wedding dresses? Danielle Bruneau, the friendly manager of this shop, explained to me that red stands for happiness. It is customary, also, to place wedding gifts in red lacquered boxes. Annam Heritage carries such boxes, which could themselves make an original gift for your sweetheart. They are round and come in three sizes, and can also be covered in subtle silver or gold lacquer. Everything is tasteful in this showcase of Vietnam's arts and crafts, lovingly selected by Thanh Thai, himself a native of Annam in central Vietnam. The vases, boxes, dishes, trays, crockery to match the embroidered table wear, photo albums, and more are lovingly displayed by Danielle. She will let you browse in peace or will guide you patiently through her shop should you wish. As it is located on the edge of a neighborhood's bustling street market, you might enjoy winding down in this spacious haven of tranquility. You will not be pressured into buying, although you will inevitably find something worth considering, as everything is stylish, often light-weight, and very reasonably priced.

Don't hesitate to take advantage of Danielle's suggestions. She has such a versatile imagination that she will show you how to turn a powder box into a designer vase and a vase into an ice box. And when she spreads out for you a hand-embroidered tablecloth, she will take you to rural Vietnam, telling you how it was embroidered by a group of village women seated around a huge table. Imagine also the village men sandpapering and lacquering up to 30 times each item to give it the perfect finish. Danielle's stories are wonderful, and she speaks fluent English.

Artisanat du Liban
30, rue de Varenne, 75007
Tel: 01 45 44 88 57
Open Monday 2 to 7 p.m.; Tuesday—Saturday 10:30 a.m. to 7 p.m.

A journey into the heart of Lebanon. Traditional crafts for both you and your home: copperware, embroidery, jewelry, paper weights, letter openers, wine bottle stoppers, napkin rings, evening bags, gowns… the choice is immensely eclectic and affordable.

Demons et Merveilles
45, rue Jacob, 75006
Tel: 01 42 96 26 11

Open Monday—Saturday 10 a.m. to 7 p.m.; may be closed August
A thousand tales of a 1,001 nights are conjured up in this bewitching showcase of central Asia, the Orient, and North Africa. Golden embroidery on flamboyant velvet coats, gorgeous shawls, and ethnic jewelry studded with striking semi-precious gems are on display in this treasure trove. Watch out, though. Nothing is cheap.

Galerie Triff
35, rue Jacob, 75006
Tel: 01 42 60 22 60

Open Monday 2 to 7 p.m.; Tuesday—Saturday 10:30 a.m. to 7 p.m.
This is one of my favorite shops in Paris—if you can call it a shop. You first walk through an exquisite old courtyard of St-Germain-des-Prés, brimming with greenery and a profusion of flowers come spring, framed above by picturesque old Parisian roofs. When you eventually enter the beautiful premises, the array of gorgeous kilims and the trickling fountain will stun you. The 30-year-old store is the passion of Henri and Jacqueline Daumas and their son Eric, who was away during my last visit, unearthing more treasures in Turkey, the main kilim supplier since the 1970s.

Henri discovered kilims (or gilims, "woven tapestry") in 1971 at the Hôtel Drouot auction house and succumbed at once. Before he knew it, he gave up his dealings in 18th-century French antiques, and along with his wife and son, turned this secret recess of St-Germain into a gem of a backdrop for a fabulous collection. Whether you buy an old kilim (19th century) or a modern one (some are specially designed for their shop), you are sure to find nothing but the best and the most beautiful here. Just wander around the way you would in a museum—they are very hospitable. You can even browse through their superb coffee table books and pick up a great cushion for less than €27.

Last but not least, you may be as amazed as I was to discover that the landscape gardener of this neighborhood's most exquisite courtyard is no other than Henri himself, a man of versatile passions and talents, and of charming modesty.

Kazana
40, rue St-André-des-Arts, 75006
Tel: 01 43 29 10 09
Open Sunday 11 a.m. to 8 p.m.; Monday—Thursday 10 a.m. to 8
p.m.; Friday & Saturday 10 a.m. until midnight
Also at 47, rue Mouffetard, 75005
Tel: 01 43 36 19 02
Open 10 a.m. to 8 p.m.; Saturday until midnight
This affordable favorite of mine has several outlets, but I
particularly like the above locations—include them in a leisurely
stroll. Scarves, jewelry, and handbags from India and Thailand,
often in cheerful, flamboyant colors. Backpackers are sure to find
here some token of love for their sweethearts. And at weekends you
can do so until midnight!

Mohanjeet
21, rue St-Sulpice, 75006
Tel: 01 43 54 73 29
Open Monday 2 to 7 p.m; Tuesday—Saturday 11 a.m. to 7 p.m.
Also at 10, rue de Turenne, 75004
Tel: 01 42 74 27 00
Open Sunday & Monday 2 to 7 p.m.; Tuesday—Saturday 11 a.m.
to 7 p.m.
Sensuous India with a touch of Parisian style—the blend is
exquisite. Josiane, the shop manager, will tell you that a piece of
clothing has to breathe. It sways and moves to the rhythm of your

Above: Kazana

body. Amber and ruby red, emerald green and sapphire blue, layer upon layer of silk and velvet or cotton and wool, to be wrapped in throughout the cold winter or to be peeled off in summer time. The person behind these beautiful garments is Mohanjeet Grewal, a longtime Parisian Indian, who declared to me: "Being an Indian and a woman is a combination I would give up for nothing."

Mohanjeet arrived in Paris in the early 1960s, from New York, where she had been working as a journalist for the *New York Times*. On a drizzling Armistice Day (November 11th), when she saw President de Gaulle coming down the avenue des Champs-Elysées, she instantaneously fell in love with Paris, which became her adopted motherland.

Back in the 1950s, she graduated from UCLA in political science (something very few women did then). Her true passion, though, was writing, dancing, and painting. Her designs reflect her thoughtful love of movement and color. The garments have a living fire, which would have been appreciated by the likes of Isadora Duncan or Loïs Fuller. Her understanding of Hinduism also shapes her designs, for, as she explained to me, it excludes nothing and is receptive to everything. It sets no rules. It guides you, but the thinking is yours. So she leaves it up to you to combine and blend her garments, creating for yourself your own harmony.

HOUSE AND HOME

La Cornue
18, rue Mabillon, 75006
Tel: 01 46 33 84 74
Open Tuesday—Saturday 10 a.m. to 1 p.m. & 2 to 6:30 p.m.,
Monday 2:30 to 6:30 p.m.; closed August
In the motherland of culinary devotion, it is impossible not to mention La Cornue. Famous for their handcrafted stoves, they also take pride in their exclusive kitchen utensils and tableware, which can now be bought in their Parisian outlet in St-Germain-des-Prés. These make wonderful gifts for anyone who cares about food. Each piece

combines elegance and common sense, warmth, comfort, and beauty. I have noticed in particular their silver-lined copper saucepans with nonconductive cast-iron handles, stainless steel tools with solid rosewood handles, carving knives for every carving need, spoons and boards of beech wood with brass hanging rings, chopping blocks of horn wood, marble mortars and pestles, and authentic leather aprons.

You might also like their French bistro crockery, cutlery, and linen, or, for more festive occasions, their French château items, such as crystal decanters and glasses, handcrafted cutlery in sterling silver and boxwood, silver candlesticks and candelabras, linen with *fleur-de-lys* patterns against a blue background... a truly regal dinner party is in store.

Deux Milles et Une Nuit
13, rue des Francs-Bourgeois, 75004
Tel: 01 48 87 07 07
Open daily 11 a.m. to 7:30 p.m.; closed Christmas & New Year's Day
Welcome to Aladdin's cave, hidden at the back of a picturesque courtyard in the historic Marais. It overflows with so many dazzling treasures that you can't help noticing it even from the street. You are as likely to be compelled to walk in as you would be to hear the end

of Scheherazade's story. To make matters even more tempting, the shop is open practically every day of the year.

Once inside, the interesting wares are from places as varied as Morocco and Holland, a surprising combination—until you find out that behind this fabulous shop is a love story between a Dutch woman and a Moroccan man. I fell for the magical Fortuny lamps from Venice; I also loved their great collection of cozy cushions from India and their dinner set from the South of France, beautifully displayed on a dining table with stylish wine glasses. At close scrutiny, I noticed a tiny, delicate red heart discreetly tucked between the stem and the cup—a great gift for the pair of you!

Maison de Famille
29, rue St-Sulpice, 75006
Tel: 01 40 46 97 47
Open Monday — Saturday 10:30 a.m. to 7 p.m.
This house caters to the best of country living but with the added French touch, which makes all the difference. You may buy here a lovely doormat for your winter mountain hideaway... or a comfy bulky sweater to wear as you sip whisky by the log fire. Or perhaps two identical fresh white waffle cotton bathrobes. They have so much to choose from—soaps, candle sticks, leather goods—all in very good taste, and for every section of your home.

La Paresse en Douce
97, rue du Bac, 75007
Tel: 01 42 22 64 10
Open Monday 2 to 7 p.m.; Tuesday — Saturday 11 a.m. to 7 p.m.
You are invited to indulge in a permanent honeymoon between your sheets, unless you'd rather lounge on your couch wrapped up in cashmere, alpaca, or velvet throws. This shop also carries all the necessary accessories for luxuriating in your bathroom. Everything is of exquisite taste and refinement and starts at very reasonable prices. You can pick up small, light items such as candles, house scents, and

Left & Above: Deux Milles et Une Nuit

charming crochet slippers in ravishing colors. But what made me melt was the variety of gorgeous nightdresses at the back of the shop—you could practically buy a different one for every night of the year.

Porthault
18, avenue Montaigne, 75008
Tel: 01 47 20 75 25

Open Monday 9:30 a.m. to 1 p.m. & 2 to 6:30 p.m.; Tuesday — Saturday 9:30 a.m. to 6:30 p.m., Saturday 10 a.m. to 1 p.m. & 2 to 6 p.m.

You will love browsing in the spacious premises of this two-story shop on the glamorous avenue Montaigne. The walls were paneled by Jansen with warm, luminous oak and the floors muted with thick soft carpets. The place overlooks a lovely flowery garden, and a wonderful feeling of well-being prevails, halfway between a discreet museum and an opulent, private home.

The house was founded by Daniel and Madeleine Porthault back in the 1920s and enjoyed widespread recognition right away. The "Rolls Royce of house linen" it was dubbed in the United States, where it was even celebrated by a Rizzoli book called *White Dreams*. (A paradox of a title, since Madeleine Porthault was the daring young woman who had first introduced colored patterns to bed linen. Today we take color for granted, but in 1920 this was quite a revolution.)

Since the beginning Porthault has always kept under its control all the stages of production—the weaving, confectioning, and printing, as well as the designs of the patterns. Since the beginning, too, their watchword has been quality and perfect craftsmanship,

which accounts for their prestigious customers, including the Duchess of Windsor, who became Madeleine's personal friend, and for whose love Edward VIII gave up the throne. The little graceful hearts that have become the trademark of Porthault and are still sprinkled on many of the fabrics and articles, were first commissioned by the Duchess as the emblem of the Windsors' burning love, except that the hearts came in twos at the time, and were passionately interlaced. The four-leaf clover, traditionally a lucky charm, was also deposited as a household signature, this time by Louise de Vilmorin, another of Madeleine's friends.

Jackie Kennedy commissioned from Porthault all the linen for the White House. Many other celebrities have been among their clientele over the years, including Maria Callas and King Hassan II of Morocco. Yet Porthault's most impressive, albeit most ephemeral, contribution to history was a 100-meter long tablecloth commissioned for the bi-Millennium of the Iranian Empire.

Today Porthault has branched off to other household goods, especially involving breakfast, which is, after all, the conclusion of the night. The patterns on the dishes seem to echo delightfully those decorating the sheets. Prices are obviously high, but they also sell smaller items such as scent candles and home scents, aprons and gloves for the kitchen, tea cozies, table mats, and breakfast trays, and those can be surprisingly inexpensive. I love their gorgeously embroidered bed linen, as well as some of their printed linen, sprinkled romantically with tiny flowers, thin leaves, or little hearts. Those of you with a more dramatic taste may prefer the very contemporary spirit of their black linen and the contrasting strong colors of their geometric patterns. They are actually quite stunning and perpetuate Madeleine's avant-garde determination. I suspect that the strength of Porthault lies largely in the balance they strike between maintaining old traditions and adjusting to new trends, and also in the fact that though they are open to the outside world and export 80 percent of their goods, they have somehow managed to stick to their slogan, "Made in France"—no meager feat in this day and age.

Sous le Soleil
89, rue Mouffetard, 75005
Tel: 01 45 35 35 83
Open Sunday 11 a.m. to 6:30 p.m.; Tuesday—Saturday 11 a.m. to 7:30 p.m; closed September

This is a small shop on a famous, bustling market street, on the eastern edge of the Latin Quarter. Everything is sunny here—first of all Alain himself, the proprietor who has brought to Paris from his native Bandole a delicious southern accent, and also wonderful merchandise from Provence. It's so cheerful that while I was looking around and chatting with Alain, I completely forgot that it was raining miserably outside. I also forgot about the junk that much of the rest of rue Mouffetard offers for sale these days. At Sous le Soleil, quite to the contrary: everything is pretty and of good quality. I have bought here armfuls of gifts for American Francophile friends and filled their hearts with the Mediterranean sun. All the aroma and hues of Provence are printed in lovely patterns into table cloths, napkins, bread bags, kitchen gloves, what have you—sunflowers, poppies, mimosa, olives. There is so much choice that most of it has to be kept folded up on the shelves. Once spread open in all their beauty, you will find it even harder to pick and choose and resist temptation—be forewarned! All the more so as Alain's prices run truly low. If you are not unwilling to carry home some weight, you will also find here very fine ceramics from the southern village of Vallauris.

JEWELRY

Only four stones have been granted the status of gems—the diamond, the emblem of power, wealth, and eternal love; the emerald, the emblem of happiness; the ruby, the emblem of love, purity, and courage; and the sapphire, the emblem of wisdom. If that's what you have in mind for your sweetheart, then head for place Vendôme, where the container is as much of a jewel as the contained. For not only is the place Vendôme Paris's glamorous showcase of the trade, but it is also an architectural gem in its own right and a sparkling jewelry box after dark. All the big names have outlets here—Boucheron, Bulgari, Cartier, Chaumet, Dubail, Holemans, Mauboussin, Piaget, Repossi, Van Cleef & Arpels. Some also spill into rue Castiglione and rue de la Paix, respectively to the south and to the north of place Vendôme, and into rue St-Honoré, where you will find the Danish gold- and silversmith, Georg Jensen, at no. 239 and Fabergé at no. 281.

But don't feel disheartened if this neighborhood is beyond your means: Paris has many affordable, tasteful jewelery shops where you may find pieces that are just as becoming as the most precious of gems. I have found some marvelous places, in all price ranges. I offer them all to you as part of your sightseeing adventure, for the sheer pleasure of the eye, even if you end up buying nothing.

Cipango
14, rue de 'Echaudé, 75006
Tel: 01 43 26 08 92
Open Tuesday—Saturday 11 a.m. to 7 p.m.; closed August
Tucked away in one of the most romantic spots of St-Germain-des-Prés, behind the rue du Fürstemberg, this wonderful shop escapes many a passerby. But those who find it can't help but marvel at the lavish necklaces of amber, amethyst, lapis lazuli, coral, pearls, emerald, jade, and other such bounties of the earth and the deep. The previous owner of this place was clearly thinking of the earth's far reaches when she named it Cipango in homage to "World's End," the Japan of Marco Polo's time.

Recently Sylvie Tissot-Schneider has taken over, keeping intact the spirit of the place and designing jewelry of the same character. While most jewelry-makers I interviewed spoke of beauty and seductiveness, Sylvie spoke of talismans, which may be why she incorporates archeological artifacts into many of her pieces. She also sometimes joins forces with her husband Christophe, who designs and carves striking metal pieces for her jewelry that enhance the natural beauty of the stones. He, incidentally, is a sought-after painter, whose 126-meter-long frieze of the Murlion, Singapore's emblematic lion of the sea, decorates that city's regal Brass Bassah Road.

If you are the kind of woman who looks good in jewelry with strong character, and if you can afford the average price of €1,000, you will be delighted to discover this gem of a hidden place.

Cooch Behar
12, rue Jacob, 75006
Tel: 0143 25 50 99
Open Monday—Saturday 11:30 a.m. to 7 p.m.; closed 3 weeks in August
This extraordinary jewelry shop, hidden at the back of an old, shady courtyard, pays homage to the native province of its "godmother," Gayatri Devi, the widow of the maharajah of Rajastan. Ever since her husband's death, she has devoted her life to the promotion of their province's arts. Here, you will find showers of the famous Kasliwal emeralds and rubies from the Gem Palace of Jaipur (the capital of Rajastan). The Kasliwal jewelers, who settled in Jaipur in 1852, were once jewelers to the Moghul emperors and, in more contemporary history, to a string of royal princesses from England, Japan, Sweden,

and Spain. Don't let this intimidate you—I was greeted just like a queen myself when I visited this newly opened establishment and was allowed to try on every splendid item my heart craved. The prices are as head-spinning as the magic—in the main nothing less than prohibitive, although they also carry affordable rings, earrings, and other smaller items.

Jean Vendome
352, rue St-Honoré, 75001
Tel: 01 42 60 88 34

Open Monday—Saturday 11 a.m. to 1 p.m. & 2 to 7 p.m.; closed August
When I first walked past this shop, I was so overwhelmed by the glamour of the window display that I had to brace myself to actually enter. But once inside, I met the most unassuming jeweler and two other friendly faces, Jean Vendome's sons, now jewelry-makers in their own right.

More than a jeweler, Vendome is a sculptor, an artist whose works are celebrated in museums worldwide and have been entered in the Larousse dictionary. He does not subordinate a stone to a design, which is what jewelry-making is usually about; on the contrary, he starts from the stone itself. The stone is his inspiration, and he celebrates it with the utmost respect, turning it into a living, mobile, fluid sculpture—a match for the living, mobile, fluid woman who will wear it. His stones are mostly stunning minerals, sometimes crystals—"flowers of the earth" that astonish their beholder. Like flowers, like women, each piece is unique—he has never made two alike. But whereas the flowers of nature fade, Vendome's "flowers" are fragments of eternity.

I asked the man who is called the "father of contemporary jewelry" how he defines "contemporary." "Jewelry that lives with its times," came the reply. How extraordinary to have remained eternally young at age 71, always moving on, always looking ahead. What better example than his astounding gold-and-diamond compact pendant that comes apart and turns into a bracelet, a pair of earrings, two smaller pendants, and a ring, all gracefully enhanced by rubies, sapphires, and emeralds. In this speedy age of ours, when women often rush out for the evening straight from work, this piece offers an ingenious, Cinderella-like transformation. This spectacular piece is on display at the Musée des Arts Décoratifs.

During your meanderings in the Tuileries gardens, don't hesitate to wander off into this shop, just east of place Vendôme. You may not be able to afford some of the spectacular creations that cost several thousand euros, but never mind... you are not going to buy anything at the Louvre either! Just step in and delight in the miraculous treasures of our earth—amethysts, tourmalines, cobalto-calcite, opal, and agate, delicately enhanced by diamonds, pearls, rubies, gold, and silver. Besides, some pieces are much more affordable.

"Rejoicing is extremely important," Jean Vendome said to me earnestly. Life is full of tragedy and the moments of joy help us bear the cross. Creating jewelry is his way of emphasizing the joy.

Mikimoto
8 place Vendôme, 75001
Tel: 01 42 60 33 55

*Open Monday—Saturday 10 a.m to 6:30 p.m.; closed Saturdays
in August & daily 1 to 2 p.m.*

Legend has it that the Tibetans were in possession of a "pearl of
seduction" that increased the amorous appetite of women caught in
its luster. Whether or not they have the same effect on you, pearls are
inarguably timelessly splendid, dignified, and discreet. Richard
Burton thought so when he gave a very precious pearl to Elizabeth
Taylor. It was 500 years old and had belonged to Mary Queen of
Scots. Unfortunately, Taylor's dog liked it, too—and by the time he
had finished chewing, the pearl had lost much of its value.

Mikimoto's story goes back to July 11, 1893, when Kokichi
Mikimoto produced the first cultured pearl ever, a spherical one. It had
taken him years of hardship and had cost him all his meager savings.
Only his supportive and courageous wife believed in him and followed
him devotedly—everyone else in the family thought he was out of his
mind! After the early death of his beloved wife, creating perfect
cultured pearls became his only goal. At a time of growing demand on
the international market and an increasing shortage of oysters,
Mikimoto benefited from the authorities' enthusiastic support, who
quickly realized that his invention might become a huge economic
asset to their country. This created one of the first commercial links
between Japan and the West. Mikimoto ensured that only the best
pearls would reach the West, and still today only five percent are
retained for export. The strict criteria take into account shape, size,
smoothness of surface, color, and, above all, luster.

If you are a Cancer, the pearl is your gem, or if you just love them
and can afford the splurge, Mikimoto is your destination. His pearls
are unsurpassed.

Othello
21, rue des Sts-Pères, 75006
Tel: 01 42 60 26 24

Open Monday—Saturday 10:30 a.m. to 7 p.m.

This jewelry is as passionately dramatic as the Shakespearean hero
the shop is named after. Annie-Paule Malaval, the proprietor, loves
the bard. She also loves ethnic jewelry, which she collected way back
in the 1960s, when it first swept over Europe. Eventually she gave up
teaching Spanish for her present trade: designing or commissioning
ethnically inspired, high-quality jewelry. A piece of jewelry, she
claims, is the one item devoid of any utilitarian function, the one you
crave for the mere pleasure of seduction. According to the type of
woman you are, you will crave a different type of jewelry. Are you a
domineering Cleopatra or an enticing Queen of Sheba? A graceful
Botticelli? To each her weapon. Annie-Paule provides for all.

Don't let the spectacular window display intimidate you. Although the Princess of Kent, Farah Pavlavi, Rudolph Nuryeyev, and members of the French nobility have been among her glamorous clientele, I was astonished to find some inexpensive pieces. Take your time, browse, and allow yourself to indulge.

Parthénon
54, rue des Ecoles, 75005
Tel: 01 43 54 26 04
Open Monday—Saturday 10:30 a.m. to 7 p.m.
Located across the street from the Sorbonne and by the Museum of the Middle Ages at the Hôtel de Cluny, this outlet of Didier Germain's workshop is not to be missed. I have been shopping here for years, enjoying both the harmony and the eclectic nature of their merchandise. Everyone can find something here. Germain's charming wife, Margid Kupfer, is the hostess of the shop, and it's a well-run business that allows the couple to keep prices as low as possible. Didier started out as a graphic designer in the advertising world, and has kept his penchant for graphic design in the jewelry he's been making since 1973. Many of his pieces successfully combine a pure, graphic line and the warmth of semi-precious stones, such as lapis lazuli and amber, with bronze and silver (I have bought pieces of each).

I love Didier's knack for adding a subtle ethnic touch to his overall contemporary spirit; I love Margid's aesthetic sense and beautiful window displays; I love their amazingly reasonable prices. I am sure you will, too.

Simone d'Avray
14, rue de l'Echaudé, 75006
Tel: 01 44 07 11 69
Open daily 12 to 7 p.m.; closed August
These teeny premises, on a tiny back street of St-Germain, are inhabited by a lovely, ebulliently creative jeweler. She also happens to be a talented sculptor—time permitting. Take the time to discover her huge choice of inexpensive goods, some her own, some made by others. She also carries out repairs, which might prove handy some day.

Virginie Monroe
30, rue de Charonne, 75011
Tel: 01 43 73 86 72
Open Sunday & Tuesday—Friday 11:30 a.m. to 8 p.m., Saturday 12 to 8 p.m.
Close to the place de la Bastille, this is the trendy young area of Paris, and Virginie Monroe's jewelry is both trendy and affordable. She uses glass beads, ceramics, enamel, feathers, and muslin, and lovely colors. It is all very feminine and seductive. You can also find

soothing oriental body lotions and oils from a Parisian Spa whose name alone—la Sultane de Sabah—evokes exotic lands, enhanced by Oriental music played in the background. And try their mint tea, with jasmine and orange blossoms.

LINGERIE

Like flowers, gorgeous lingerie can be found everywhere in town, even in the most out-of-the-way neighborhoods. In fact, the average annual spending on lingerie is higher in France than in any other European country. That is precisely why I have only given you one address under this section, where they carry goods the likes of which I have seen nowhere else in town.

Vannina Vesperini
60, rue des Sts-Peres, 75007
Tel: 01 42 84 37 62
Open Monday—Saturday 10 a.m. to 7 p.m.; closed August When Hungary and Corsica were wed, they gave birth to red-haired, blue-eyed Vannina. And as if she weren't blessed enough by nature, she also happens to be the most creative and artistic young lingerie designer around. So much talent—and barely 30 years old!

Here you can find all you need for seduction. The fabrics are fabulous, with microfiber as the basic layer, over which are layered muslin, tulle, or a bouquet of silk. Everything is fluid and undeniably sexy. Some of the designs are perennial, others more contemporary; all are carried out with a perfect finish, including the smallest detail. Vannina's lingerie is designed also as evening wear, suitable for a restaurant, a dinner party, or a ball. But you may prefer to reserve it for the exclusive pleasure of your lover and wear it only at home.

MEN'S ITEMS

While writing the shopping section of this book, I was severely reprimanded by a close friend for a female chauvinist attitude, as I had completely overlooked the male half of the human couple in providing my recommendations. Rather than sexist, I was simply self-centered, projecting my own desires for chocolate, champagne, flowers, and scents. And the occasional piece of jewelry.

Of course plenty of men enjoy all that too, but if you absolutely want to make your man happy, according to my above-mentioned friend, take him to the least romantic place in Paris, namely the do-it-yourself section in the basement of the BHV department store, at 52, rue de Rivoli. On weekend afternoons it is a bedlam of human congestion, but your man will have the time of his life messing around with his favorite toys. Ideally you will split up on that occasion, and you can meanwhile do some of your own shopping in the Marais or the Ile St-Louis, both of which are only a short walk away.

Cassegrain
422, rue St-Honoré, 75001
Tel: 01 42 60 20 08
Open Monday—Saturday 10 a.m. to 7 p.m.; closed Sundays
If you are still among those old-fashioned poets who shun the electronic age and want to express your love the old way, this is the place for you. Cassegrain specializes in all the items you might need for your correspondence: wonderful pens, leather goods, and superb writing paper, including your own gilded letterhead—at prices that can make your head spin.

Drapeaux de France
14, galerie de Montpensier, 75001
Tel: 01 42 97 55 40
Open Monday—Saturday 10 a.m. to 7 p.m.

I mean to offend no one, but they say that men never grow up. Those who are still into electric trains and toy soldiers should head to this shop, located in one of the utterly romantic arcades of the Palais-Royal. It is a collector's paradise—the world's biggest collection! Ten foundries from different parts of Europe work for the company, creating miniature, minutely-wrought treasures. Soldiers of Napoleon's First Empire are in particular demand, but my soft spot went to the colorful knights of the Middle Ages, with or without their horses. There was even a miniature Round Table in the shop. Ancient Greece, Ancient Rome, the American Revolution, the Scottish Guards in their kilts, the India of the Maharajahs, moving about on elephant backs… the entire history of the world is on display in this small shop. Twenty-thousand pieces are stocked, and many more can be ordered.

Once you start looking, you will also discover the feathered dancers of the Lido, Moulin Rouge cancan dancers, and strip-tease artists from one of the less glamorous dives of Pigalle. In their much more touristy annex, you will find models of romantic Paris landmarks, such as place des Vosges, the Palais Royal, the Tuileries, and also some of the street fittings, such as the Art Nouveau Métro stations. You'll be amazed at what you unearth here.

Dupont
58, avenue Montaigne, 75008
Tel: 01 45 61 08 39
Open Monday—Saturday 10 a.m. to 7 p.m.

Some objects become mythical. Dupont's lighter is one of them.

The founding father of this company, Simon Tissot-Dupont, started out selling luxury leather goods back in 1872. In the 1920s, the golden age of leisure travel, Dupont's travel cases, with their assortment of equally refined accessories, were indispensable to kings, maharajahs and princes. The one made for the Maharajah of Patiala in 1941 contained a novelty—a small pocket lighter made of gold. It was reproduced in aluminum and sometimes covered with China lacquer. Dupont has been the world standard in luxury lighters ever since.

In 1973 Dupont began to bring out luxury pens for men, and in 1977 re-introduced leather goods again, but only small items such as wallets. Rectangular wristwatches were added to their range in 1981. They too were decorated in China lacquer and have been much sought after.

Men's fashion followed in 1989, when Dupont took up residence on the glamorous avenue Montaigne, now its sole showcase in Paris. All their traditional articles are on sale here, and also cufflinks, belts, accessories for smokers, glasses, and now men's scents too.

If you are looking for a stylish but mainstream gift for your man, and if you want it to be French, Dupont is certainly the place you should head for first.

Jorg Hysek
45, rue Pierre Charron, 75008
Tel: 01 49 52 09 89

Open Tuesday — Saturday 10 a.m. to 7 p.m.; closed 2 weeks in August
The famous Swiss-Czech watch designer has now moved on to designing pens as well and has opened his first outlet. He chose Paris for the location and you will find the shop just south of the Champs-Elysées. His designs are resolutely modern in the best sense of the word, elegant and stylish and even revolutionary (the clip is fixed to a leather holder rather than to the pen itself so as not to affect your balance while you are writing, as clips will do). They come in lots of colors in the spirit of our times, bright but never gaudy. Just as revolutionary is his use of carbon fiber for his pens, unless you look to the future with his dipping pen, inspired by the quill pen of yore. Sounds paradoxical? Not really—you can write a full page with just one dip. And it looks so smart on its sleek, steel support. So go visit. His watches are here too, of course, and they are irresistibly elegant.

Milliaud (Jaeger-le-Coultre agent)
8, rue Royale, 75008
Tel: 01 42 86 96 16

Open Monday — Saturday 10 a.m. to 6:30 p.m.
Le Sentier, Switzerland. Picture a village nestling in a valley surrounded by the wooded Jura mountains. Among the Huguenots who escaped here from France in the mid-16th century was Pierre LeCoultre, an ancestor of Antoine LeCoultre. Born in 1803, Antoine learned the art of clockwork from his father, and by the age of 30 he and his brother Ulysse had set up a factory for making clock mechanisms. Pocket watches soon followed. In 1903 LeCoultre, still a family business, produced the flattest pocket watch in the world (1.38 mm). This is also when they struck up a partnership that would propel the company to staggering heights, with Edmond Jaeger, a chronometer manufacturer from Paris. Great efforts went into miniaturization and mechanical precision, culminating, in the 1920s, in their tiny rectangular wristwatch. The smallest one they ever made was studded with diamonds and worn by Queen Elizabeth on the day of her coronation. The launching of the Atmos pendulum in 1928, which required no winding, was just as sensational. This classic object has been presented by the Swiss government to VIP guests since 1936 (by now, however, it has been surpassed by the Millennium Atmos, which creates a quasi perpetual movement, indicating the years, months, and phases of the moon over the next 1,000 years). The Atmos is available here for €2,744.

The legendary art deco Reverso, brought out in 1931, was the first wristwatch designed for sporting activities. Its strap is mounted on a cradle in which the watchcase can flip over so as to protect the face of the watch from any shock. In 1932 the maharajah of Karputala ordered 50 of them, all with his own enameled effigy. Other Reverso watches bear enameled miniatures inspired by Art Nouveau paintings, notably those of Mucha. They are simply stunning.

A Reverso watch is one of the most superb (and expensive) gifts you can give the man in your life. You can make it very personal by having his initials or his astrological sign chiseled on the reverse side, or any other symbol for that matter. If you are fascinated by the mystery of space, you may consider lavishing on him the Sun Moon Reverso, truly of celestial beauty. In this age of quartz watches, they also carry a Reverso Memory, the keeper of personal time.

Another great gift which I saw in their shop was a desk globe of a perfect size, covered with lapis lazuli and other semiprecious stones, which goes for €1,448. A world map version for the wall costs about €562.

Patek Philippe
10, place Vendôme, 75001
Tel: 01 42 44 17 77
Open Sunday—Friday 10 a.m. to 12:30 p.m. & Saturday 2 to 7 p.m.;
closed Saturdays in July & August
Since 1839, this famous Swiss watchmaker has had one ambition—to make a perfect watch. Five hundred craftsmen and 240 watchmakers pursue this goal in the company's workshops in Geneva.

Giving your man a Philippe Patek watch is like receiving from him the most precious diamond ring or a string of pearls—an *objet d'art* of flawless beauty that will last forever. Their discerning customers realized this soon enough and included such illustrious figures as Queen Victoria, Peter Tchaikovsky, and Albert Einstein.

Today the Calatrava remains their most popular style—a classic round watch going back to 1932, but you may want a more complicated face, with dates, moon phases, and time zones. They also carry more contemporary designs, some of which are downright sporty, like the leisure watch, Nautilus, which also comes in stainless steel. It is water-resistant, yet stylish and elegant.

Point Plume
21, rue Quentin-Bauchart, 75008
Tel: 01 49 52 09 89
Open Monday—Saturday 10 a.m. to 7:15 p.m.
The realm of ballpoint and fountain pens and all things needed for your love letters. Here you will find an extraordinary array of collector's items to be seen nowhere else in the world. Besides the most prestigious labels, Point Plume is the only outlet of the extraordinary

sculptured pieces by Michel Audiard, purveyor of the Elysée presidential palace—what grander recommendation? His clients from the political sphere have not distracted him from romance, and you will find here unique items to offer your man (or woman), such as Audiard's sophisticated champagne bottle, his graceful *femme oiseau*, and his romantic roses, not to mention the new creations he brings out for each Valentine's Day. I was amazed by a specific pen that had a pair of Marilyn's legs sculpted on its clip, to be worn and exposed on your lapel. I thought it might look cheap, but quite the contrary—it was both exquisite and witty! Other than pens, the shop also carries superb wrist watches and boxes to keep them in safely, as well as jewel boxes, tea boxes, music boxes… all of them gorgeous and hand finished. Prices of course rocket to the heavens, but the shop is definitely worth exploring for the pleasure of the eye. It is only a short walk off the Champs-Elysées and avenue George V.

Tabac Journaux
16, rue des Sts-Pères, 75007
Tel: 01 42 60 20 54
Open Monday—Saturday 8 a.m. to 7 p.m.; closed August
A genuine neighborhood tobacconist that has been in business for over a century. The two charming ladies who run the shop are just as genuine. They don't speak much English, but you are sure to understand one another. At long last a place where you can buy him a gift, and they are all French made, in pure regional tradition— beautifully made pipes from St-Claude in the Jura mountains or knives from the picturesque town of Laguiole in the Aveyron. You can find here an attractive paper knife for under €40 and a traditional screwdriver combined with a knife in its elegant box for about €87. They also carry several excellent brands of cigars, but those come directly from Havana.

MISCELLANEOUS

Alice au Pays des Artistes
73, rue de Monceau, 75008
Tel: 01 42 25 44 55
Open Monday—Friday, 10:30 a.m. to 7 p.m.; Saturday 11 a.m. to 5:30 p.m.; may be closed August
Within minutes of the bejeweled Parc Monceau, you will find here an impressive choice of sculptures, jewelry, and household items, by rotating artists, both French and foreign. Many of the works are affordable and the choice is eclectic.

Right: Mélodies Graphiques

Mélodies Graphiques
10, rue du Pont-Louis-Philippe, 75004
Tel: 01 42 74 57 68
Open Monday 2 to 7 p.m.; Tuesday—Saturday 10 a.m. to 7 p.m.
If you find our e-age totally devoid of romance, make your way at once to this address, located in one of the most romantic spots of Paris. This is a place for those who long for bygone days when one waited with palpitating anticipation for the arrival of the postman, when one's hands trembled as they tore open the envelope that contained the most-treasured gift, and when love letters were placed religiously under one's pillow for the journey of the night. At Mélodies Graphiques love is woven into paper and cloth. Here you will sing your love with the poetry of your pen, enhanced by baroque music in the background. In the stack of greeting cards, you might unearth a subtle watercolor of Juliet's balcony. Look for a tiny envelope with little bits of paper inside and ask owner Eric de Tanguy to unveil to you its mystery. Or ask Eric for his guest book where you may scribble something for your other half. You may also enjoy leafing through it—it contains a bouquet of love missives that clients have written to each other. Two clandestine lovers once used this shop and this book in lieu of any other mailbox.

Orphée
8, rue du Pont Louis-Philippe, 75004
Tel: 01 42 72 68 42
Open Monday—Saturday 2 to 7 p.m.
If you understand Orpheus's loss of Eurydice, or if you love old musical instruments, walk into this exquisite museum-turned shop, where you might find a romantic guitar or a mandolin to accompany your love songs, as the guitar was used in the 19th century. In the classical age, the gift of a violin was symbolic of the harmony of the souls. Not long ago, Paul McCartney walked in here with his daughter and bought her an earthenware ocarina. She was doing a fashion show in Paris to his music.

Robert Capia
24-26, galerie Véro-Dodat, 75001
Tel: 01 42 36 25 94
Open Monday—Saturday 10 a.m. to 7 p.m.
The enchanting world of antique dolls is tucked away in one of the least known marvels of Paris, an early 19th-century arcade, all mirrors framed in brass, with imitation marble and checkered flooring. You don't have to travel far to find this hiding place. It is right in the heart of the city, just off rue du Louvre, though unknown to most.

Robert Capia is the man you want to find if you love antique dolls. His collection of both dolls and archives is surpassed by none on the Paris scene. His renown has crossed the borders and his contribution has even been rewarded by the Legion of Honor. The 1967 exhibition he organized triggered an interest in antique dolls that hasn't waned since.

Don't be inhibited by any of this—although his shop is deliciously crowded with museum pieces, Capia is most charming and personable, and will lavish upon you a warm welcome. His antique dolls date from the 19th and early 20th centuries and come with houses and furniture.

Sartoni-Cerveau
15, quai St-Michel, 75005
Tel: 01 43 54 75 73
Open daily 11 a.m. to 7 p.m.
This shop, located along the Left-Bank quai of the Seine, across the river from Notre Dame, is inevitably on your romantic trail. Walk in and take your time to browse through their old books, maps, and prints, from the 17th through 19th centuries. I have unearthed here wonderful treasures of old Paris, at very reasonable prices, and they make wonderful souvenirs to take back home.

PERFUME

The quintessential weapon of seduction. So much so that only women of easy virtue applied it directly to their skin in 19th-century France. Respectable women would only apply it to their handkerchiefs or clothes, although on certain occasions a small, single drop would be tolerated, if applied to the hollow of the neck, or behind the ear.

Annick Goutal
12, place St-Sulpice, 75006
Tel: 01 46 33 03 15
Open Monday—Saturday 10 a.m. to 7 p.m.

The late Annick Goutal started out as a pianist, but she had always loved scents. For her own pleasure, she blended jasmine and tuberose oils into what was to become her first scent. She named it simply "Passion," which said it all and marked the beginning of a new career. Today Annick Goutal's trademark is part of the Tattinger empire, owners of the famous champagne, the Baccara crystal, the Crillon, and the Michelin three-star restaurant, Le Grand Véfour, a guarantee of luxury, quality, and prestige. All these perfumes are made out of natural oils and are sure to make your lover drift to heavenly spheres. My personal favorite is Hadrian, an astonishing blend of lime, cedrat, grapefruit, and mandarin. It is also suitable for men.

Caron
34, avenue Montaigne, 75008
Tel: 01 47 23 40 82
Open Monday—Saturday 10 a.m. to 6:30 p.m.

Visiting this venerable establishment is a journey into history.

In 1903 Ernest Daltroff set up shop at 10, rue de la Paix, then the city's most fashionable street. Success came immediately with the launching of several topically-inspired scents: Radiant, a tribute to the discoveries of electricity and radium, and London-Paris, an homage to the 1904 *entente cordiale*. These two scents, along with Royal Caron and Royal Emilia, gained Daltroff quick admission into the world of perfumery.

A love story catapulted Caron to further heights. It began on the staircase of 10, rue de la Paix, where Ernest met Félicie Wanpouille, a successful *couturière* who worked in the same building. Their perfume Bel Amour may have been an allusion to their honeymoon period, which alas, was not to last. Felicie swapped the designing of ladies' clothes for the designing of perfume bottles, for which she displayed as great a talent. Like Paul Poiret and René Lalique, she drew her inspiration from cultural life, notably Diaghilev's Ballets Russes. With her talent and Ernest's unwavering drive, Caron was a dazzling success, crowned by Narcisse Noir in 1911. But why did the Narcisse Noir have a black anemone on its stopper, so out of keeping with the bottle? Apparently something kept them from achieving the perfect love they craved, though they expressed hope the following year in their new scent, Infini. It was Narcisse Noir, though, that became Caron's trademark. In 1913 Ernest gave it to the young Colette, who was acting at the Olympia. "The originality and talent of this young person is in harmony with the perfume," he wrote to Félicie from Grasse.

Despite threatening competition from the *haute couture* houses, which after the war started producing their own scents, Caron's success continued to grow, Félicie and Ernest having been able to separate their private lives from their common professional goals. In 1918 they carried their success across the Atlantic and received the prize for perfumes during the New York fashion show. Five years later they even opened a shop on Fifth Avenue. The same year they brought out a bath essence that came in a bottle of champagne and had an antique-style bas-relief label designed by Félicie. It was simply and appropriately called Champagne, and was inspired by and reflected on the orgiastic endings of many a night during the Roaring Twenties.

Today you will find Caron on glamorous premises on the avenue Montaigne. Their array of products has increased infinitely, but if you were to try just one, let it be N'aimez Que Moi (love but me), a mix of bergamot, iris, amber, and musk, in a quirky, asymmetrical bottle.

Guerlain
68, avenue des Champs-Elysées, 75008
Tel: 01 45 62 11 21
Open Monday—Saturday 10:30 a.m. to 8 p.m.

In 1828, Pierre-François-Pascal Guerlain, a young doctor in chemistry, opened the first Parisian shop of what would become this world-famous company. The small factory where he was creating his experimental fragrances was way out in the country (now the corner of place de l'Etoile and the avenue Kléber). During the Second Empire he created his famous Eau de Cologne Impériale, which is still on sale today in its original bottle. Empress Eugénie was delighted and Guerlain was granted the title, His Majesty's Official Perfumer. Parfum Impérial, Parfum de France, Bouquet de l'Impératrice, Bouquet Napoléon, and Délice du Prince followed and brought new clients, among them Queen Victoria and the Empress Sissi of Austria.

A new era began in 1900, when Guerlain's nephew Jacques expanded to the full range of beauty products we now take for granted—lotions, creams, and powders, and even makeup. His most celebrated client was the divine Sarah Bernhardt, the Belle Époque's most adulated actress.

And new scents kept coming, including the exquisitely romantic l'Heure Bleu, designed to celebrate the moment when the sky has lost its sun but hasn't yet found its stars, and le Mouchoir de Monsieur, to be used by men as part of their courtship strategy. (It was customary to offer a coveted lady a delicately perfumed handkerchief, with the hope that she would have occasion to use it to wipe away a tear, be it of joy or sadness.)

In 1925 Guerlain came out with Shalimar ("temple of love" in Sanskrit), which was the place where the great emperor of India, Shah Jahan, would meet his favorite, Mumtaz Mahal. When his beloved died, he replaced it with a mausoleum worthy of his love— the famous Taj Mahal. The perfume conquered the United States immediately, both for the sensual delight of the scent and for the beauty of the bottle. It is still Guerlain's household name.

Many others followed... Vol de Nuit, which pays tribute to the poet aviator Antoine de St-Exupéry, author of the unforgettable *Little Prince*; Nahéma, entirely dedicated to the rose; Jardins de Bagatelle, as exquisite as the Parisian gardens in the Bois de Boulogne (see page 242); and Samsara ("eternal rebirth" in Sanskrit), a combination of jasmine and sandalwood. And Guerlain's latest creation, Champs-Elysées, celebrates its present home address. It is the first scent to have "tamed" the mimosa blossom, and blended it with rose petals and almond blossoms. Today Jean-Paul Guerlain travels the world over in quest of the best of scents—sandalwood and jasmine from India, bergamot from Calabria, orange blossom from Tunisia, benjamin from Ethiopia, the one-time kingdom of the Queen of Sheba, and more.

Guerlain remains in the family after nearly 200 years, a reference in itself. So is the fact that they have sustained their adventurous creativity and produced 626 different perfumes. Discovering Guerlain is like embarking on a never-ending journey. Their landmark shop on the Champs-Elysées is the place to begin.

Salon du Palais Royal Shiseido
142, galerie de Valois (the eastern arcade), 75001
Tel: 01 49 27 09 09
Open Monday—Saturday 10 a.m. to 7 p.m.
This is a unique place, my very own favorite, to be approached in silent awe. You first climb up one floor before penetrating a dim, silent sanctuary permeated with fabulous, subtle scents. You have stepped into a dream of marble floors, lilac walls, and rosewood paneling, where Parisian chic meets Japanese refinement. On our visit, the priestess in charge of the ceremony was a gorgeous, exotic-looking shop assistant who kept producing samples of bewitching fragrances. Some are suitable for both men and women and you can even have your initials engraved on the bottles.

WINES & SPIRITS

Passant par Paris vidant ma bouteille,
Un de mes amis me dit à l'oreille:
Le bon vin m'endort,
L'amour me réveille.

Passing through Paris, my bottle runs dry
One of my friends whispered in my ear:
Wine makes me sleepy,
Love wakes me up.

Long before the first Bishop of Paris, Saint Denis, came to die as a martyr on the hill of Montmartre, the jovial Dionysus had taken up residence on that very same hill. Some believe that Denys, as his name was once spelled, was no other than Dionysus, reborn into a new Christian identity. When Denis was beheaded by the Roman heathens, he simply picked up his head and continued walking up the hill where he washed off the blood in a fountain before resuming his journey to what is now the suburb of Saint Denis, north of Paris. Could it have been that earlier pagan god had lost his head after too much merry drinking? Did he need to refresh himself a bit in the fountain because he suffered from a hangover?

Be that as it may, wine has always been the lifeblood of Paris, the fuel of its revolutions and the aphrodisiac of its feasts. Up until the French Revolution the Paris area was France's first wine-growing region. The heights of Belleville in eastern Paris, the slopes of Auteuil and Passy to the west, Vaugirard further south, the hill of Montmartre north of the city, and the stretches of fields south of the Latin Quarter, even patches of St-Germain, were all covered with vineyards. All went with the arrival of industry. Yet the vineyards of Paris have been resurrected in recent years, to locals' delight. Paris now numbers nine such patches, which produce 2,310 bottles per year. If you happen to be in Paris in the autumn, you may enjoy taking part in a grape-picking celebration, especially the one on the hill of Montmartre.

L'Antiquaire du Vin
12, rue Mallar, 75007
Tel: 01 47 05 01 02
Open Tuesday—Saturday 12 to 9 p.m. & by appointment; closed 3 weeks in August
Roland Marzari is an Italian Swiss who started out as a mechanical engineer. He likes to refer to himself as a 1943 vintage. A few years ago, he felt he needed a career change and he became an old wine dealer. His bottles go back to 1780—*before* the French Revolution. He became a member of the wine committee of Montmartre, which presides over the destiny of its pocket-size vineyard, and stocks some of its wine in his shop.

The most expensive wine you will find here is a Romanée-Conti 95, a Burgundy from the Côte-d'Or in the Jura. It goes for €2,000 (plus VAT). Roland also carries amazing old cognacs, even a Napoleon vintage from 1800 (for €1,500 plus VAT). But don't be discouraged: he also carries excellent wines for as little as €20–30.

Legrand Filles et Fils
1, rue de la Banque, 75002
Tel: 01 42 60 07 12
Open Monday 10 a.m. to 7 p.m. Tuesday—Friday 9 a.m. to 7:30 p.m. & Saturday 9 a.m. to 7 p.m.

This address has been going strong as a delicatessen since 1919, when Monsieur Legrand opened shop in what was then just a little Parisian neighborhood. It was right after the Great War and good food was much in demand. Note: Walk in through the back entrance, which opens into the romantic galerie Vivienne, one of Paris's loveliest arcades.

After World War II, Paris revived once more, and Legrand's son Lucien decided to specialize in wines. The gourmet grocery is still going strong, with wonderful mustard, olive oil, jams, honey, chocolates, and so forth, but the wine department has largely taken over and is what the house is renowned for.

A team of very knowledgeable wine lovers runs the place, spending their time between Paris and the French countryside, scouring its little-known vineyards for an unknown gem. Entrust yourself blindfolded to Pascal who, before switching to the wine business, trained to become a mathematician. He will help you choose according to your budget, including the best of champagnes, notably a bottle of Gosset grand réserve at €30, but also other excellent ones that come from small producers, such as Tarlant cuvée blanc de blanc chez Legrand, for only €21 per bottle, or the house champagne, Legrand (Tarlant) for €17, which makes an excellent apéritif. Besides wines, they carry the traditional French alcohols, such as calvados, Armagnac, eau de vie, and lesser known ones too. Their only imports are whiskeys and ports, both of which are top quality.

I left the house with a Cuvée Francine, so called after Monsieur Legrand's grand-daughter, who now carries the torch of this great establishment.

Last minute post scriptum: Legrand has expanded its activities and now has a specialized bookshop!

Musée de La Vie Romantique

6

COZY MUSEUMS

*[Paris]...the civilized world's eternal
and splendid courtesan.*
—William Faulkner

CATTERED THROUGHOUT PARIS ARE MORE THAN 150 museums. Some of them are so popular and crowded that they are hardly conducive to a romantic visit. I have tried to focus on smaller, lesser known museums, some of which nestle in greenery and will provide pleasant getaways for the pair of you. The more popular among this category of museums, notably the Rodin and the Jacquemart-André, can become very crowded—visit in the early hours of the morning and avoid on weekend and holiday afternoons.

Baccarat
30bis, rue de Paradis, 75010
Tel: 01 47 70 64 30
Open Monday—Saturday 10 a.m. to 6 p.m.

If you wish to be dazzled, make your way to this down-at-heel section of Paris, where few tourists stray. Rue de Paradis is the city's stronghold of crystal outlets, a testimony to the neighborhood's more congenial past, when several royal workshops and factories stood here, alongside some magnificent townhouses. Stop too at 18, rue de Paradis, once the outlet of the Choisy-le-Roy pottery, to see a stunning display of turn-of-the-century ceramics.

Make your way through the vast elegant entrance hall, basically unchanged since the middle of the 19th century, when Baccarat first established their Parisian outlet here. Proceed up the beautiful wooden staircase to see the two stunning candelabra. Tsar Nicolas II originally commissioned ten of them, but none reached their destination due to the political upheavals in turn-of-the-century Russia. You will also be greeted by two huge vases made out of unique gold and red crystal, that initially brought Baccarat into the limelight. Hanging from the ceiling is an overwhelming chandelier of gilt bronze and streams of crystal. For safety reasons its scores of candles are kept unlit, but imagine a mirrored ball room, where their glowing flames are multiplied infinitely! For every item on display must be imagined in context to be fully appreciated. More than 1,000 *objets d'art* are housed here and exhibited in rotation, tracing the history of the factory from 1764, when it was first established in the village of Baccarat, in Eastern France.

Travel back in time to the city's 1867 World Fair, when Baccarat offered astounded visitors a 19-foot-tall fountain entirely made of crystal. Or the 1925 Fair, when Baccarat was commissioned by the celebrated fashion house, Jean Patou, to design a bottle for its new scent, Amour-Amour. Perfume bottles have been one of Baccarat's specialties for the last hundred years and many designs, including contemporary ones, are on display in the museum. Now Baccarat has even branched off into making their own scents.

Each window case is devoted to a specific period, and I personally succumbed to the display of 1909. The mindboggling beauty, luster, and grace of each design! Some seem to be covered by the finest of lace, others look like chiseled gems, or a dripping piece of jewelry. To think that such splendors were all wrought out of the same alchemy of fire and sand!

Balzac (Maison)
47, rue Raynouard, 75016
Tel: 01 55 74 41 80
Open Tuesday—Sunday 10 a.m. to 5:40 p.m.; closed holidays

Nestling in a shady garden, among beautiful old trees, this one-time home of writer Balzac has the delightful rustic look of a country cottage. After all, this was remote countryside back in the 1840s, which is precisely why he moved here. It provided an excellent hideaway from his creditors' bailiffs, as he informed his mistress, Madame Hanska, on 16 November 1840: "From the moment you receive this letter write to me at the following address: Monsieur de Brugnol, rue Basse [now Raynouard] in Passy-lès[near]-Paris. I am well-hidden here for a while."

His new identity was borrowed from Louise, his vigilant housekeeper who admitted no one without the password, "The plum season has arrived"—followed by, "I am bringing lace from Bruges," when reaching the first floor.

Balzac's correspondence with Madame Hanska also gives us a clear idea of his timetable: "Working, dear Countess, is to get up each night at 12 and write till 8, to breakfast in a quarter of an hour, work till 5, dine, go to sleep and start all over the following day." This accounts for his vast output during those seven years, which included such masterpieces as *Le Cousin Pons*, *Les Illusions perdues*, and *La Cousine Bette*, not to mention revising the entire *Comédie Humaine*. It also accounts for the omnipresence of his notorious coffee-pot, which never left his desk and is on view in the museum.

If you love Balzac, you will be moved to be where he lived, looking out on the garden or peering into his study, which has been preserved almost intact. You will see the faces of those who accompanied him through his life, above all, Evelyne Hanska, the wife of the Polish Count Hanski, who sent the author a fan letter in 1832 that sparked off a sixteen-year correspondence and a passionate love. Despite the distance that separated them, they managed to meet the following year in Neuchâtel, Switzerland, then again in Geneva the year after, and again the following year in Vienna. After a separation of eight years, they finally met once more in Saint Petersburg, in 1843. By then Madame Hanska was widowed, but she kept evading and rejecting Balzac's persistent proposals. In order to accommodate her lavish tastes, he bought an apartment by the fashionable Parc Monceau, which he could barely afford, and had it decorated sumptuously for her sake, but she never came to live there. The impassioned Balzac himself ended up moving to the estate, where they were finally married on March 14, 1850. Eighteen months later, Balzac was back in Paris. Madame Hanska did not accompany him on his journey and was not by his bedside when he passed away, shortly after, in the palatial apartment he had so wished to offer his beloved countess, and which she had never even seen.

You, who are happy to be together and are looking for secluded getaways, will enjoy the lovely gardens overlooking the one-time palace of Marie-Antoinette's close friend, la Princesse de Lamballe (now the Turkish Embassy).

From Balzac in Passy to Madame Hanska in Wierzchownia, the Ukraine

Must I then repeat to you that ever since I received your dear portrait, I've looked at nothing else whilst working, and that no one has been allowed into my study without the divine image first being withdrawn, and that ever since I received Wierzchownia, my eyes have constantly been gazing upon this landscape, and upon you. So much so that I haven't altered a phrase, searched for an idea or found a subject that I didn't see in your eyes or in the pond of Wierzchownia.

10 April 1842

Bourdelle
16, rue Antoine, 75015
Tel: 01 49 54 73 73
Open Tuesday—Sunday 10 a.m. to 5:40 p.m.

Tucked away on a side street off commercial Montparnasse, this museum is a miraculous survivor from old times, when many artists lived in what was then both a "village" and the artistic center of the world. Antoine Bourdelle actually lived and worked on these very extensive premises, which he bought up little by little. He needed all that space for his gigantic sculptures, and some for his parents, too.

You will not find here the palatial elegance of the Musée Rodin and the lovely grounds that go with it: Montparnasse was a poor man's neighborhood. But Bourdelle, who was Rodin's distinguished student, deserves discovery. The place is uncrowded and atmospheric, with its two charmingly unkempt gardens, overgrown with rambling creepers and filled with Bourdelle's works.

Bourdelle moved here from his native Montauban in 1885 and, like Rodin, dreamed of having his own museum. After his death in 1929 the city of Paris rejected his widow's donation of the property and its content, but fortunately revised its opinion in 1949, when it was turned into a museum.

During your visit you can follow Bourdelle's artistic growth, which is displayed with great clarity from his academic beginnings, through expressionism's obvious influence, and on to the architectural style he achieved by 1900. His contribution to the Théâtre des Champs-Elysées (1913) is one of his masterpieces, and if you attend a concert there, you will also discover his beautiful wall paintings. Bourdelle became an inspiration to scores of aspiring sculptors from the world over who came to learn under his wing, Alberto Giacometti and Vieira da Silva among them.

Bourdelle taught at the famous Académie de la Grande Chaumière in Montparnasse, but some of his students liked to come to work here, on the Impasse du Maine, as the street was then called. One of them, Léon Indenbaum, considered Bourdelle "a great master" and "a marvelous teacher," and admonished his students: "Don't do what I am doing—sing your own song."

Sometimes his Russian protégés from the Ecole de Paris would do precisely that, filling the studio with nostalgic songs from their motherland. They say Bourdelle would wait behind the closed door and listen, before stepping in to critique their work. As you visit, try to imagine the place as it was back in those livelier days.

Carnavalet
23, rue de Sévigné, 75003
Tel: 01 44 59 58 58
Open Tuesday—Sunday 10 a.m. to 5:40 p.m.

There are two unusual love affairs connected to the Carnavalet mansion: First, the love between its 17th-century tenant, my much admired Marquise de Sévigné, and the house itself, and then, the Sévigné's passion for her daughter, which sparked one of the most famous of epistolary writings in French literature. Both passions thrived in harmony when the Sévigné acquired the lease of this coveted place, and brought her daughter's household to it as well, to the satisfaction of all.

Today this is the museum of the history of Paris and a great favorite of mine. I love it for its content but also for its architectural beauty, for it is the oldest and only surviving Renaissance palace in the Marais (albeit much restored by Mansart in the 17th century). Its gorgeous front courtyard was decorated by the king's sculptor Goujon, and deserves attention in itself. The inner garden is wonderful, too, with its exquisite profusion of rose bushes.

The museum traces the history of Paris from its very beginning, but if you are especially seeking the romantic, you should visit the rooms of Marcel Proust, the poet Anna de Noailles, and of course, the Sévigné.

Recently, the newly restored orangery, located in the square Gaston-Cain, became home to the oldest boats ever found in the river Seine. They bear witness to human presence in the Paris area

back in the third millennium B.C. The charming little square that serves as a depository for the museum's ancient stones is overlooked by most. So is the adjacent square Léopold-Achille—a good reason for the two of you to escape to one of its benches.

> *Thank God, we have the [lease of the] Hôtel Carnavalet. It is an admirable affair; there will be room for all of us and we shall have good air. As one cannot have everything, we shall have to do without parquet floors and without the small fireplaces that are so in vogue; but we have at least a beautiful courtyard, a beautiful garden, a beautiful neighborhood and good little "blue girls" [from the neighboring orphanage] who are very well behaved.*
> —*Madame de Sévigné*

Cognacq–Jay
8, rue Elzévir, 75003
Tel: 01 40 27 07 21

Open Tuesday—Sunday 10 a.m. to 5:40 p.m.; closed holidays

Located in the late-16th-century Hôtel Donon, one of the earliest mansions in the Marais, this museum contains the Ernest Cognacq and Marie-Louise Jay collection of 18th-century French art.

Cognacq was born in 1839, one of eleven children. Instead of becoming a painter, as he dreamed, he became an orphan and a peddler on the Pont Neuf, struggling to survive. By 1869 he owned a shop on the Right-Bank edge of the bridge, which he named La Samaritaine, after the river's old water pump. Within a couple of decades it became one of the early department stores of Paris... quite a head-spinning climb! Driven by ambition, he collected art in the pursuit of social status. Ernest was by no means a true connoisseur, but he hired art dealers to build up what was to become an outstanding collection. His wife Louise had little to do with his venture, although her name graces the museum. (As a matter of fact, she thought it was a waste of money and time.) Like Cognacq, she came from a modest background and was working in a draper's shop when Ernest first met her.

Ernest Cognacq bequeathed his collection to the city of Paris in 1928. Besides paintings by the most representative artists of the time—Fragonard, Boucher, Watteau, Nattier, Greuse, Quintin La Tour, to name a few—it contains beautiful decorative arts as well, such as woodcraft, porcelain, snuff boxes, perfume bottles, Aubusson tapestry, and an extraordinary bed in the Louis XVI room, which once belonged to the king's aunt, Madame Adélaïde.

Left: Carnavalet

Delacroix
6, rue de Fürstemberg, 75006
Tel: 01 44 41 86 50
Open Wednesday—Monday 9:30 a.m. to 5 p.m.

Tucked away behind an old cobbled courtyard, opening into one of the prettiest of little squares, set off by the pink-and-white brick-and-stone wall of the one time palace of the abbot of St-Germain, this is one of the most romantic addresses on the Left Bank. It may look vaguely familiar, if you've seen Vincente Minnelli's *Gigi*.

Try to make it in the early morning, when you can appreciate the same light that the painter himself loved here, at his last home. (See page 27.)

Edith Piaf
5, rue Crespin-du-Gacst, 75011
Tel: 01 43 55 52 72
Open Monday–Thursday 1 to 6 p.m. by appointment only; closed in September

If you are an Edith Piaf fan, take a sentimental journey to this out-of-the-way working-class neighborhood. This is the world into which Piaf was born back in 1916, where the true heart of Paris throbs. Piaf grew up on the then-destitute rue de Belleville a little further east. Today the neighborhood is changing fast; nearby rue Oberkampf is a trendy street crowded with young people, especially at night and on weekends.

Piaf was a great, but—as you will see in this miniscule apartment-come-museum—tiny woman. A life-size picture reveals all four feet and nine inches of her. On display, too, are a pair of size 4 shoes, a handbag, a pair of gloves, the celebrated black dress she wore on the stage, and a huge Teddy bear. Her voice and songs play in the background, and the shrine is lined with sculptures, paintings, and writings that have been deposited here by admiring friends and fans. Among them a homage by Jean Cocteau:

> *Et voila qu'une voix qui sort des entrailles, une voix qui l'habite des pieds à la tete, déroule une haute vague de velours noir.*
> When lo, a voice emerges from her guts, a voice that fills her from top to toe, unrolling a wave of black velvet.

Piaf died on the morning of October 11, 1963. Shattered by the news, Cocteau had a heart attack a few hours later and died the very same day.

Eroticism
72, boulevard de Clichy, 75018
Tel: 01 42 58 28 73
Open 10 a.m. to 2 a.m.

How symptomatic that Paris should be the world's only capital to devote a cultural institution to erotica! The museum is located in the infamous neighborhood of Pigalle. This, and the fact that it stretches opening hours until two in the morning—I bet no other museum beats that!—was off-putting. I would never have bothered to visit, if it had not been for this book, and the fear that some reader might accuse me of prudish narrowmindedness. So I got a male friend to accompany me and was actually pleasantly surprised. The museum definitely fulfills its cultural ambition and puts on view a vast panorama of erotic artifacts and *objets d'art* from all parts of the world. The references to the Hindu love manual, the *Kama Sutra*, actually provide food for thought and can be very touching.

Fan Museum
2, boulevard de Strasbourg, 75010
Tel: 01 42 08 90 20
Open Monday—Wednesday 2 to 6 p.m.; closed August & holidays
Although the fan began its career as the ancestor of the air-conditioner, it quickly became a weapon of seduction, allowing women to engage in teasing games of hide-and-seek. When the Portuguese brought it back from China in the 16th century, it became fashionable among European ladies of the court right away, especially in Catherine de Medici's France. An elaborate code was soon part of the game, and by the way they handled their fans, the ladies signaled acceptance, rejection, or other love messages. In 17th-century Spain, for instance, a fan held in the left hand meant, "We are being observed;" if rolled in the right, "My heart belongs to another." As the fan's popularity grew, Louis XIV's minister, Colbert, organized the craft of fan-making into a thriving business. Demand grew as fans were ordered by the same client for different occasions, to be appreciated both as *objets d'art* and marks of social status.

The popularity of the fan peaked in the 19th century, during the Belle Epoque, when Parisian society shifted its "catwalk" from mansions to the *grands boulevards*, the theater, and the opera. These were the days when Anne Hoguet's great-grandfather made fans.

Hoguet is the last surviving fan-maker in France, and it is her father's collection of 800 magnificent fans that are on display in the private little museum she has set up in a regular Parisian apartment building, in a rather unappetizing neighborhood close to the Gare de l'Est. In the 19th century, the area was a stronghold of luxury crafts, with 60 workshops employing some 1,200 artisans who worked for the domestic market and for export, predominantly to Spain, Holland, and England.

Women's emancipation knocked the fan over and barged into the 20th century with the cigarette, which framed the face with provocative sophistication, if still providing the occassional screen of smoke.

Back in the 18th century, fifteen craftsmen designed and made a single fan, but today Anne Hoguet does everything herself. She works predominantly for the cinema, the theater, the opera, and the *haute couture* houses. Karl Lagerfeld, Christian Lacroix, Nina Ricci, and Christian Dior are among her clients. In 1998, Jean-Paul Gaultier commissioned a pink satin wedding gown, entirely made of fans. It took 2,000 hours to complete.

The museum's collection spans nearly four centuries, from the 17th to the present day. Some items are sumptuous, some are more discreet, some fold, others are mounted on screens. Some bear paintings of scenes of courtship, proposal, and bethrothal. All are magnificently crafted, using materials as varied as kidskin, silk, lace, satin, or organdy for the mounts, and fine woods, mother-of-pearl, tortoise-shell, ivory, horn, or bone for the sticks. There is also a gift shop with reasonably priced items.

Fragonard (Museum of Perfume)
9, rue Scribe, 75009
Tel: 01 47 42 04 56
39, boulevard des Capucines, 75009
Tel: 01 42 60 37 14
Open 9 a.m. to 6 p.m.; Sundays in summer & holidays 9:30 a.m. to 4 p.m.

The only link between perfumes and the famous 18th-century painter is the fact that both were natives of the world's capital of scents, Grasse, which perches on the flowery hills of Provence. The perfumery goes back to the 18th century, but changed hands in 1926. Its new owner, Eugène Fuchs, renamed it Parfumerie Fragonard, in homage to Grasse's celebrated son. In 1968, his grandson Jean-François Costa, a passionate art collector, decided to open his collection to the public, and it became a museum in 1975. In 1983 the museum moved to this magnificent Napoleon III mansion on rue Scribe, by the Palais Garnier. The museum extended its premises in 1992 to the neighboring Théâtre des Capucines, a magnificent 1900 hall. Now 3,000 years of perfume-making history come to life through engravings, photos, displays of laboratory utensils, and even a miniature factory.

The museum houses gorgeous perfume bottles and documents nicely different historical uses of perfumes—therapeutic, ritualistic, hygienic—before they became a stimulus for voluptuous pleasures among the privileged of 18th-century France.

You are sure to succumb in their shop to the refined beauty of the bottles and to the exquisite scents they contain.

Gustave Moreau
14, rue de La Rochefoucauld, 75009
Tel: 01 48 74 38 50
Open Monday & Wednesday 11 a.m. to 5:15 p.m.; Thursday—Sunday 10 a.m. to 12:30 p.m. & 2 to 5 p.m.

Located in the charming neighborhood of La Nouvelle Athènes, this used to be the painter Gustave Moreau's home, bought for him by his parents, who lived here too. It was Moreau's idea to turn his home into a museum, to keep his works under the same roof and prevent them from being dispersed. The substantial alterations this required were entirely financed by the artist himself, and caused no small disturbance in the neighborhood, as this letter from a close lady friend tells us: "I have thought a lot about you during the entire summer! I shall not say that it was always with the same sentiment of good humor. Oh, what a racket! Oh, so much dust… and it is not over yet."

The museum, which opened in 1903, a few years after the artist's death, gives you the cozy feel of a private home. A stunning spiral staircase leads to the upper floors. One section of the museum, designated as *"le boudoir,"* is devoted to his lifetime friend, Alexandrine Dureux. The two met in 1859 and their friendship lasted until her death in 1890, when she was just 54. Gustave was devastated, especially as he had always taken it for granted that he would die first.

S hould I become unwell or seriously ill, the following are my specific instructions. I let it be understood and I order that Mademoiselle Adélaïde Alexandrine Dureux, my best friend, to whom I have been united for twenty-seven years by the deepest, the most respectful and the most tender affection, be free to come and visit me and enter my room at any time of day and night. I desire to be nursed by her alone or under her sole supervision. My close friends are fully aware of my attachment to her and of her boundless devotion, of which she gave me frequent and noble proofs during the terrible days that followed the loss of the person whom I cherished most in the world [his mother]… I also desire that on my last hour her hand be in mine and that we should be left alone.

Paris, 10 January 1886
Gustave Moreau
Painter of history, residing in Paris
14, rue de La Rochefoucauld

Alexandrine had lived on the nearby rue Notre-Dame-de-Lorette, and the two saw each other every day, but the nature of the relationship was never clarified. His painting *Orphée pleurant sur la tombe d'Eurydice* (Orpheus weeping on Eurydice's tomb), one of the museum's masterpieces, was painted a year after her death, and is explicitly autobiographical. The painting echoes the suffering on the cross as Orpheus's arm is stretched against the thunderstruck trunk of a tree by Eurydice's tomb. The martyrdom of Saint Sebastian also comes to mind, and so does the penitent monk in the desert as represented by the Italian Quattrocento.

Among the thousands of works housed here, of which only a small number can be displayed, there are several paintings of femmes fatales, such as Delilah, who symbolize the fall of modern-day Babylon, the Paris of his age. His painting of Salomé inspired both Oscar Wilde and Richard Strauss. (Unfortunately, it is often on loan.) Another of the museum's highlights is *La fée aux griffons* (The fairy and the griffins). It radiates with such an astonishing glow that the fairy truly seems to inhabit a dream world. Apparently this painting had a great impact on André Breton, who often came over from his home on the neighboring rue Fontaine.

Jacquemart–André
158, boulevard Haussmann, 75008
Tel: 01 42 89 04 91
Open Wednesday—Monday 11 a.m. to 6 p.m.; closed holidays
When the 48-year-old Edouard André married the 40-year-old Nélie (Cornélie) Jacquemart, in 1881, people's tongues wagged. He had been born into a fabulously wealthy banking family, while Nélie, albeit a renowned portrait painter of society, came from an obscure background. She was a Catholic and royalist; Edouard, a Bonapartist and Protestant. They had met nine years earlier, when he commissioned from her his portrait, and their relationship grew steadily into deep friendship. Whether theirs was a marriage of love or a marriage of reason, it was certainly one of great happiness and harmony—and an immense contribution to the world of art, for the childless couple channeled their passion and energy into building an exceptional art collection.

It is not surprising that this, one of the sumptuous dwellings of the Plaine Monceau (Paris's most desirable neighborhood in the second half of the 19th century), has become one of the most visited museums in Paris, combining as it does the splendor of a Parisian mansion with a display of exceptional masterpieces. The discerning pair collected art during extensive travels, and Nélie continued on her own after her husband's death. Among the highlights are Italian primitives, works from the 18th-century French school, the Italian Renaissance, the 17th-century Flemish school, and paintings by the English masters Reynolds and Gainsborough. At the end of your visit make your way to the exquisite old-fashioned tea room. Or if the weather is warm, relax on one of the garden's benches and dream of the *beau monde* alighting from their *coupés* and *landaus* along the driveway, about to attend a reception or a concert.

Dazzling enchantment at Monsieur André's ball

No more admirable setting could be imagined. Attending were all the celebrities of fashion and elegance: the Countess Portalès, the Duchess of Mouchy, Countess Tolstoy, Countess Petrowska, Countess Viel-Castel, Baroness Vuitry, Baroness Alphonse de Rothschild, the Duchess of La Rochefoucauld Bisaccia, Mesdames Eugène Waritoff, de Janzé, de Gouy, d'Acry, and many more who all dazzled with equal intensity. We were, however, spared the abuse of diamonds, a blunt instrument often used to batter the other ladies and whose glitter is often a mask for a lack of taste and genuine elegance.

—**Housewarming reception described in** *L'illustration*, 1876

Maillol
59–61, rue de Grenelle, 75007
Tel: 01 42 22 59 58
Fax: 01 42 84 14 44
Open Wednesday—Monday 11 a.m. to 6 p.m.; closed holidays

Dina Vierny was fifteen when she met Aristide Maillol. At long last, the ageing sculptor (by then in his seventies) had found his muse. Their ten-year collaboration was among the most creative in his career, and culminated in such masterpieces as *The River*.

During World War II, Maillol moved with Vierny to a mountain retreat, where he focused on his famous sculpture *Harmony*. The work was left unfinished when he died in a car crash in 1944.

After the war, Vierny, urged on by Henri Matisse and Jeanne Bucher, opened an art gallery in St-Germain. Her gallery became a mecca of modern art. In the 1960s she brought Soviet avant-garde artists to Europe.

It took Dina 30 years of determined battle to have a museum devoted to Maillol's works. The beautiful building, located in the heart of Faubourg St-Germain, was the property of the Recollets order until the French Revolution. Bouchardon's famous fountain of the four seasons decorates its front.

At the end of your visit, you can wind down at the pleasant cafeteria in the basement and savor a dish of smoked salmon and blinis, *l'Assiette Dina*, a tribute to the Russian-born muse of this great sculptor of the female body. Better still—complete your visit with a stroll through the Carrousel Gardens by the Tuileries, where several of Maillol's sculptures are on display.

Montmartre Museum
12, rue Cortot, 75018
Tel: 01 46 06 61 11
Open Tuesday—Sunday 11 a.m. to 5:30 p.m.

This charming old Montmartre house is located blissfully on the other slope of the hill—the one less trodden on by tourists. Drowning in the greenery of its own garden, it looks out on the hill's famous vineyard. This used to be the home of many of Montmartre's artists, Utrillo and his mother, Suzanne Valadon, among them (see page 49). Renoir had his studio here, and it was in this very garden that he painted his famous work, *The Swing*. The composer Erik Satie, at some point Suzanne Valadon's impassioned lover, lived nearby.

The Montmartre museum is a great place for a visit down memory lane, as it contains many relics of the artistic life on the hill in its heyday. Temporary exhibitions are organized occasionally, often focusing on a specific artist.

Montparnasse Museum
21, Impasse du Maine, 75015
Tel: 01 42 22 91 96
Open Wednesday—Sunday 1 to 7 p.m.

Don't miss this place! This delightful cobbled alley, bathed in greenery, one of the last remnants of old Montparnasse, was sentenced to death and to be replaced by concrete high rises, when the opening of this museum gave it a new lease of life. It is deliciously romantic and celebrates the heyday of this neighborhood in the first half of the 20th century, when Montparnasse was the artistic and cultural center of the world. It's a small, humble museum, which survives as best it can and runs on a tiny budget and immense willpower. Several interesting, even very interesting, exhibitions are held here every year, devoted to the great artists who made Montparnasse. Kiki was their queen, the model and friend of many, and a talented painter in her own right. Her enflamed love affair with Man Ray lasted from 1921 to 1929, the longest to be recorded in the history of Montparnasse.

From Man Ray to Kiki

My heart is heavy at the thought that tonight you will be alone in your bed, because I would love to hold you in my arms while you're asleep. I love you too much; in order to love you less I would need to be with you more. That would be good because you are not made to be loved, you are too calm...Well, I must take you as you are, because you are nonetheless my lover whom I adore, the one who will make me die of pleasure and pain and love... I bite your mouth till it bleeds and I am intoxicated by your indifferent and wicked look.... See you on Monday, my great sweetheart, your KikitadoresMan.

Musée National du Moyen Age (Hôtel de Cluny)

Moyen Age (at the Hôtel de Cluny)
6, place Paul-Painlevé, 75005
Tel: 01 53 73 78 15
Open Wednesday — Monday 9:15 a.m. to 5:45 p.m.

Only a few steps away from the Sorbonne, in the heart of the Latin Quarter, the beautiful Hôtel de Cluny was once the Paris *pied-à-terre* of the famous Burgundian abbey's clergy. Today it is home to the medieval treasures of Paris, and also to the Roman baths that stood here some thousand years earlier. Of late the adjacent garden has been redesigned in a medieval spirit. You might wind down there after your visit. It is made up of juxtaposed square sections, each devoted to a specific kind of vegetation—medicinal herbs, flowers, vegetables, and even one filled with coronation and thyme, devoted to courtly love.

The highlight of the museum are the celebrated tapestries, *The Lady and the Unicorn*, which, like the Hôtel de Cluny itself, date from the late 15th century. These splendid pieces were brought to the attention of the world in the 19th century through the writings of George Sand. The Lady is exquisitely graceful and is seen in each of the tapestries, seated between a lion and a unicorn in an enchanting garden of love. The garden is of deep blue hue, sprinkled with delicate pink and crimson flowers, a deliberately non-realistic presentation of nature that enhances the sense of magic, and has to be understood allegorically: five of the tapestries depict the five senses, through the lady's different occupations.

The sixth (or first) tapestry, however, seems to indicate that earthly pleasures have been renounced by the lady for the sake of the true love of Christ. The unicorn can be read emblematically as the presence of Christ, (or the lover). The unicorn was thought to be a fast, dangerous creature that could only be captured and tamed by a virgin, as the tapestries reveal.

Nissim de Camondo
63, rue de Monceau, 75008
Tel: 01 53 89 06 50
Open Wednesday — Sunday 10 a.m. to 5 p.m.

Unrequited love brought about this wonderful museum on the edge of the lovely Parc Monceau. Moïse de Camondo, who came from a leading Jewish banking family of the Ottoman Empire, had married Irène Cahen d'Anvers who, likewise, came from an upper-class family. The receptions given by her mother Louise were among the most fashionable in the city, and were attended by such society writers as the Goncourt brothers and Guy de Maupassant. Like all bourgeois marriages, theirs was a *mariage de convenance*, meant to secure for the family and their social class economic, social, and moral stability. Alas, Irène fell head-over-heels in love with the Italian head of the stables, the Comte Sampieri, and ended up walking out on her husband and marrying the Count, an audacious act for a bourgeois woman in the second half of the 19th-century, when marriages were arranged as a matter of fact.

Moïse was devastated by the 1902 divorce and never remarried. He put his heart into the upbringing of his beloved children, Nissim and Béatrice, and into collecting 18th-century decorative arts, the century when the *art de vivre* had reached its peak, it seemed to him. In order to sustain its artistic coherence, he pulled down the townhouse inherited from his father and replaced it with the present one, inspired by the 18th-century Petit Trianon in Versailles.

Moïse's sorrows, however, were not over. His son, who served as a pilot during the Great War, perished in action, after which his devastated father lived only for his art collection, which he turned into a museum named after his son. Further disaster was brewing, but Moïse was fortunate not to see it. He died in 1935, happy to bequeath the museum to the state. It opened in 1936 with its furniture and other items left practically in their original position, in accordance with his wishes.

Meanwhile the skies were darkening over Paris and the Germans were about to begin their four-year occupation, during which Moïse's daughter, Béatrice; her husband, Léon Reinach, and their two children, Fanny and Bertrand, were deported to the camps. Not one returned.

Don't let these sorrows keep you from the museum. Besides viewing a fabulous art collection, you will also gain an insider's view into the private areas of a home that was a model of modernity in the early decades of the 20th century.

Rodin
77, rue de Varenne, 75007
Tel: 01 44 18 61 10
Open Tuesday — Sunday 9:30 a.m. to 4:45 p.m.
The Rodin museum offers a rare opportunity to enter an 18th-century palatial townhouse—most such mansions now serve as embassies or ministries. Make your way through a lovely, rose-filled courtyard, with the Dome of the Invalides to your right, glowing with its 50,000 gold leaves against a blue sky.

This house, the Hôtel Biron, was built for a wigmaker, apparently a profitable profession in the 18th century. In any case, this wigmaker made such a fortune that he was able to hire the king's architect, Gabriel, to design his mansion. Louise de Bourbon, the daughter-in-law of Louis XIV and of his mistress, the Duchesse de Montespan, later bought the place from the wigmaker. After the French Revolution, it fell into the hands of the Dames de Sacré Coeur, but was confiscated from them in 1904, when state and church were separated by law. The last nun was expelled in 1907. About that time Clara Rilke, whose husband, the poet Rainer Maria Rilke, was Rodin's secretary, discovered this godsend, and the following year both Rodin and Matisse got permission to move in. Rodin rented four

rooms on the main floor, to which he moved his furniture and some of his sculptures. Other artists followed—Isadora Duncan, who used the gallery against the garden wall for rehearsals; Clara Rilke, who was herself a sculptor and worked on the main floor. There was also Jean Cocteau, who left some moving descriptions of his stay here in *Portrait-Souvenirs*: "It was hard to imagine that Paris lived, walked, rode and worked around such a pool of silence."

Rodin's mistress at the time was the Duchesse de Choiselle and the pair spent many a blissful hour listening to the novel sound of the gramophone. "At 70, he is in love once more," we are told by Rilke on November 3, 1909, "and his mistress keeps everyone away: 'No use disturbing him since I am here. I handle everything. I am Rodin.'"

When the state bought the mansion in 1910, Rodin was given a life lease, with the agreement that the place would become a museum for his works after his death. Not everyone was happy with this decision, as quickly became apparent in 1912, after the premiere of Diaghilev's *l'Apres-midi d'un faune*. To Calmette from *Le Figaro* the performance was all about "vile movements of erotic bestiality and gestures of heavy shamelessness." Rodin, on the other hand, defended it: "… nothing could be more soul-stirring than the movement at the close of the act… when he throws himself down on the discarded veil, to kiss it with all the pent-up force of passionate *volupté*."

Then came Calmette's response on the pages of *Le Figaro*:

> I admire Rodin deeply as one of our most illustrious and able sculptors, but I must decline to accept his judgment on the question of theatrical morality. I feel it necessary to recall that, in defiance of common propriety, he now exhibits in a former chapel of Sacré Coeur, as well as in the former rooms of exiled nuns, a series of objectionable drawings and cynical sketches, which with great brutality depict the same kind of immodest gestures as those

of the faun who was justly booed yesterday at the (théâtre du) Chatêlet… It is inconceivable that the state—that is, the French taxpayers—has paid 5.000,000 francs for the Hôtel Biron, simply to house our richest sculptor. This is the real scandal, and it is the business of the government to put a stop to it.

Be that as it may, we ordinary lovers from all over the world are most appreciative of the gift of this, perhaps the city's most romantic museum, where love is celebrated with so much voluptuous passion that it makes the stone come alive. Granted, the women in Rodin's life did not have it easy… neither Camille Claudel who sank tragically into madness, nor his wife Rose, who could hardly have suffered less. Though how moving to see Rodin, like the prodigal son, return to the reassuring bosom of his wife at the end of his life's journey:

24 August 1913, Le Pressoir, Pargnan, par Beaurieux, Aisne

𝓜y good Rose,
I am sending you this letter like a reflection I am having about the immensity of the gift that God has given me by putting you next to me. Put this in your generous heart. I am coming back on Tuesday.

Your friend, Auguste Rodin

The museum and the garden contain many of Rodin's masterpieces—*The Thinker, Balzac, Eve, Eternal Springtime, The Kiss, The Gates of Hell,* and also some of Camille Claudel's passionate works—*Sakuntala, The Dancers,* and *Vertumne and Pomone,* which responds to Paolo and Francesca of Rodin's *Kiss.*

End your visit in the wonderful tree-filled grounds at the back of the museum and enjoy a coffee break, snack, or tea in their cafeteria.

𝓜y poor head is all mixed up and I can no longer get up in the morning. This evening I ran around (for hours) to all our spots without finding you. Death would be sweeter! And how long is my agony. Why didn't you wait for me in the atelier, where are you going? to what agony have I been destined… Camille, I feel the madness take hold of me, which will be your doing if this continues, why won't you believe me? I abandon my Dalou, the sculpture, that is. If I could go to any place, to some country where I could forget, but there is none. In a single instant I feel your terrible force. Have pity, mean girl. I can't go on. I can't go another day without seeing you. Atrocious madness, it's the end. I won't be able to work anymore. Malevolent goddess and yet I love you furiously… Don't let this slow and hideous sickness overtake my intelligence, the ardent and pure love I have for you—in short, have pity, my beloved, and you will be rewarded.

—Rodin, 1883

Victor Hugo (Maison)
6, place des Vosges, 75004
Tel: 01 42 72 10 16
Open Tuesday — Sunday 10 a.m. to 5:40 p.m.

This was the home of the great writer Victor Hugo between 1832 and 1848, the time of his passion for the actress Juliette Drouet, whom he first met in 1833, when she was playing the role of Princess Negroni in his play *Lucrèce Borgia*. Juliette became his lifelong mistress, even following him into exile on the Isle of Guernsey, where he set her up in a separate house within sight of his own family home. The furnishing and decoration of that house, entirely designed and made by him, are reproduced in the museum (see the *salon chinois*). They reveal Victor Hugo to be a gifted craftsman. His initials can be seen on much of the furniture. At close examination, Juliette's own initials too can be detected, often camouflaged playfully in a game of hide-and-seek. In 1878, when Hugo was a widower, Juliette moved in with him on the avenue Eylau in the 16th arrondissement (now avenue Victor Hugo). She died first, on May 11, 1883, passionately in love with him to the very last. Victor Hugo lived on for another two years, until May 22, 1885. Their love affair was legendary—Auguste Rodin considered it one of the great loves of all times.

Juju/JJ (Juliette Drouet) to her Toto (Victor Hugo)

Je t'aime, c'est ma vie; je t'aime, c'est mon souffle: je t'aime, c'est ma pensée; je t'aime, c'est mon passe; je t'aime, c'est mon présent; je t'aime, c'est mon avenir; je t'aime, c'est mon âme... il me faut toi, il ne me faut que toi, je ne peux pas vivre sans toi.

I love you is my life: I love you is my breath; I love you are my thoughts; I love you is my past; I love you is my present; I love you is my future; I love you is my soul... I need you, I need but you, I can't live without you.

La Vie Romantique (Musée de)
16, rue Chaptal, 75009
Tel: 01 48 74 95 38
Open Tuesday — Sunday 10 a.m. to 5:40 p.m.; closed holidays

A driveway lined with trees leads to a flowery cobbled courtyard where nothing seems to have changed since 1830. An Italianate house, a profusion of wisteria, rose bushes, and a few tables and chairs where tea is served in the summer months—this is the blissful welcome that awaits you here. Don't let the name mislead you, however: this museum is not about romance. Instead you will glimpse into the lives of those who made the 19th-century Romantic movement, most of whom lived in this bucolic neighborhood of La Nouvelle Athènes.

For nearly a century this house remained in the hands of the same family and was the meeting place of literati and artists, especially when Ary Scheffer, the Dutch-born portrait painter of the royal family and other prominent members of society, lived here (1830–1858). All the famous names that come to mind used to gather here, in what was the neighborhood's social hub—Géricault and Delacroix, who lived a few steps away, Liszt, Rossini, Turgenev, Dickens, Lamartine, and, of course, George Sand and Chopin, the most celebrated couple of the time. George Sand was only a guest here, like all the other artists, but she did live in the neighborhood. When her granddaughter, who had inherited her estate wanted to donate it to the the city's Musée Carnavalet, city hall was not particularly interested. Luckily Sand's memorabilia found a more suitable environment here. As you wander around, notice some portraits of hers, some furniture, *objets d'art*, and scores of documents and letters. Her home in Nohant has been recaptured in the yellow and blue salons, thanks to contemporary engravings, so you cal stroll through, imagining her life with all its ingredients of a tale of romance.

Sand to Mme. Marliani, as Chopin traveled from Paris to Nohant

My little Chopin is on his way: I entrust him to you. Look after him, even though he may not want you to. He is so careless of himself when I am not there, and his servant, though a good creature, is stupid. I am not worrying about his main meals, because I know he will be asked everywhere, but I am so terribly afraid that, in the mornings, in his haste to go off to his teaching appointments he may forget to drink the cup of chocolate or broth which I insist on him taking before he goes out, in spite of all his protests...

Zadkine
100 bis, rue d'Assas, 75006
Tel: 01 43 26 91 90
Open Tuesday—Sunday 10 a.m. to 5:40 p.m.

This is a tiny, adorable museum located by the Luxembourg gardens, on the one-time premises of the cubist sculptor. Zadkine moved here from La Ruche, the humble residence on the eastern edge of Paris that he escaped as soon as times improved. He was delighted to land here and wrote to a friend: "Come and see my house and you will understand how a man's life can change because of a pigeon house, because of a tree." There are excellent sculptures to enjoy, and also the pleasure of viewing some of them in a little garden filled with birdsong.

SENTIMENTAL TRAILS

Nobody has ever measured,
even poets, how much a
heart can hold.
—Zelda Sayre Fitzgerald

ARIS IS A WALKER'S PARADISE. PUT ON COMFORTABLE shoes and start out early: the city, barely awoken, is uncrowded and awash with golden light.

How would you like to be,
Down by the Seine with me?
Under the bridges of Paris with you,
I'll make your dreams come true.

If you can take but one romantic walk, it must be along the river Seine. You will have to come back, in all seasons and in all kinds of weather, at sunrise, sunset, and by night. You will never tire of it and you will never cease to be moved. The Kingston Trio felt the same way in the late 1950s, when they were famous for their hit "Tom Dooley." The same album contained a song called "The Seine," a great romantic favorite of mine in my teens. In it, American tourist meets local French girl in front of Notre Dame. They stroll hand-in-hand along the Seine through the night, and part with a kiss, washed in tears, at the break of dawn, at the foot of the Eiffel Tower.

I. THE SEINE

For this walk, start out far enough east to include the **Ile St-Louis** (it had not yet been spotted by most tourists at the time of the Kingston Trio). You will alternate between street level and down by the water (where once upon a time there were no motorways and the river belonged entirely to those who walked beside it). Most importantly, you will cross bridges, and enjoy spectacular and ravishing views.

Start out as early in the morning as you can, when the sun is behind you and spreads its splendor to the west. (If you walk at sunset, then reverse the itinerary). Pack a snack and picnic by the water. And definitely repeat this walk at night.

Make your way to Métro station Sully-Morland, east of Ile St-Louis, and head for the **Pont de Sully**, the island's easternmost bridge. Cross over and enjoy the spectacular view of the tip of the island. Turn right along the **quai de la Tournelle** and right again onto **Pont de la Tournelle**. To your right, the patron saint of Paris, Geneviève, stands protecting the city's eastern gateway. To your left, a magnificent view of the back of **Notre Dame**.

BY BIKE OR SKATES
Bike'N Roller rental
6, rue St-Julien-Le-Pauvre, 75005; Tel: 01 44 07 35 89
137, rue St-Dominique, 75007; Tel: 01 44 18 30 39
38, rue Fabert (by the Invalides), 75007; Tel: 01 45 50 38 27

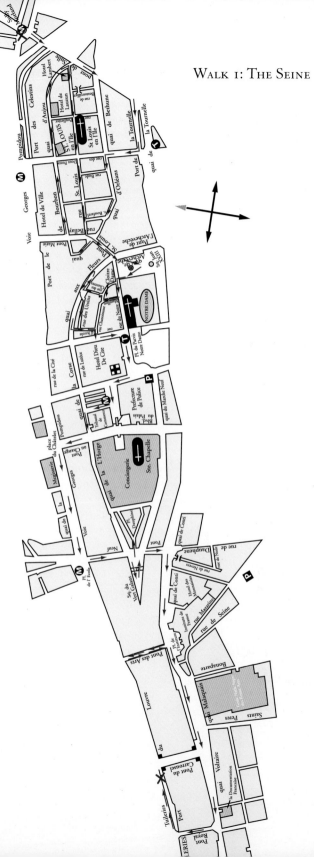

WALK 1: THE SEINE

Turn left into **quai d'Orléans** and circuit the island, either down by the water or along the quai. It is more romantic by the water, but on street level you will see magnificent 17th-century townhouses. The island was built up almost overnight, which accounts for its architectural homogeneity. Some houses merit special mention, such as 19, quai de Bourbon, once the **home of Nicolas de Jassaud**, the secretary of Louis XIV. At the back of the courtyard was **Camille Claudel's studio**, where she lived from 1899 until 1913, when she was interned definitively in a mental home after a tragic descent into insanity.

The **Hôtel de Lauzan** at 17, quai d'Anjou, is one of the most prestigious addresses on the island. The one time home of the Duc de Lauzan, it is more famous for its 19th-century tenants, notably Baudelaire, who wrote here the first poems of *Les fleurs du mal.* He and his friends turned the premises into *le club des hashishins*, in honor of their drug of choice. When the neighbors complained, Baudelaire wrote back, "Sir, I chop up wood in my living-room; I drag my mistress about by her hair; this is done in everybody's home and you have no right to interfere." You will recognize the building with its stunning gilded wrought-iron balcony and the gilded fish-scales on its water spouts. Today it is the property of the city of Paris where guests of honor are hosted. In general, no one else can enter the place—alas, for it truly is a place of splendor, decorated as it was during the reign of Louis XIV. The house is sometimes open to guided tours (check through your hotel).

The **Hôtel de Lambert**, at 1, quai d'Anjou, is perhaps the island's best-known landmark, but it's better from the river. If you've taken a boat ride, you are bound to have seen it overlooking the eastern tip of the island. This was once the home of the celebrated French actress Michèle Morgan, whose gorgeous blue eyes made Jean Gabin utter one of the legendary sentences of French cinema: *"T'as de beaux yeux, tu sais."* (You've got nice eyes, you know.)

Before you leave the island, make your way to its main street, **rue St-Louis-en-l'Ile**, lined with splendid boutiques, galleries, eating places, food shops, hotels,

Hôtel de Lambert

and, above all, several outlets of the island's famous ice cream maker, **Berthillon**, for the sake of which people make pilgrimages in warm weather.

Walk across the **Pont St-Louis footbridge** to the **Ile de la Cité** and stroll through the garden behind Notre Dame (**square Jean XXIII**). At this time of day, with few people around, you will find it even more romantic—so enjoy the benches. When you leave the garden, explore the streets to the north. I like in particular to approach the **quai aux Fleurs** by way of **rue des Chantres**. If you can do this at night it is perfectly silent and quintessentially romantic, and even more so in the heart of winter. At 9, quai aux Fleurs, to your right, is the city's most emblematic landmark of romance, the **home of Canon Fulbert**, where the secret love affair between Héloïse and Abélard began. Walk around to the front of **Notre Dame**. Walk in and take in the splendor. If you happen to fall upon a lucky day when visitors are scarce, you may want to climb its famous tower for a spectacular view. Spare a compassionate thought for the Hunchback, Quasimodo, whose home this was, and for his beloved gypsy girl, Esmeralda.

As you walk west, heading north toward the **Pont au Change**, you may enjoy the profusion of colors in the city's **flower market** (closed Mondays). Cross the river on the Pont au Change, which will afford you a magnificent view of the **Pont Neuf** to the west and the **Conciergerie** to the southwest. Back in the Middle Ages, this was the prison adjacent to the king's palace. Its westernmost tower was used for interrogations and the screams of the tortured could be heard outside. The easternmost tower features the oldest clock in the city, installed in the 14th century, at the time of Charles V, restored in the 16th, at the time of Henri III, and totally mute at present. The quai, where the entrance to the Conciergerie is situated, is named after it. It is worth a visit for the beautiful remains of Gothic architecture it contains. The Conciergerie remained an active prison until the end of the French Revolution, during which it was the guillotine's antechamber. You can view the cell where Marie-Antoinette was jailed before her execution at place de la Concorde.

The bridge leads to **place du Châtelet**, which was opened by the Baron Haussmann. Two of the city's well-known theaters were part of the project and face each other on either side of its central fountain, **Théâtre de la Ville** (once Sarah Bernhardt) and **Théâtre Musical de Paris** (once Châtelet) respectively to the east and to the west.

Turn left along **quai de la Mégisserie**, which has another colorful flower market and a pet market on its right, and bookstalls on its left. Take the **Pont Neuf** back to the island. Enjoy the spectacular view to the west, framed by the Louvre on your right and the **Mint** and the **Institut de France** with its famous dome on your left. Right before you is the **Pont des Arts**, the city's oldest iron bridge (1804). Take it all in, then walk down the steps to the tip of the island. This has got to be the city's most romantic spot. Either this, or the tip of the Ile St-Louis.

Though perhaps you'll find inside the little garden just as pleasing. The garden bears the suitable name of **Vert Galant** (gallant youth), in honor of the young Henri IV, a notorious philanderer. He seems to have scattered some seventy children throughout the kingdom, several of whom were a great menace to the stability of France. But his true love was Gabrielle d'Estrée (see page 6).

Henri IV to Gabrielle d'Estrée, 4 February 1593

My beautiful angel, if at each moment I could take the liberty to trouble you with the memory of your subject, I believe the end of each letter would be the beginning of another one. Therefore presently I shall write to you again, since absence prevents me from doing so otherwise. But business, or should I say the importunities are in greater number here than they were in Chartres. They will detain me here tomorrow, when I was meant to leave. Souvray honors us today with a feast, which all the ladies will attend. I for my part am clad in black, for I am bereaved of all that may bring me joy and contentment. There is no devotion so pure as mine. Rejoice in it, as it is for your sake… Let me kiss your hands a hundred times, as heartily as I kissed them yesterday.

Retrace your steps up to the bridge, past the Vert Galant's equestrian statue, and walk east into the tree-filled **place Dauphine**. It was built by Henri IV and was lined with the same brick-and-stone houses that still surround its contemporary **place des Vosges**. Whereas place des Vosges is a perfect square, place Dauphine is a triangle. Few of the original houses stand, unfortunately, and the architectural unity is gone, but the spot is still blissfully romantic (this was the home of the celebrated Simone Signoret and Yves Montand) and visited by few.

Walk south along the Pont Neuf to the **Left Bank**. Turn right into **quai de Conti**, up to the **Pont des Arts** where you may even find some entertainment. This footbridge has become a draw to artists and musicians, and a mix of strollers, vendors, and lovers, and occasionally a picnicking party, especially on a summer night. You can spend quite some time here, with the splendid view in either direction of the bridge, notably the view overlooking the **Ile de la Cité**. Anchored safely between the two sections of the Pont Neuf, it looks like the bow of a majestic vessel, all ablaze at sunset. Make sure to come back at that time. As you look west, remember that you are standing on the western boundary of medieval Paris. Picture to your right the old Louvre fortress and its tower, and the notorious Tower of Nesle (see page 5) to your left, now replaced by the dome-capped Institut de France.

Return to the Left Bank and continue west along **quais Malaquais and Voltaire**, a treasure trove for book lovers, who may

unearth rare finds among the green stalls (see page 54). Quai Voltaire is world-renowned for its antique dealers and has the further bonus of affording a superb view over the **Louvre**, the **Tuileries gardens**, and the magnificent **Pont Royal**, which was thrown between the two banks by Louis XIV's glorious architect, Jules-Hardouin Mansart. The quai was home to some prominent figures, not least Voltaire, who spent his last few years at no. 27. As many as 500,000 over-wrought Parisians packed into the quai there to pay him a last homage at his funeral. It was the **Hôtel de Mailly-Neslé** next door (no. 29), on the other side of rue de Beaune, that drew the attention of Louis XV. Five fair sisters dwelled here, all of whom were seduced by the king, except for the third one, who was kept under jealous guard by an uncooperative husband. The last sister became the notorious Duchesse de Chateauroux, his official favorite between 1740 and 1744. Her sudden and mysterious death (in her room upstairs, which still exists) at the age of 27, has never been explained. But the king did not seem much shaken by her loss—in no time the Pompadour took her place, and was set up officially in Versailles.

Cross over the **Pont Royal** and feast your eyes once more on stunning views, notably those of the **Tuileries** and the **Musée d'Orsay** on either side of the Seine, as you look west. Walk down to the water along the **quai des Tuileries**, a great, romantic spot for your midday picnic, especially as hardly anyone seems to be aware of this, at least for the time being.

2. ILE DES CYGNES — EIFFEL TOWER — MUSÉE RODIN

If you are adventurous and eager to do things differently, here is a way of including the river and the **Eiffel Tower**, while maintaining a spirit of romance.

Start out as early as you can and head for the **Bir-Hakeim Métro station**. Take the **Bir-Hakeim bridge** and walk down the flight of steps leading to water level and to a strip of an island known as the **Ile des Cygnes** (the Island of Swans). The island has never had any swans, nor any architectural glamour. And it is not even a natural island but a paltry strip of concrete that looks out on the sprawl of installations of the Paris port, and also on a boring motorway on the other side of the Seine. Yet, for some inexplicable reason, the Ile des Cygnes (officially allée des Cygnes)—has a magic all of its own. I can't put my finger on it, but there is something utterly atmospheric about it. I love to walk through the serene rows of poplar, lime, and chestnut trees to its tip, then sit down by the water. Behind, a small-scale model of the Statue of Liberty, looks west (to where her bigger sister was shipped in 1884). The tower-dented skyline of today's Paris sets me ruminating over the passing of time. When my eyes rest on the bridge of Mirabeau to the west, I recall Guillaume Apollinaire's lines:

> *Passent les jours , passent les semaines*
> *Ni temps passé ni les amours reviennent*
> *Sous le Pont Mirabeau coule la Seine...*
> Days go by, years go by,
> Neither time past nor love returns
> Under the bridge of Mirabeau flows the Seine...

When you are ready, return to the Left Bank and head to the Eiffel Tower. Go as early as possible, to miss the crowds. After you climb this landmark, wander through the lovely gardens of the **Champ de Mars**. Tourists tend to overlook these gardens, despite the wonderful flowers, secluded nooks, and even a romantic grotto.

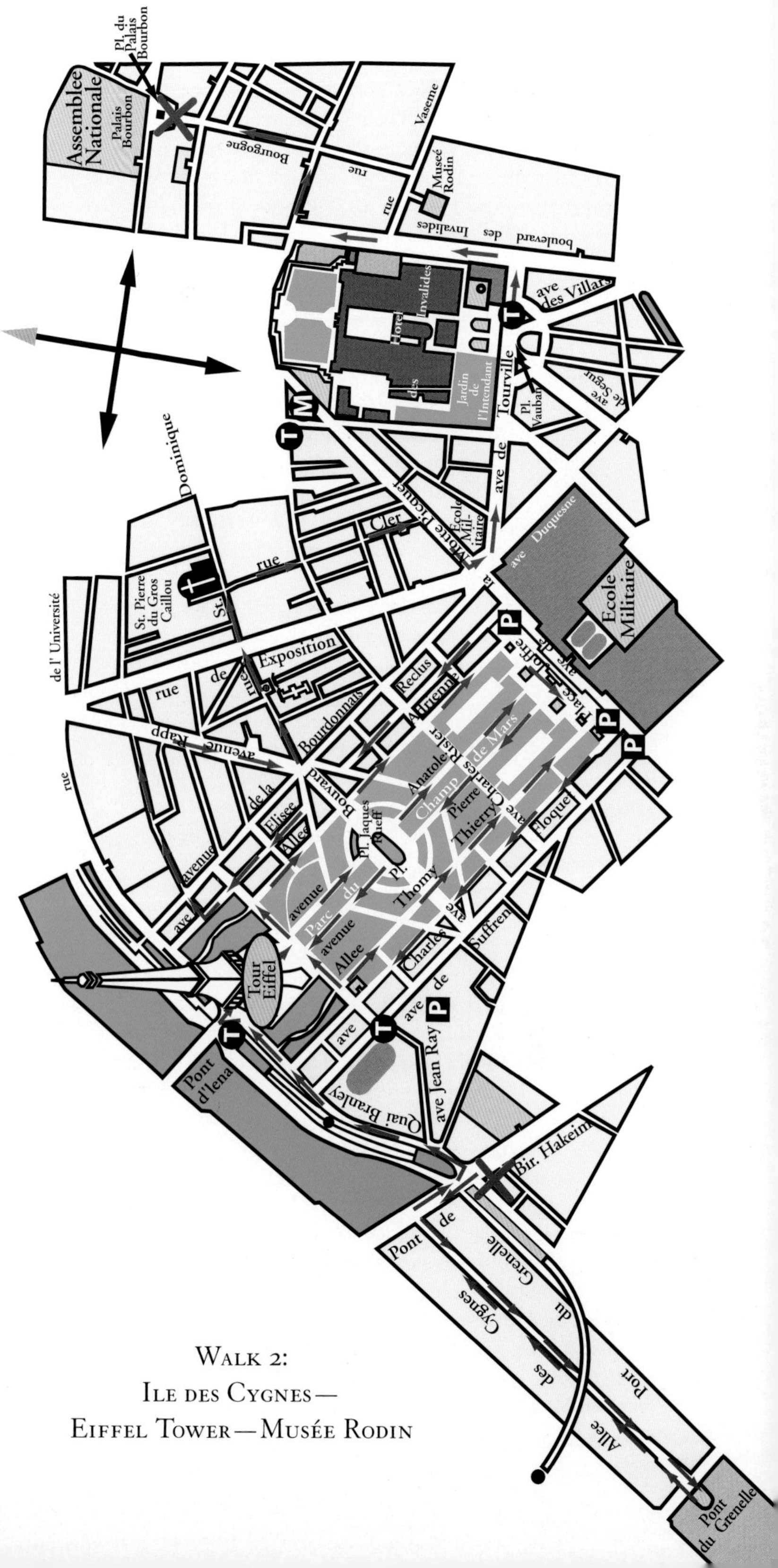

WALK 2:
ILE DES CYGNES—
EIFFEL TOWER—MUSÉE RODIN

Leave the gardens on their northeast edge, into **rue de l'Université**. Stop at **Les Deux Abeilles** for your morning coffee (see page 115). Once restored, continue to **29, avenue Rapp**, one of the most spectacular Art Nouveau façades in the city, and certainly the most romantic one, featuring Adam and Eve, and also the beloved wife of the architect above the doorway. You may want to stop next door at **Puyricard** (see page 134) for a fresh supply of mouth-watering chocolate.

Turn left into rue **St-Dominique**, filled with neighborhood shops and genuinely Parisian atmosphere. A fountain dedicated to the god of war (bequeathed by Napoleon), stands on the corner of **rue de l'Exposition**, a charming, arcaded spot with a picturesque bistro, appropriately named **La Fontaine de Mars**. Rue de l'Exposition is named after the World Fair, which was held at the Champ de Mars, and is lined with good, inexpensive eating places.

Continue along **rue St-Dominique** and turn right into **rue Cler**, a colorful street market that has enjoyed worldwide publicity in recent years. Dive into the depths of culinary and gourmet France here, before continuing the walk. Stop at **place Vauban**, for a magnificent view of the **Invalides Church of the Dome**, Jules-Hardouin Mansart's ultimate masterpiece, dating from 1700.

Your next stop is the **Rodin museum** at 77, rue de Varenne (see page 197). After your visit, walk along **rue de Bourgogne**, a neighborhood street lined with enticing shops of all sorts. It leads to the exquisitely discreet **place du Palais-Bourbon**, an elegant 18th-century piece of architecture. The florist **Moulié** (no. 8) contributes a patch of magnificent hues to this otherwise understated spot. Step in and buy a bouquet for your sweetheart. It will be made up of some of the city's most ravishing flowers.

3. THE LATIN QUARTER

If you can do this walk on a Tuesday, Thursday, or Saturday morning, you will enjoy the extra pleasure of the **street market of place Maubert**.

Make your way there in the early morning. Stroll through the market stalls and settle for a *café* and a croissant on the terrace of **Le Métro** (no. 18, on the northern side). Soak up a truly Parisian atmosphere with no frills. Picture the open air university located here in the Middle Ages, when Maître Albert, after whom the place is named, was one of the university's great masters. In later years, this was a place of public executions. It remained a seedy neighborhood until the latter part of the 19th century, referred to as a "cesspool" by the famous 18th-century writer, Restif de la Bretonne. Today this has become an upscale neighborhood, with an intellectual bent, naturally.

Leave the square on its northern side and walk along **rue Frédéric Sauton**. It leads to an enclave of picturesque old side-streets, graced with pleasing greenery and arty boutiques. On your right is the **impasse Maubert**, a silent dead-end alley, home to a laboratory of gruesome associations in the 17th century: this is where the notorious

WALK 3:
THE LATIN QUARTER

rue de l'Hôtel Colbert
rue des Grãs Degas
rue des Trois Portes
Maubert Albert
rue Lagrange
rue des Anglais
rue Galande
rue de Bièvre
Pl. Maubert
M
P
Maubert Mutualite
des
Bernardins
Sts. Archanges
Rue du Carmel
Musee de la Pref. de Police
St. Ephrem
rue de la Montagne
rue St. Etienne du Mont
Pl Genevieve
ace du Pantheon
éon
Clovis
rue
St. Etienne du Mont
Descartes
Thouin
Lycee Henri IV
rue
rue de l'Estrapade
M
Sq. de Arénas de Lutéce
Arénes de Lutéce
Arenes
rue des
rue
Cuvier
Monge
rue de Navare
Lacepede
Linné
M
Jardi d'H
rue
Nouveau Théâtre Mouffetard
Mouffrand
Clin. Geoffrey St. Hilaire
Clin. C.A. Colliard
rue de
Quatrefages
Institut Musulman Et. Mosquee
Geoffroy
rue
Mouffrand
rue Daubenton
M
St. Médard
Censier

Les Amoureux des Bancs Publics
Lovers on the Public Benches
by Georges Brassens

Les gens qui voient de travers
Pensent que les bancs verts
Qu'on voit sur les trottoirs
Sont faits pour les impotents ou les
  ventripotents
Mais c'est une absurdité
Car à la vérité
Ils sont là c'est notoir'
Pour acceuillier quelque temps les
  amours débutants.

Refrain
Les amoureux qui s'bécott'nt sur les
  bancs publics,
Bancs publics, bancs publics,
En s'foutant pas mal du r'gard
  oblique
Des passants honnêtes
Les amoureux qui s'bécott'nt sur les
  bancs publics,
Bancs publics, bancs publics,
En s'disant des "Je t'aim'" pathétiqu's
Ont des p'tit's gueul' bien
  sympathiqu's.

…Quand les mois auront passé
Quand seront apaisés
Leurs beaux rêves flambants
Quand leur ciel se couvrira de gros
  nuages lourds
Ils s'apercevront émus
Qu' c'est au hasard des rues
Sur un d' ces fameux bancs
Qu'ils ont vécu le meilleur morceau
  de leur amour.

People who can't see straight
Think that the green benches
That you see on the pavements
Are made for the weak and the obese.
But this is absurd,
For in fact
They are there, as everyone knows,
To welcome apprentice lovers from
  time to time.

Refrain
The lovers who kiss on the public
  benches,
Public benches, public benches,
Not caring about the sidelong
  glance
Of the upright passerby
The lovers who kiss on the public
  benches,
Public benches, public benches,
Saying their pathetic "I love you's"
Have something rather nice about
  them.

…When the months have passed
When the heat is gone
From their flaming dreams
When their sky is covered with
lowering clouds
They will realize, moved,
That it was by chance on the streets
On one of these famous benches
That they have lived the best part
of their love.

mass poisoner, the Marquise de Brinvilliers, and her lover, Monsieur Godin, experimented with the concoctions that were to dispatch to other worlds several members of the Marquise's family. They planned to get rid of them and run off with the inheritance, but Godin died prematurely and the Marquise was caught and burned to ashes at the place de Grève (now Hôtel-de-Ville, across the river). Her father must have had a robust constitution, since it took ten attempts to dispose of him, but her husband proved to be altogether immortal. (Though rumor has it that Godin, not actually eager to don the noose of matrimony with the future widow, removed the poison on the sly, at her each attempt to kill him.)

Follow the map to **rue de Bièvre**. The street commemorates the one-time river Bièvre, which now flows underground. Pollution chased away the beavers and instead brought epidemics, so the river had to be covered up. The filth was such that by the 18th century, the above-mentioned Restif de la Bretonne claimed that rue de Bièvre was the public latrine of the university. There is certainly no remnant of this at present. It's all been cleaned up, painted fresh, and also has some exquisite boutiques. Go and snuggle in the tiny little nest of a garden on your right, a well-kept secret where one hardly ever sees a soul. Make it your own. It's lovely and is surrounded by picturesque old houses. The one looking out on you from the south was the home of President Mitterrand until his death in 1996.

Continue to the eastern edge of **place Maubert**, cross over and continue uphill, along **rue de la Montagne-Ste-Geneviève**. Its junction with **rue de Polytechnique** and **rue Laplace** makes for a romantic stopping spot, complete with a café terrace. The famous Polytechnique school, where France's elite mathematicians and other brainy people are trained, was located behind the gate on your left, at 5, **rue Descartes**, until 1977. Only the garden has survived (and welcomes both neighbors and visitors). Continue diagonally to the right, along rue Descartes, then turn right into rue **St-Etienne-du-Mont**, a charming, narrow alley along the church by the same name. It will unfold a pocket-size garden on the right, shaded by a clump of birch trees.

Skirt the church to the left and enter for a visit, since it is home to the reliquary of the city's patron saint, Geneviève. It is one of the city's finest churches, noteworthy for its astonishingly asymmetric structure, its beautiful 17th-century organ, and its magnificent chancel screen, the only one in Paris to have survived. You should also make your way to the **Chapelle des Catéchismes**, where stunning 16th- and 17th-century stained glass is on display.

At the end of your visit, see if you may climb up to the dome of the **Panthéon**, facing you to the west. (It has been closed for security reasons of late.) You are in the heart of the city's oldest neighborhood and will be afforded one of its most romantic bird's eye views, complete with a jumble of old roofs and chimney pots.

The Panthéon is the nation's official mausoleum, where such heroes as Victor Hugo rest, and also now a woman—Marie Curie.

But it was first built as a church to Sainte Geneviève, to replace the old abbey church of which only the gothic belltower has survived. You will see it if you look east from the Panthéon, or as you skirt the **church of St-Etienne-du-Mont**, after your visit, and enter **rue Clovis**. On your right is the prestigious **lycée Henri IV**, on the site of the former abbey, a few vestiges of which are still standing inside the school. The new, gigantic church was built by Louis XV, or rather was extorted out of him by the monks of Sainte Geneviève. When, due to his debauched philanderings, Louis came down with a fatal disease, he vowed to build a new church and renounce his mistress, the Duchesse de Châteauroux, if only God would restore his health. No sooner did he recover, than he flew back to the arms of his duchess and would surely have forgotten his pledge to build the new church, had it not been for the tenacious monks.

Before turning into rue Descartes, turn back for a superb view of the abbey's belltower, against the dome of the Panthéon. Continue past **39, rue Descartes**, where Verlaine once shared a seedy room with a wretched street girl. Hemingway rented a studio in the same building. Ahead is **place de la Contrescarpe**, the social hub of the neighborhood, where you may relax with a drink on a café terrace facing the central fountain. Continue east, down **rue Mouffetard**, one of the city's famous street markets. It gets better as you reach the bottom of the street, and altogether bursts with bright hues along rue de l'Arbalète. Walk downhill past the **church of St-Médard**, on your left, and turn around. Delight in the picture-postcard view of the colorful hill slope and the church framed by shady trees.

Follow the map to the **Paris Mosque**, and stop for a glass of mint tea under a shady fig tree, to the delightful sound of the fountain's trickling water. The Mosque was built in the 1920s and hosted the wedding ceremony of Rita Hayworth and Ali Khan in 1949 (yet another marriage that was not to last long, alas). The main entrance to the mosque is opposite the pretty **place du Puits-de-l'Ermite**, where on Friday mornings you will see Muslim faithfuls gathering for their weekly prayer. Skirt the mosque by way of **rue Daubenton** heading west, then **rue G. Desplas** heading north. Peep into the garden: you will love the Moorish architecture, the colorful tiles, and the rose beds. Head north toward the **Arènes de Lutece**, the heavily restored remains of a Roman amphitheater that was once the scene of gladiator fights and is now surrounded by a lovely garden. Linger here, then head for the **Jardin des Plantes,** and enter on the corner of **rue Cuvier**. This is the romantic bit of the garden, hilly and untamed—which is not to say that the French gardens that cover most of the area are not pleasing. My favorite bit is the Alpine garden, a rock garden filled with a stunning variety of flowers and a wonderful blend of balms and scents. The entrance is located opposite the tropical greenhouse and it is open from 8 to 11 A.M. and 1:30 to 5 P.M., from Monday to Friday. On my last visit, in the heat of the tourist season, I didn't walk past a single person.

The Jardin des Plantes was originally laid out for the cultivation of medicinal plants and herbs at the initiative of Louis XIII, which accounts for its ongoing scientific vocation and the presence here of the **Museum of Natural History**, as well as a small zoo. The first Parisian giraffe, offered to Charles X by the Pasha of Egypt on July 9, 1826, was paraded to its zoo along streets packed with cheering crowds. In the winter of 1870, during the Prussian War, the starving Parisians proved less friendly to their four-legged fellow creatures: they ended up storming the zoo and eating up all its inmates.

There is a pleasant **open-air café** within the precincts of the menagerie, where you can lunch in a bucolic environment (after buying an entrance ticket). Another café for lighter fare such as crêpes and waffles is situated outside the menagerie, facing the kangaroo patch and the children's playground.

Jardin des Plantes

4. AROUND THE BASTILLE

For centuries this was the stronghold of working-class Paris (hence the storming of the Bastille on July 14, 1789). The First of May workers' procession still gathers at the **Bastille**, but this is a hangover from the past—since the 1980s the area has become young and trendy. Its main landmark is the new **Opera House**, which sprawls on the eastern side of **place de la Bastille**, a controversial piece of architecture inaugurated on July 14, 1989, to coincide with the bicentennial of the official beginning of the French Revolution. The fortress actually stood on the other side of the vast traffic circle. Since no trace of it is left, people look up to the gilded **Spirit of Liberty**, perched on top of the central column, in their subconscious quest for historical references. Yet both the Spirit and the column belong to another, later insurrection, the one that erupted on July 28, 1830 and brought Louis-Philippe to the throne three days later. Inside the column are the remains of the heroic victims of the *Trois Glorieuses*, as the revolt has come to be known.

Today the neighborhood pulsates with nightlife, especially around **rues de la Roquette and Lappe**, northeast of the place de la Bastille. But by day you may explore undisturbed bucolic courtyards, until recently home to woodworkers, now to dot-coms, graphic designers, and other off-shoots of modern times. Avoid coming here on weekends, when most courtyards are hermetically sealed. On the other hand, Thursday and Sunday mornings offer the open market on **boulevard Richard-le-Noir**.

Turn into the **passage du Cheval Blanc**, on the northeastern edge of place de la Bastille, where some of the old trades have survived among bright geraniums and fragrant lavender bushes. Stroll through the successive courtyards that celebrate several months of the year—*janvier* (which even has a fig tree), *février, mars, avril*—and come out on **rue du Faubourg St-Antoine**, the neighborhood's main artery. Step into no. 33—a secret paradise is tucked away behind its closed door, bursting with greenery and draped in creepers.

Cross over and walk to **56, cour du Bel-Air**, undoubtedly one of the neighborhood's gems. It has two successive cobbled courtyards and a ravishing assortment of creepers, flowers, and bushes. There is also a great bookshop here, if you can read French, and a photographer's gallery.

Cross over again and peep into **71, cour de Shadox**, displaying a spectacular glass canopy and a bunch of skipping children in the afternoon. There is a great little shop of embroidered linens at the back of the courtyard, but I have never seen it open and wonder how it stays in business.

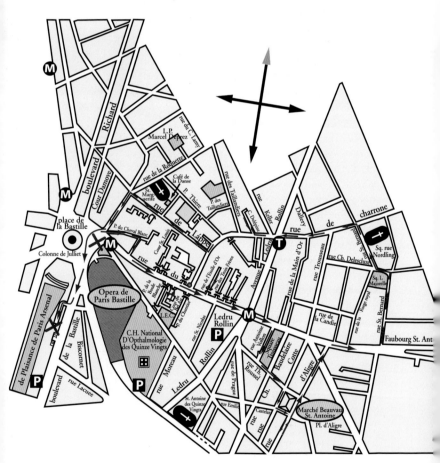

WALK 4: AROUND THE BASTILLE

Walk into **75, cour l'Etoile d'Or**—an astonishing alley in a world of its own. Ahead is a bright pink, green-shuttered house, of the kind you would expect to see in an operetta set of Montmartre. It even has a charming *trompe-l'oeil* of dubious taste. On your right as you enter is a pretty 18th-century house that must have belonged to a prosperous craftsman; beyond, an old rustic house, straight from the heartland of rural France, complete with pocket-size patches of gardens. At the end of the alley is another 18th-century house with a sundial. Back on **rue du Faubourg-St-Antoine**, look into **83, cour des Trois-Frères**—its spectacular iron-and-glass structure provides a view of a different time.

Cross over and continue east to the charming **square Trousseau**, prettily decorated with a Belle-Epoque kiosque that seems to serve no other purpose than please the eye. Walk through the square and come out on **rue Théophile Roussel**, on its southern edge. Head east to **place d'Aligre**, where one of the city's best-known streetmarkets lies, **Marché Beauvau St-Antoine**. It is especially known for its secondhand clothes, a hangover from the past when the market came under the jurisdiction of the Abbess of St-Antoine, who stipulated that every vendor must also sell cheap clothing to the poor. Today this is still a wonderful slice of genuine old Paris. On sunny mornings, you may even be greeted by the nostalgic sound of a street organ on the corner of **rue Théophile Roussel**. Just hang around and soak up this moment of romantic magic, as the musician's hand and the organ's handle turn around and around in unison, pouring out of the perforated scroll old French favorites.

Head north along **rue d'Aligre**, back to 173, **rue du Faubourg-St-Antoine,** yet another countrified courtyard with a mix of workshops and private homes and the feeling of a sleepy village. And step into the

ravishing no. 179, too: the whitewashed houses, the lovely vegetation, the great smell of varnish (yes, the traditional trades of Faubourg St-Antoine have not died out here) will fill you with pleasure.

Head north on **rue St-Bernard**, for the **church of Ste-Marguerite**, a rural-looking church with a picturesque slate belltower topped by a weathercock and prettily framed by trees. Few Parisians besides its neighbors have ever heard of this church, yet it contains one of Paris's best kept secrets, the tomb of the "Temple Child," the supposed King Louis XVII, who died in a dark cell in the tower of the nearby Temple and whose remains, in all probability, were exchanged for another's. The tomb is tucked away in the garden (ask a member of the church to unlock the door leading to it). Surmounted by a little white cross, the tomb bears the inscription Louis XVII 1785–1795. If you have a love affair with history, this will be a moving and edifying experience.

Peep into the astonishing courtyard at **42, rue St-Bernard**. It has the usual mix of geraniums, lavender, and creepers, plus a sunny terrace rimmed with flowers and shaded by a single umbrella.

Turn onto rue de Charonne and look into the **cour Delépine**, lush with greenery and a profusion of bamboo. Then proceed to **rue de Lappe**, the stronghold of the neighborhood's nightlife since the early 20th century. This was the birthplace of the *bal-musette*, Parisian dance music played to the accordion. The **Balajo**, the street's historical landmark, once frequented by the likes of Edith Piaf, is still going strong at no. 9, having adjusted to contemporary trends.

This street was also the center of the hard-working Auvergnat community, who developed Paris's café and hotel industry. The city's oldest Auvergnat food shop, **Aux Produits d'Auvergne**, still stands at 6, rue de Lappe, where it opened over 100 years ago.

You can't miss the more recent restaurant, **La Galoche d'Aurillac**, at no. 41, because of the profusion of clogs (*galoches*) dangling from the ceiling. (Aurillac is the name of an old town of the Cantal, in the Auvergne.) Consider buying some food at the Produits d'Auvergne and having a picnic. Before leaving the area, check the pretty courtyards concealed behind the doorways at nos. 34, 26, and 24, provided the doors are unlocked. Just try your luck. Then follow the map to your picnic spot in the **Arsenal gardens**, along the marina of the **Bassin de l'Arsenal**. The gardens are pretty and sprinkled with secluded nooks, where the two of you will be alone in the world. Forget Paris for a while—it may be around the corner, but you are miles away....

5. CANAL ST-MARTIN — BUTTES CHAUMONT — MOUZÄIA NEIGHBORHOOD

This is going to be a long stretch, designed for those who know central Paris well and are looking for something different. Reserve it for warm weather, as flowers and greenery are an essential part of the treat. Make sure you are fit and wearing comfortable shoes, as the **Buttes Chaumont** is a hilly park with lots of steep slopes and flights of steps.

I have divided the walk into three parts—the **Canal St-Martin**, the **Buttes Chaumont** proper, and the neighborhood around **rue de Mouzäia**. You can pick and choose, according to your energy and time. Grant yourself a good part of the day, if you want to do it all leisurely and throw in a pastoral lunch at **Le Pavillon Puebla**, which I recommend wholeheartedly (see page 105). It is located inside the Buttes Chaumont and is a well-deserved prize after an exerting outing. Reserve your table beforehand and keep in mind that the restaurant is closed on Sundays, Mondays, and for three weeks in August.

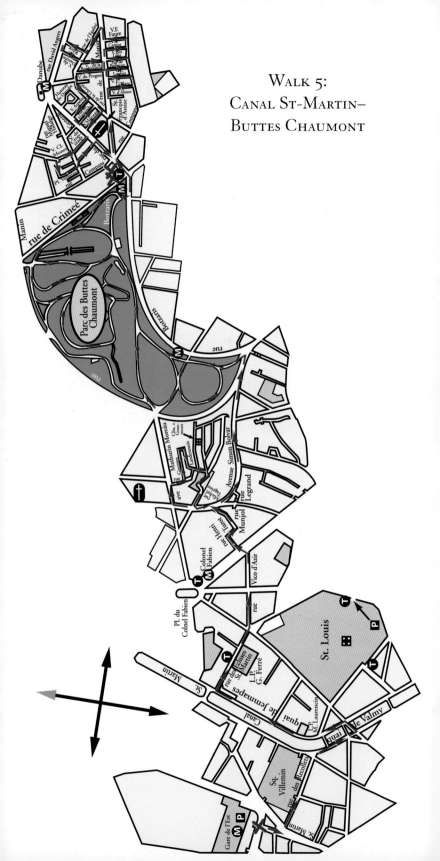

WALK 5:
CANAL ST-MARTIN–
BUTTES CHAUMONT

The Canal St-Martin

Start out in the morning at the **Métro Gare de l'Est**. Follow the map past the Jardin Villemin toward the canal. On my last visit the sun was shining to the sound of a street organ wheeled along the water by a wandering father and son. It made my day and I wish you the same stroke of luck.

The **Canal St-Martin** has none of the glamour displayed by the monuments along the Seine. If anything it has been marred by the construction of modern blocks of flats, so out of keeping with its melancholic, northern atmosphere, which craves red brick and shrieks for Flemish gabled roofs. But never mind! Just focus on the banks of the canal and its wonderfully arched iron footbridges. And, of course, the slow passing barges. The opening and closing of locks happens by way of an antiquated mechanism. So much ado about so little, and it seems to take forever—but what a moment of grace, when time is suspended and our crazed racing from dawn to dusk comes to a brief halt. Locals (myself included) stop to watch this monotonous sameness with fascinated concentration. As the barge reaches the turning bridge, it brings all traffic to a momentary stop. It is the one spot in Paris where I have never seen drivers lose their temper nor heard them hoot. Unbelievable! I suppose the Canal St-Martin could be prescribed as alternative medicine to stressed-out citizens of modern times.

Turn right along **quai de Valmy**, and walk as far as the turning bridge, a picturesque spot with an old-fashioned café and a restaurant complete with a cheerful red awning. This is a great place for hanging around and waiting for a barge, after which you can cross the bridge and make your way north to 102, quai de Jemmapes, home of the mythical **Hôtel du Nord**, which inspired Marcel Carné's classic of the same name (see page 258). Today you can bask on its sun-drenched terrace—which was certainly not there in its seedier days.

Continue along the canal and turn right along **rue des Ecluses St-Martin**. Now follow the map until you get to the long, steep flight of steps known as **rue Michel Tagrine**. This commemorates a young violinist who was killed in World War II, and makes for a picturesque shortcut to a steep enclave of eclectic houses and lush greenery. At the top of the steps you will be back on **rue Georges Lardennois**, where you will turn right and be gratified with a breathtaking surprise, which I will leave you to discover for yourselves. There is also a wonderful hill slope covered with colorful flowers and vines, the very one you must have noticed from down below. Continue walking along rue Georges Lardennois until you reach its end, and walk down the steps to your right. They will take you back to **avenue Simon Bolivar**, where you will turn left and continue to the gardens of the Buttes Chaumont.

The Buttes Chaumont

The Romantic gardens of Paris—here you will find all the trimmings of the clichéd, tormented landscape that a Byron or a Chateaubriand would have loved—dramatic cliffs… wilderness… grottoes… a lake… a mighty waterfall…. There is also a spectacular Second Empire folly, perched conspicuously on top of the highest cliff—you really must make the effort to climb for the reward of a romantic kiss and a magnificent view. The folly is a copy of the Temple of the Sybils at Tivoli, a reminder that this extraordinary sample of nature was revisited by the artisans of Napoleon III, who took over a sinister gypsum quarry lying on the seedy, northeastern edge of Paris, and turned it into a patch of beauty, "*les Tuileries du peuple,*" the Emperor said. It was a generous gift: The gardens cover 61 acres. Admittedly, land was cheap here, but this doesn't take away from the fact that these remain among the city's largest gardens, all for the visitor's pleasure. With so many hidden corners, you can truly feel you own the place if you come in the morning. The Pavillon de la Puebla is on the side of the park where you have entered, but if you started out early, come back at the end of your outing.

On the northern side of the park, at the intersection of rues du Rhin, Laumière, and Armand Carel, stands the **19th arrondissement's monumental town hall**. This is where the painting featuring the notorious courtesan Valtesse de la Bigne presides over the wedding hall (see page 15). (It is usually kept locked when not in use, but you can give it a try. Who knows? Perhaps you'll be lucky.)

When you leave the gardens, make your way to the southeastern exit by **Métro Botzaris**, a wonderful, curving Art Nouveau gateway, the legacy of Hector Guimard. It blends beautifully into the leafy alley that runs along the southern side of the gardens, the territory of timeless *boules* players.

The Mouzaïa Neighborhood

This enclave lying east of the Buttes Chaumont also stands on the site of the gypsum quarries, whose stone was used for the construction of the sockle of the Statue of Liberty and also the White House, which is why, many believe, the quarries were called *les carrières d'Amérique* or *du Mississippi*. (Though it seems that the name goes back to the 17th century, which leaves its origin an enigma.) The neighborhood was built up in the 1920s as a modest working-class garden-city, hence such ideological names as rues de l'Egalité, Liberté, Fraternité, and Solidarité. Today many privileged Parisians would be willing to pay a high price for a pocket-sized patch of garden and the clean air here. The area is immersed in rambling greenery and cascading blossoms—wisteria, lilac, roses, clematis, according to the time of year. Explore slowly, the way you enjoy a good wine. A new surprise greets you at every turn. Wonderful smells hang in the air. Linger and soak it all up. You are in an unpretentious neighborhood and will not be frowned upon as an unwelcome intruder. Take advantage of this opportunity, which is not always afforded the stranger in snootier parts of the city.

Meander through the alleys between **rue de Mouzaïa** and **rue de Bellevue** until you come level with **rue de l'Egalité** at a hairpin bend on your left. Stroll up and down the streets on either of its sides, turning back if you reach as far north as **rue David Anger**. Continue exploring as shown on the map, until you are ready to head back to Métro Botzaris, where your walk will end.

6. HEADING FOR MONTMARTRE

North of the *grands boulevards* lies an unspoiled neighborhood, a serene slope that climbs up gently to the hill of Montmartre. This is Paris's best-kept secret, entirely tourist-free and, more surprisingly, known to few Parisians who don't live or work here. Fewer still are aware that in the 19th century, this *was* Paris, the tiny area that contained everything and everyone that counted—the world of finance and politics, art, literature, music, passion, and high society prostitution, too. Everyone convened daily on the *boulevards*, that ribbon of glamour and temptation to the south. This was the stage of the Paris of "365 Sundays," streaming with carriages and sweeping gowns, top hats and sunshades, and everything else you recall from the movies and the Impressionists' paintings. This was the frivolous playground where the likes of the Prince of Wales found an escape from the puritanical England of his mother.

When urban development spread into the countrified slope in 1821, it became a magnet for the Romantic artists, musicians and writers, all of whom lived at some point in this new neighborhood,

which came to be known as **La Nouvelle Athènes** (New Athens). A few years later, a new cluster of streets mushroomed just as fast to its east, and was named after the **place St-Georges**, which stands in its center. Today, they are really one neighborhood, designated indiscriminately by either of these names.

If understated old-world charm and the pleasure of treading an unbeaten track appeals to you, make your way to **Métro Trinité**, at place d'Estienne d'Orves, the pretty little garden south of the **church of Ste-Trinité**.

Walk into the leafy courtyard at **54, rue St-Lazare**, and conjure up the carriages of four of Paris's long gone idols, who shared this back entrance to their four houses—the great actor, Talma, to your left,

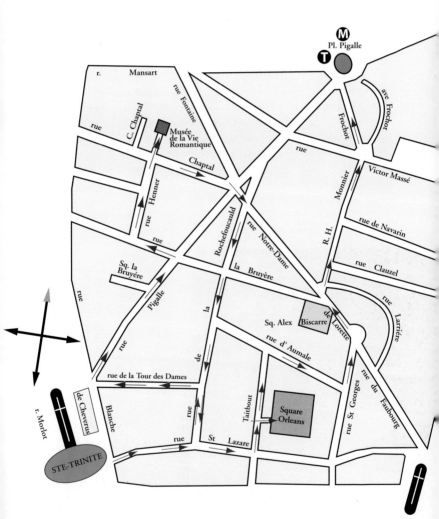

WALK 6: MONTMARTRE

the great actresses Mlle Mars and Mlle Duchesnois to the right, and Horace Vernet, Napoleon's official painter, who lived and had his studio in the house in front. Occasionally this quiet alley would be filled with the drumbeats of troops of infantry and cavalry on their way to Vernet's studio, where they would pose for posterity to the glory of the Emperor. Walk around to the fronts of their houses on **rue de la Tour-des-Dames,** so called after the tower of the windmill that stood at no. 4, belonging to the abbesses ("dames") of the famous abbey of Montmartre. It is said that wine from the reign of Henri IV was found on the site. Mlle Mars once lived at no. 1 (try to peek inside the house, which was decorated by the famous Visconti); Mlle Duchesnois at no. 3; Vernet at no. 5–7; and Talma, the greatest actor of his time by all accounts, at no. 9.

Cross the street to see, too, the sheer architectural pleasure at nos. 2 and 4, with the exquisite rolling gardens that testify to the heavenly past of these parts.

Continue on to **rue Pigalle.** Balzac had this to say on March 15, 1841, to his beloved Comtessa, Madame Hanska, about one of the street's most famous residents, George Sand:

> She is living at the bottom of a garden, at no. 16 rue Pigalle, over the coach-house and stables belonging to a mansion facing the street. She has a dining-room furnished in carved oak. Her boudoir is done in café-au-lait, and the drawing-room, in which she receives, is filled with flowers in superb Chinese vases….
> There is a side-table covered with odds and ends of bric-a-brac, and there are pictures by Delacroix as well as a portrait of herself by Calamatta… The piano is a magnificent square upright in rosewood. Chopin is always there. She smokes only cigarettes—nothing else. She doesn't get up till four. At that hour Chopin is finished with his lessons…. She sleeps on two mattresses laid on the floor, Turkish fashion. Ecco, contessa!"

You may wish to stroll along rue Pigalle just for the sake of its past tenants, who also included painters Pierre Bonnard and Emile Vuillard, who shared a studio at the top of no. 28; Victor Hugo at no. 55; and Charles Baudelaire at no. 60.

Follow the map to the leafy alley at 16, rue Chaptal, for a visit to the **Musée de la Vie Romantique** (see page 200).

I have had three further meetings with her. She gazed deep into my eyes while I played. I had chosen some rather sad music, Legends of the Danube. My heart was dancing with her in a country scene. What were her eyes saying, those dark, those curious eyes, so intently fixed on mine? She leaned on the piano, and her gaze was like a fiery flood..... Flowers all about us. My heart was captured! Since then I have seen her twice again....She loves me..... .Aurore, what a lovely name!...

—Chopin's Journal, October 1837

After your visit, head to 14, rue de La Rochefoucauld, for a visit to the **Gustave Moreau** museum, the one time home of the symbolist painter (see page 191).

Follow the map to 80, rue Taitbout. Stop, walk in, and enjoy your amazement: You could never have suspected such a gem behind the street! You have stumbled upon the celebrated **square d'Orléans**, the living quarters of some of the most prominent Romantic artists and writers, notably Sand and Chopin, who moved respectively to nos. 9 and 5 in 1841 (the square was built up the previous year on a plot belonging to the actress Mars). What an enchanting nook to live in, surrounded by elegant Italianate architecture and a graceful fountain in the center. No wonder several of their friends moved here too—the famous singer Pauline Garcia-Viardot, whom Sand had actually introduced to her husband, the writer Louis Viardot, and Alexandre Dumas. Everyone else gathered here—Delacroix, Balzac, Heine, Marie Dorval, Mickiewicz, and also Betty and James de Rothschild. Viardot would sing Mozart's *Don Giovanni*, while Chopin (Chip, Chipette, or Chopinsky, to Sand) would play to them with his "velvet fingers." It was quite a communal life, according to Sand, and certainly a lot of fun: "We have even arranged to do only one lot of cooking, and to have our meals in common, which is much cheaper and more amusing than each of us living separately...."

> *George Sand is beautiful: but she is not very dangerous even for the wicked cats who stroke her with one paw and scratch with the other; not even for the dogs who bark most fiercely at her. Like the Moon, she is a gentle queen, and looks down on everyone from a great height."*
> —Henrich Heine

At **82, rue d'Aumale**, you can glimpse the garden of the apartment once occupied by George Sand. Turn left into **rue St-Georges**, which has some interesting antique and second-hand dealers. You will come to the picturesque **place St-Georges**, the landmark of the neighborhood. In its center stands the cartoonist Gavarni's elegant fountain. The artist, who lived on rue St-Georges, devoted much of his work to the neighborhood's female celebrities of easy virtue, the *lorettes* (see page 14). According to Baudelaire, they owed their existence to Gavarni. The most notorious courtesan of her day, the Marquise de la Païva, lived at no. 28 (which flaunts a fabulously ornate façade) while she waited for the completion of her palatial townhouse on the Champs-Elysées.

An adventurous temperament took this daughter of poor Russian-Polish Jews across both social and geographical boundaries, all the way from Constantinople to London, a long way in those days. She gained the title of Marquise by marrying the Portuguese Franco

Aranjo, the Marquis de la Païva, for whom she soon had no use as she continued her social ascent. In order to marry the Count Henckel of Denmark, a multimillionaire and a much better catch, she had her marriage to the Marquis annulled, following which the desperate husband is believed to have shot himself. This was during the sensitive times of 1871, and it is not impossible that the rumors about the courtesan's spying activities are justified, especially since Count Henckel was Bismarck's cousin. Be that as it may, it was definitely Count Henckel who financed the extravagant mansion that still stands at 25, Champs-Elysées. Despite its questionable taste, a reflection of its parvenu tenant, the best society of literati were more than happy to attend the sumptuous receptions lavished here by the courtesan—money talks! Among them was Edmond Goncourt, who would then go home and tear her to shreds in his *Journal*. At present the townhouse belongs to a private club and is therefore generally inaccessible to outsiders. If you live in Paris, or spend some time here, you may have the opportunity to visit with a guided tour.

The **Hôtel Thiers** at 27, rue St-Georges, is a replica of the home of France's celebrated head of state during the Prussian War. Thiers married the daughter of the chairman of the company that had financed the development of the neighborhood, which is why the couple moved here. In 1871, during the Commune, the house was burned down by the Parisian working classes, who were infuriated by his humiliating capitulation to the Prussians.

Head northwest along **rue Notre-Dame-de-Lorette**. On your left is a pretty neighborhood little garden, **square Alexandre Biscarre**, filled with flowers and foliage, and lots of benches. Turn right on **rue Henri Monnier**. On your right is a drowsy shaded spot, the tiny **place Gustave-Toudouze**, barely a speck on the map of Paris. Whatever the time of day, I always stop at **Tea Folies**, at no. 6 (see page 119), when in this neighborhood. You deserve a rest by now, so why not do so in this timeless corner of the city?

If you still have some energy left, make your way north along rue Henri Monnier to the intersection of **rue Victor Massé** and **rue Frochot**. A resplendent oasis of greenery, called avenue Frochot, lies to the northwest, teasing from behind an unyielding wrought-iron gate. It comes with a cheerful, flowery chalet, the home of the lucky, happy, almighty concierge. Even the little you will see is worth the extra stroll. I shall say no more. Except that one immaculate blue morning, I happened to pass by when the concierge was watering the alley and the gates were wide open. I just stood there, gaping, and then, plucking up my courage, I put on my cutest of smiles and somewhat coyly asked him if he would let me in. He did, and very kindly so, and of course I thanked him profusely. I wish you the same pot of luck, because from outside the gate it is impossible to even begin to picture the slice of heaven that lies at the back of the alley. Even if you don't make it beyond the gate, you will glimpse enough to have an idea why the avenue Frochot has always attracted the artists who either frequented it (Victor Hugo, Alexandre Dumas) or actually lived here (Jean Renoir, the film director and son of the painter; Toulouse-Lautrec). **Place Pigalle** is just behind the alley, a very short way from the painter's headquarters, the **Moulin Rouge.**

7. PARC MONCEAU

Parc Monceau is not just one of the city's loveliest gardens, it is also surrounded by mansions of glittering opulence, where two bejeweled museums are sheltered, the **Musée Nissim de Camondo** (see page 196) and the **Musée Cernuschi** (7, avenue Velasquez), which specializes in Far Eastern art. This is all in the 8th arrondissement. It was north of the park, in the 17th arrondissement, where the newly moneyed classes settled in the second half of the 19th century, gravitating around the **place Malesherbes** (now Général Catroux). Venus, of course, picked up on this in no time and set up little sanctuaries where the voluptuous curves of her pink, scented flesh could be worshipped at leisure, provided one could afford it. When Alexandre Dumas (the younger) asked to be admitted into "Comtesse" Valtesse de la Bigne's boudoir, Her Highness, albeit his neighbor and friend, flatly sent him packing: "It is not within your means, *cher maître!*" Start out from **Métro station Monceau**, where the north entrance to the park is located. Several streets fan out north from here, with **rue de Prony** lying further to the west. Stroll along rue de Prony and enjoy the

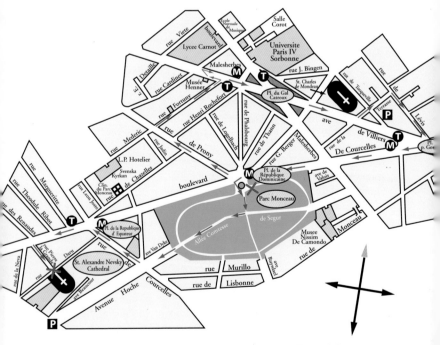

WALK 7: PARC MONCEAU

delightfully exuberant and decadent façades on display, once the preserves of courtesans. The Americans among you might be interested to know that a lady of a different sort was conceived nearby, namely the Statue of Liberty, who came out of the foundry and workshops at **25, rue de Chazelles**.

Turn right into **rue Fortuny**, also the one-time home of the *demi-monde*, as can be gathered from the extravagant façades. Among them lived two eminent writers, Edmond Rostand at no. 2, where he completed *Cyrano de Bergerac*—what better environment for a passionate tale of love—and Marcel Pagnol, at no. 13. The notorious Caroline Otero lived at no. 29; next door (at no. 27) lived her sworn rival, Geneviève Lantelm, who put an end to her existence by drowning herself in the Rhine in 1918. A woman of greater merit lived at nos. 35–37, on the corner of **avenue de Villiers**: That extraordinary mansion (built by the famous architect Jules Février and decorated by the no-less- famous Chéret) was the home of none other than Sarah Bernhardt, one of the greatest actresses of all times, or "*monstre sacré*," as Jean Cocteau put it. No. 35 still stands, but no. 37 was scandalously allowed to be torn down in the 1960s and replaced by the drab building now standing.

Turn left on avenue de Villiers, past the **Musée Jean-Jacques Henner** at no. 43, a period mansion displaying Henner's paintings. Continue west to the **corner of rue Cardinet.** You have come to the site of Nana's home, where Emile Zola set up his celebrated heroine, "in that luxurious district being developed in the middle of the wastelands of what used to be the plain of Monceau. It was a palatial, Renaissance-style building with a fantastic interior arrangement of rooms and furniture...."

Retrace your steps and head for the **place du Général Catroux**, made up of stretches of shady chestnut trees and green lawns, ablaze with azalea blossoms in June. This is the meeting point of avenue de Villiers and boulevard Malesherbes, the home of those who could afford it. One palatial mansion survives, at 100, **boulevard Malesherbes**. Now the Banque de France, it was built (1878–1882) for Emile Gaillard, then head of the **Bank of France**, by the same Février who had built Sarah Bernhardt's home, as well as the Renaissance-style residence of Valtesse de la Bigne, which stood next door at no. 98. (If you want to know what it looked like, detour to Zola's *Nana*.)

Place du Général-Catroux is now adorned with the sculptures of the neighborhood's famous residents, Alexandre Dumas *père* (on the western edge) and *fils* (eastern edge), and Sarah Bernhardt dressed as Phaedra, her icon role. She has replaced an earlier statue of Grandfather Dumas.

If you can spare the time and crave some local color, continue along avenue de Villiers, turn left into **rue de la Terrasse** and right into **rue Lévis**, a well-known street market where you can also buy yourself provisions for a picnic in Parc Monceau. If you'd rather spoil yourselves, stop at **Chocolat Viennois** at 118, rue des Dames (from midday on).

Follow the map back to enter Parc Monceau at the rotunda. It was initially one of the 60 tollhouses built by Nicolas Ledoux around Paris, just a couple of years before the outbreak of the French Revolution. The upstairs was used as a *pied-à-terre* by Louis-Philippe, Duke of Chartres and cousin of Louis XVI, the proprietor of the gardens, for whom they were laid out before the Revolution. From here he enjoyed a lovely view of what was then countryside, as well as abundant female company, apparently. The gardens as we see them now were largely remodeled under Napoleon III, which is when the sumptuously gilded wrought-iron gates were added. Stroll through the exquisitely romantic gardens, with their English-style follies and grottoes, their mishmash of ruins—tombs, pyramid, obelisk... whatever, from wherever. The *naumachia*, an elegant colonnade reflected in a water basin along which it curves gracefully, is one of the park's loveliest features and is located on its northeastern side. The pool is filled with lily pads and comes with the requisite romantic weeping willow—a ravishing sight.

Exit on the western side, along **avenue Van Dyck**. The fabulous mansion at no. 5 was built for the chocolate manufacturer, Emile Menier. Now, follow the map up to rue Pierre-le-Grand and turn left. Read no more until you've done that... and don't cheat!

Wow!...right? This is what I get from every visitor I bring here for the first time. All the more so when the golden onion-shaped domes of the **St Alexandre Nevsky cathedral** (1860)—which is what you are seeing—are set against a bright blue sky. This is where Pablo Picasso got married for the first time, to Olga Khoklova, a member of Diaghilev's Ballets Russes. Their bliss, alas, did not last long.

8. SAVE FOR A RAINY DAY

If you have landed in Paris in the midst of a horrific downpour that seems unstoppable, and if you are done with museums and departments stores, don't despair: there are some patches of romance to be found under shelter, slices of timeless Paris at its most atmospheric, where you might even brush against an elusive shadow from the past. And the duller the day, all the more atmospheric. These are the **shopping arcades** of central Paris, which flourished in the 19th century (there were more than 150 of them in 1870), the glamorous forerunners of today's shopping malls. At the time these were the first and only places to be lit by gas and where you were not splashed by mud. During the day they enjoy soft daylight filtering through their glass roofs. As you stroll, browsing through faded postcards of a world that is no more, old posters, old prints, dusty old books, antiquated cameras, and antique dolls, try to conjure graceful ladies sweeping the floors with their rustling skirts... especially after dark, when the arcades bathe in an amber glow.

> *G*o on, lovers of Paris, go from passage Brady all lined with fur to the passage du Grand-Cerf all lace and feather-weight iron, from passage Ste-Anne whose keeper is a cat, to the passage du Havre where one strolls past pictures of hair and displays of buttons and detachable collars... Go under these clear glass roofs, away from the din of the streets, and listen through the passing of time to the heartbeats of the city that you love.
>
> —Maurice Bedel, *Les Passages parisiens* (1947)

Here are my favorites, listed by arrondissements. Note that the *galérie* was originally more elegant than the *passage*, which still holds true to a certain degree.

Galérie Véro-Dodat, off rue J.J. Rousseau, 1st arr.
Galérie Colbert, off rue des Petits-Champs and rue Vivienne, 2nd arr.
Galérie Vivienne, off rue des Petits-Champs and rue Vivienne, 2nd arr.
Passage du Grand-Cerf, off rue St-Denis, 2nd arr.
Passage Jouffroy, off bd Montmartre, 9th arr.
Passage Verdeau, beyond Passage Jouffroy, 9th arr.
Passage Brady, off bd de Strasbourg, 10th arr. (The odd one out, where romance is played out on an exotic miniature stage of the Indian subcontinent.)

9. ROMANTIC GRAVES

The **Père Lachaise** in eastern Paris is certainly the largest and most famous of the city's cemeteries. It is by no means the only one worth mentioning—others contain tombs that are just as famous. I point you to the graves most associated with romantic love, and also to their location within their respective cemeteries. Maps are available at the entrances to the main cemeteries.

Abélard (1079–1142) and Héloïse (1101–1164)
Père Lachaise, division 7

The celebrated medieval lovers have shared the same grave for most of their afterlives, close to a thousand years, and were brought together to the Père Lachaise in 1817 (see page 5). Their impressive monument is neo-gothic rather than gothic and the sentimental epistle engraved in the stone is, likewise, pure fabrication.

Epître adressée à Héloïse

*Si la mort après moi vient vous
fermer les yeux,
Que le même tombeau nous
enferme tous deux.*

Epistle to Héloïse

*If after I am gone, death comes
to close your eyes in turn,
Let the same tomb
enclose us two*

Réponse d'Héloïse

*Si, dans ces tristes lieux, par
l'amour amenés,
Quelques amants, un jour, y
visitent nos cendres,
Courbés sur notre marbre et les
fronts inclinés,
Ah! diront-ils, baignés des
larmes les plus tendres,
Puissions-nous, en aimant, être
plus fortunés!*

Reply from Héloïse

*If, in this sad place, brought
here by love,
Some lovers, some day,
visit our ashes,
Bent over our marble, their
heads slightly bowed,
Oh! will they cry, bathed in
tender tears,
May we be more fortunate in
our love.*

Hector Berlioz (1803–1869): Montmartre, division 20

How extraordinary! Only in France have I seen a grave containing a threesome of husband, wife, and mistress. If you don't believe me, go and check the great 19th-century composer's tombstone, on which you will see engraved the name of his extramarital companion, Harriet Smithson, side by side with him and his wife.

Frederick Chopin (1810–1849): Père Lachaise, division 11

More than any other musician, Chopin embodies the outpouring of the Romantic soul. His burial site enjoys great popularity and is surmounted by a beautiful sculpture.

Oscar Wilde (1854–1900): Père Lachaise, division 89

The one-time victim and outcast of forbidden love, has since become a cult figure; his grave is among those most visited. Exiled to Paris, he died alone in a hotel in St-Germain-des-Prés (see page 69).

Alphonsine Plessis (1824–1847): Montmartre, division 15

When you come in through the main entrance at 10, avenue Rachel and turn left, you will notice an old tomb, surprisingly adorned with fresh flowers. On closer examination you will read:

Ici Repose
ALPHONSINE PLESSIS
Nee le 15 Janvier 1824
Decedee le 3 Fevrier 1847
De Profondis

If you wonder why the grave of a stranger from nearly two centuries ago still receives caring visitors, the answer is simple: Alphonsine Plessis, or Marie Duplessis (later du Plessis) as she renamed herself, was no other than Marguerite Gauthier, La Dame aux Camélias, the one time lover of the impassioned author, Alexandre Dumas *fils*. She was also known as Violetta in Giuseppe Verdi's operatic version, *La Traviata*. She was so real that you can walk past her two Parisian homes, at 28, rue Thabor, by the Tuileries gardens, and later at 15, (then 11) boulevard de la Madeleine.

Her most passionate love affair was actually with Franz Liszt, to whom "she was the most complete incarnation of womankind that has ever existed."

She certainly turned the heads of all Paris and when she died the obituaries in the Paris newspapers overflowed with emotion, as summed up to the point in *Le Siècle*: "No matter who saw [her face], be he monk, octogenarian or schoolboy, he could not but fall hopelessly in love with her."

Victor Noir (1848–1870): Père Lachaise, division 92

The famous journalist was shot dead by Prince Pierre Bonaparte, Napoleon III's cousin, in the heat of a political argument over the capitulation to Prussia. This is why you see him in effigy represented at the moment when he fell on his back, his top hat lying next to him, where it dropped off. His funeral, attended by 100,000 angry mourners, led to a riot on the Champs-Elysées.

Things have quieted down since, but his bronze effigy has become the object of a fetishistic cult among sterile women who come here to be granted fertility by touching the phallic region of his trousers (note the gleaming patch around his fly, caused by multitudes of anonymous caresses). At times the worshippers picnic by his side and deposit a rose on the sacred, protruding place. The origin of the ritual has not been determined, but he was a handsome man, if we are to go by his effigy….

The Kiss: Montparnasse, division 19 (beyond rue Emile Richard)

This is the "brainy" and "artsy" cemetery of Paris, suitably located on the Left Bank, where many members of its community are resting, notably the celebrated couple Simone de Beauvoir and Jean-

Paul Sartre in division 20. But its most poetic site is this early Brancusi, all the more moving as it surmounts an empty tomb.

10. FURTHER AFIELD

Parc de Bagatelle, Bois de Boulogne, 75016; Tel: 01 40 67 97 00; Bus 43

If you've done it all in central Paris, the Bois de Boulogne is an ideal destination for romantic outdoor activities—strolling, biking, picnicking, or rowing. Do fit in the enchanting Parc de Bagatelle—an absolute must in June, when its rose garden is at its peak. Opening hours vary according to times of year and should be checked by phone.

It may not have been a straightforward love affair that triggered the construction of the exquisite Pavillon de Bagatelle, but there were certainly flirtatious innuendos underlying the relationship between Marie-Antoinette and her brother-in-law, the Comte d'Artois, later to become Charles X. In the autumn of 1777, for the fun of a bet with the Queen, the Comte had his *pied-à-terre* demolished and replaced by this "trifle" (*bagatelle*) in just two months. He must have worked his 800 workers to the ground! This was the kind of self-indulgence the spoiled children of France allowed themselves less than two years before the Revolution.

Château de Malmaison, Avenue du Château, Rueil-Malmaison, 92500; Tel: 01 41 29 05 55; Bus 258 from La Défense

The one-time home of Josephine de Beauharnais, where Napoleon would come to relax after the battle, became his ex-wife's permanent residence after their divorce. It is outside Paris, in Rueil-Malmaison, but it is so much part of their love story that it deserves a mention and is worthy of your visit. The gorgeous veranda, the lovely theatre, Josephine's Imperial bed and, above all, her ravishing rose garden are all still there. Open daily except Tuesday from 10 A.M.; closing hours vary according to season.

11. AND CLOSER TO HOME

I couldn't forego the **Parc de Montsouris**, just south of the Latin Quarter. It is the one I call my own, since its forest of trees is level with my balcony and it makes for a glorious extension to my home. This lovely miniature of an English garden, ornamented with sculptures of amorous couples, is delightfully hilly and a draw to many a Parisian bride and bridegroom who come here for their wedding photos against the backdrop of rolling lawns and lake. On sunny Saturdays I often see several couples being photographed simultaneously, blissfully unaware of the other couples' presence as they pose for the future, thinking, like all true lovers, the day is theirs alone.

A Madame du Châtelet, from Voltaire to his mistress

Si vous voulez que j'aime encore,
Rendez-moi l'âge des amours;
Au crépuscule de mes jours
Rejoignez, s'il se peut, l'aurore.

Quoi! pour toujours vous me fuyez,
Tendresse, illusion, folie,
Dons du ciel, qui me consoliez
Des amertumes de la vie!

On meurt deux fois, je le vois bien:
Cesser d'aimer et d'être aimable,
C'est une mort insupportable;
Cesser de vivre, ce n'est rien.

Ainsi je déplorais la perte
Des erreurs de mes premiers ans;
Et mon âme, aux désirs ouverte,
Regrettait ses égarements.

Du ciel alors daignant descendre,
L'Amitié vint a mon secours;
Elle était peut-être aussi tendre,
Mais moins vive que les Amours.

Touché de sa beauté nouvelle,
Et de sa lumière éclairé,
Je la suivis, mais je pleurai
De ne pouvoir plus suivre qu'elle.

If you wish me still to love,
Return to me the years of romance
To the twilight of my days
return a touch of dawn, if you may.

What! Do you fly from me forever,
Tenderness, fond hopes and folly
Heaven's gifts that brought me solace
For the bitterness of life.

One dies twice, I see it well:
To cease to love and to be loved,
Is an unendurable death;
To cease to live, is nothing.

Thus did I bemoan the passing
Of the errors of my younger days;
And my soul, still open to desire,
Longed for the digressions of my
youth.

When, deigning to descend from heaven,
Friendship came to save me;
She may have been as sweetly tender
But was less impassioned than Love

Touched by her fresh beauty,
And illumined by her gentle light,
I followed her, though still I wept
For having none but her to follow.

8
ROMANTIC NIGHTS

Unable are the loved to die
for love is immortality.
—Jean Pierre Claris de Florian

...[Y]ou also know what a fortnight in Paris means...it makes the blood grow hot. The theater every evening, women's dresses rustling up against you and continual excitement; one goes almost mad with it. One sees nothing but dancers in tights, actresses in very low dresses, round legs, fat shoulders, all nearly within reach of one's hands, without daring or being able to touch, and one scarcely ever tastes an inferior dish. And one leaves it with a heart still all in a flutter and a mind still exhilarated by a sort of longing for kisses which tickle one's lips.

—Guy de Maupassant, from *That Pig of a Morin*

 OONLIGHT LOVERS, BEFORE YOU GET CARRIED AWAY by Maupassant, go out into the city and wander its streets all night. It doesn't matter if the moon or stars don't shine, or if it's cold and drizzling—just wrap yourselves up and go! Paris is utterly romantic after dark and gets better after midnight, when the city's glamorous floodlights give way to the soft golden gleam of its streetlamps. Plunge into old neighborhoods, stroll along the river, up to the Sacré Coeur, even later into the night and deeper into winter, when Paris is a palette of shimmering shades of darkness and hazy amber: Nobody is about except two lingering shadows and the slow echo of two pairs of steps. And if you can—if only once, you must!—stretch the night into the morning and follow the skies from black to pale and then on to pink to see Paris shake away its sleep and stir back to life.

For the energetic, strolling can be replaced by skating and roller-blading. If you are fit, confident skaters and are not overwhelmed by crowds, you can join forces with close to 30,000 fellow skaters, who glide swiftly through 25 kilometers of Paris every Friday night. Meeting point is at place d'Italie (Métro place d'Italie) at 9:45 P.M.

You can also do it by bike, on your own, and therefore at a more leisurely pace. There are dozens of miles of cycling lanes at your disposal throughout the city, and addresses for rental of both bikes and roller blades are to be found on page 206.

For those who want to dance the night away, tango is now the city's latest rage. What better place than Paris for that most sensual of dances, especially under a lush summer sky. If the night is warm, make your way to the Tino Rossi gardens on the banks of the Seine (quai St-Bernard, in the 5th arrondissement), where crowds of Parisian couples engage again and again in what has been poetically described as "a three-minute love affair." Come even if you don't dance and enjoy watching others do so against the backdrop of Ile St-Louis, Notre Dame, and the bridges of Paris. If I were you, I would hang around after the dancing is over and wait there for the break of day.

Below are listings for a wide variety of indoor entertainments, to satisfy different tastes and budgets. None necessitate any knowledge of French. They are listed in alphabetical order following the name of the establishment rather than the category of entertainment.

Le Balajo
9, rue de Lappe, 75011
Tel: 01 47 00 07 87
Price: Starts at €10
Open nightly Tuesday—Sunday
This one-time home of the working-class accordion was once frequented by the likes of Edith Piaf. Those days are now gone, and so are the working classes. But the Balajo, in the heart of the trendy Bastille neighborhood, still holds its own as a terrific dance hall in a great setting and has preserved its warm atmosphere. Different kinds of dances alternate on different nights, including salsa for the energetic on Tuesdays, Wednesdays, and Thursdays. On Thursday afternoons sentimental elders can dance to the rhythm and music of nostalgia, while the weekend nights are taken over by disco. Lush tango brings to an end the weekly round on Sunday nights.

Barrio Latino
46/48, rue St-Antoine, 75012
Tel: 01 55 78 84 75
Price: €10 entrance fee on weekends
Open nightly until 2 a.m.
Not so long ago the Bastille area was the stronghold of France's cabinet-makers and joiners. All of a sudden, in the 1980s, Paris's young and trendy swooped down on the workshops and showrooms and little by little turned them into a haven of dot-coms, graphic designers, and others, all of whom look toward the Americas.

If you are young and trendy, if you love mingling, and if your ear drums can put up with searing decibels, Barrio Latino is one of the hottest places in Paris. This one-time four-story furniture shop, (complete with an impressive iron frame designed by Gustave Eiffel) has been turned into a Latin American enclave, exploding with fiery rhythms. Don't come here if you want a peaceful outing, for 900 to 1,500 guests come here every night, most to dance to the Latin American rhythms (10:30 P.M. to 1:30 A.M.). Dance on any floor, but the ground floor is the probably best, near the first bar, which specializes in tequila. A stunning staircase leads to the other floors; the view from the top is head-spinning.

If you like Latin American food, make your way to the first floor. Barrio Latino is also a restaurant and their food is both excellent and reasonably priced (I love their tapas). We came here once for lunch, when the place was nearly empty, which enabled me to actually appreciate the astounding decorations. The top floor is reserved for VIPs, I am afraid, and consequently goes with leather armchairs. I am not quite sure how one becomes a VIP (I think it helps if you book through your hotel), but if you do make it to this elevated position, you can sit in the armchairs and choose between fifteen varieties of champagne. Personally, I prefer the tequila at the bottom of the stairs.

Le Bilboquet
13, rue St-Bénoît, 75006
Tel: 01 45 48 81 84
Price: €20 (first drink), €50 (dinner)
Open nightly until 2 or 2:30 a.m.; dinner begins at 8 p.m.
This "temple" of jazz goes all the way back to the heyday of St-Germain in the 1940s, when this was the throbbing center of intellectual and artistic life. Opened in 1947 by the celebrated Marc Doetnitz and Boris Vian, everyone converged here—Jean-Paul Sartre and Simone de Beauvoir, of course, and Marguerite Duras, Jacques Prévert... and that's just the audience. They came to see acts like Billie Holiday and Charlie Parker.

Today things start heating up after 10 P.M., with quartets in winter and trios in summer, as a general rule (in order to keep the volume lower in warm weather, when the doors are kept open).

Dinner is decent traditional French fare, but you can also drop in later, just for a drink. You will find excellent jazz in a lovely setting of red velvet and black wood. Paintings relating to jazz hang on the walls. Those I saw on my last visit were very good—and they were for sale. Don't hesitate to ask, if you are interested. There was one of Stéphane Grapelli and Didier Lockwood I would have loved to buy.

Le Calife
5, quai de Montebello, 75005 (April to September)
7, quai Malaquais, 75006 (October to March)
Tel: 01 43 54 50 04
Open nightly unless cruising
How about stopping for a drink on the Seine? The Calife first drew my attention because of its fabulous position, looking out on Notre Dame and Ile St-Louis in summer; the Pont des Arts, the Louvre and the tip of the Ile de la Cité in winter. But I was also intrigued by the boat itself— its garland of lanterns looked so pretty and magical after dark. It all made sense once I stepped in and met its captain and owner, Nicolas Gailledrat. A man who was glued to a piano by age four, he has been through several "reincarnations," always a self-made man, always loving music. The Calife has been his "baby" for the last seventeen years.

Left: Barrio Latino

When he bought it in 1984 in Auxerre, Burgundy, it was just a basic barge that carried cereals. He worked on it continually, building and decorating, until it was ready to sail the Yonne, and then down the Seine to Paris, where it's been moored ever since. As Nicholas showed me around, I noticed a statue of Buddha surrounded by flowers. And the slogan on his brochure, from Baudelaire's *Invitation au Voyage*: "All is order, beauty, luxury, and voluptuous calm." The Calife is definitely not about package tourism and loudspeakers. But you'll find excellent acoustics downstairs, where concerts are sometimes held. Occasionally the Calife cruises along the Seine, offering guests a gastronomic dinner at a competitive price (about €75 per person, including wine). Drop by for a drink against one of the most beautiful cityscapes of Paris, or call to find out what's on while you are in town.

Caveau de la Huchette
5, rue de la Huchette, 75005
Tel: 01 43 26 65 05
Price: €9; Friday, Saturday €11; Students €8
Open Sunday—Thursday 9:30 p.m. to 2:30 a.m.; Friday until 3:30 a.m.; Saturday until 4 a.m. The later the better! No booking.
Although this pedestrian enclave of the Latin Quarter has been woven into a Mediterranean tapestry of couscous and Greek eateries, some strongholds seem perennial, such as the Théâtre de la Huchette, where Ionesco's *Cantatrice chauve* has been showing without a break since 1953, and the Caveau de la Huchette, a jazz haunt since 1946. The most legendary jazzmen have all appeared here at some point— Art Blakey, Claude Bolling, Wild Bill Davis, Lionel Hampton's Big Band, Claude Luter, Memphis Slim, and so on.

Every night, whether you want to listen to jazz or dance your socks off, the exceptional atmosphere of the club will remind you of the Cotton Club and the Savoy in their days of glory.

La Closerie des Lilas (see also page 88)
171, boulevard du Montparnasse, 75006
Tel: 01 40 51 34 50
Open daily until 2 a.m.
The very same that Hemingway made his home in the 1920s. The place has remained very atmospheric, with lots of dark, sleek wood, cigarette smoke, and history. Come here for a drink late at night, and enjoy the wonderful jazz pianist (until 1 a.m.), without whom there would be no Closerie. You can even grab the microphone and give the guests a performance of some oldies, as one of the clients did when I happened to be there yesterday. A beautiful red-head dressed in black sang French Left-Bank classics with a deep, inspiring voice. This was all in honor of her lover's birthday and came with a little cake, a candle, and a wonderfully jazzy version of "Happy Birthday to You."

La Coupole
102, boulevard du Montparnasse, 75014
Tel: 01 43 20 14 20
Price: Sunday €12, with 2 drinks; Tuesday €15 (€21 with salsa class), with 1 drink; Friday, Saturday €15, with 1 drink
Open daily until 2 a.m.

This landmark of Montparnasse has been going strong since 1927. Artists and Left-Bank literati have converged here for decades. The splendid art deco brasserie serves excellent food until 1 in the morning (1:30 on weekends), so this is a great place to drop by late at night, to snack, say, on wonderfully fresh oysters washed down by champagne.

Behind the oyster counter is a discreet door that leads to the basement, where you can dance the night away with fellow Parisians and some tourists who blend in inconspicuously.

Tuesdays are devoted to salsa and are probably the best nights. It starts at 9 P.M. with an optional class taught by the American Suzanne Sparck, who is praised as a wonderful instructor. Proper dancing starts at 10:30 P.M. and those who come are really there to dance.

Friday nights are young and loud, with techno and house music; Saturday is disco, with music from the 60s through the 80s and a mixed crowd.

Le Crazy Horse
11, avenue Georges V, 75008
Tel: 01 47 23 32 32
Dinner: before or after the show, at your discretion
Price: €90 with first drink; €110 with bottle of champagne; €125, €155 with dinner at Francis, place d'Alma, 75008; €167 with dinner at Le Fouquet's, 99, ave des Champs-Elysées
Show: 8:30 & 11 p.m.; Saturdays 7:30, 9:45, & 11:50 p.m.

This is the most sophisticated of Paris's shrines to voluptuous entertainment (and the youngest—50 years old in May 2001). The red plush auditorium is tucked into a surprisingly small basement, which creates the intimate feel of a cabaret rather than a music hall, almost a cross between a sanctuary and a boudoir. Needless to say the worship is devoted to Eros. All 280 seated worshippers enjoy a close view of the stage, almost within reach of their hands, which adds to the sensuality that hangs in the air. You will see no ostrich feathers here, just fourteen perfectly carved female nudes, wrapped in nothing but laser rays, which imprint on their stunning bodies ever-changing patterns and hues. Erotica is permanently present and on her best behavior. She is tasteful, cheerful and often accompanied by a wry sense of humor. The review is called "Teasing," and that's what you will get—no more, no less. The girls are gorgeous, between 18 and 26, all professional, wonderful dancers, from a dozen different countries.

Le Don Juan
Les Yachts de Paris
10, quai Henri IV, 75004
Tel: 01 44 54 14 70 (Ask specifically for the Don Juan)
Price: €150
Boarding: 8 p.m.; Sailing: 8:30 p.m.
I can't think of a more appropriate name for a vessel that will take you on a romantic cruise in the city of love, nor of a more romantic way to crown your visit.

The Don Juan is a genuine Dutch yacht dating from 1937, all

sleek wood and shiny brass. This is no place for assembly-line tourists: fewer than 36 passengers are on board any given night. There are no loudspeakers, no garish projectors, no headphones or live commentators. Tonight you are acting out Audrey Hepburn and Cary Grant, as seen in the charming thriller, *Charade*, gliding along the sparkling banks of the Seine.

Book your table either on the glass-covered deck, for a more expansive view but less privacy, or in the wonderfully cozy cabin with its mahogany paneling and shining copper, preferably in a quiet corner by the window, on the port side, for a full view of Notre Dame. Before settling down, sip champagne on the upper deck under the canopy of a Parisian twilight. Gérard Besson, one of Paris's leading chefs, will provide an inspired dinner of French classics such as *foie gras*, scallops, duck, fish, and imaginative sweets that are as divine as the entire evening. Before disembarking, linger on the upper deck once more and soak up Paris at its most romantic, to the west.

Le Flore en l'Ile
42, quai d'Orléans, 75004
Tel: 01 43 29 88 27
Open daily until 2 a.m.
You come here for the amazing location, at the western tip of the Ile St-Louis, facing the back of Notre Dame, and all the rest. It goes without saying that you must have a Berthillon ice cream (but they also serve very good salads and other light food, at reasonable prices).

Le Fouquet's Bar
99, ave des Champs-Elysées, 75008
Tel: 01 47 23 97 56
Open daily until 2 a.m.
This Champs-Elysées landmark (see page 35) has a very pleasant bar, if you want things quiet and comfortable. I wouldn't make the trip specially, but if you are already in the neighborhood and need a place to stop, why not? It has more historical glamour than any of its younger rivals and I have been told that it's a favorite of Bruce Willis to this very day.

Le Franc Pinot (jazz)
1, quai de Bourbon, 75004
Tel: 01 46 33 60 64
Price: €13–16
Open Tueday — Thursday from 8:30 p.m., Friday & Saturday from 9:30 p.m.; closed August
You can't miss this old timer on the Ile St-Louis, as you reach it from the Pont-Marie bridge. Due to severe subsidence, it is charmingly crooked, and looks every bit as old as it actually is, dating back to the

Courtesy Courtney Kolar

first half of the 17th century, when the entire island was built up, despite the instability of the soil. Not to worry—the houses are securely wedged against one another and have been standing firmly on their foundations ever since. Le Franc Pinot was already there, catering to passengers and boatmen alike.

Today jazz has taken over in the tiny basement, with a penchant for bebop. You can either have a drink or a full dinner, but I enjoy even more their Sunday brunch, on street level, which comes with a combination of a huge French and American breakfast. An assortment of French breads and croissants, eggs and sausages will leave you nourished for the rest of the day. A brownie topped with custard is the *coup de grace*. All along you will be entertained by jazz, whether duos of piano and guitar, or saxophone. It is all yours for the ridiculously low price of €16. Book your table, as the place only seats twenty.

Hôtel du Nord
102, quai de Jemmapes, 75010
Tel: 01 40 40 78 78
Price: €22 (set menu with wine and show)
French songs, Saturdays from 9 p.m.; dinner served from 8 p.m.
Call to ask about musical events other nights

Who cares that Marcel Carné's famous film, *L'Hôtel du Nord* (starring the legendary Louis Jouvet and Arletty), was actually shot in a studio? Still the novel that inspired Carné took place on these premises, by the quai of the atmospheric canal St-Martin. Its author, Eugène Dabit, was actually the son of the hotel-keepers, and his love story was written with the backdrop of 1930s Parisian low life. Dabit's pair of lovers check into the Hôtel du Nord planning to put an end to their lives in one of its seedy rooms—how utterly romantic! But this is film noir, and things will go wrong....

The hotel has been converted into upscale apartments, but the façade has been preserved to satisfy nostalgic film lovers, and the downstairs converted into a wonderful café restaurant. Be grateful to James Arch, a one-time assistant of Marcel Carné, who has struggled hard to perpetuate Carné's memory and the memory of his Paris. Arch put his heart into the restoration of the place, scouring the city for the period tiles that now make up the beautiful floor and the wonderful period bar. He even arranged a party for Carné's 90th birthday here, just before his death, and invited all the famous actors from his films. On Saturdays, Arch and his wife help raise the ghosts with French favorites from the 1930s, sung by an enthusiastic and very professional threesome, accompanied by an accordionist. They even wear period clothes for the occasion, and the diners sing along and enjoy themselves wholeheartedly.

Arch has been a prominent figure of Parisian nightlife since the 1960s. He knows how to imbue a place with nostalgic atmosphere, but he also knows how to respond to modern tastes. On other nights you can hear different kinds of music—jazz, country, klezmer. Call to ask when you make your reservations.

If you wonder why all the music and the full (perfectly commendable) meal comes at such a bargain price, this is part of the genuine slice of Paris *populaire* that Arch wants to preserve.

Le Lapin Agile
22, rue des Saules, 75019
Tel: 01 46 06 85 87
Price: €23 (with 1 drink); student discount available, except Saturdays
Open Tuesday—Sunday 9 p.m. to 2 a.m.
This famous old Montmartre place, once the haunt of the likes of Utrillo, Modigliani, and Picasso, is still the same little cottage that it used to be, huddling against the northern slope of the Butte Montmartre. Except that it now faces a pretty vineyard and has been altogether facelifted. It truly looks like a picture postcard of Montmartre with its pink walls, green fence, and profusion of greenery. Just on the right side of kitschy, it is charming and full of joy. Spend the night traveling down memory lane with old French songs, good humor, laughs, and jokes that you may not understand (but that doesn't matter). See also page 45.

Le Latina (Le Bistro Latin)
20, rue du Temple, 75004
Tel: 01 42 77 21 11

Open Wednesday—Monday until 1 a.m.; weekends only in August

No dance celebrates the passionate fusion of two lovers as well as tango—one body and four legs; and the place to do it is Le Latina, the mecca of tango just a few steps from the Hôtel de Ville. Véronique and Thierry Lecoq, the tango instructors, seem madly in love. Though they admit that the three-minute exchange of energy and emotion that is tango is beyond words, Thierry nonetheless speculated that "the man is the rock in the sea; his lady the wave." Véronique said, with a twinkling eye, that it makes her "feel like a flying carpet." So, if you want to say it all with impassioned legs, ladies, put on your stockings and high heels, and let your lover hold you tight, cheek to cheek, and sweep you off your feet.

Metamorphosis
55, quai de la Tournelle, 75005 (April to September)
7, quai Malaquais, 75006 (October to March)
Tel: 01 43 54 08 08
Price: dinner & show €50; show only €25

Open Tuesday—Saturday; dinner 7:30 p.m.; show 9:30 p.m.

Metamorphosis is a barge moored in the glamorous section of the Seine, with a stunning view of the Louvre and the Pont des Arts in winter, and the back of Notre Dame in summer. Yet you will see few tourists aboard—Metamorphosis caters to regular French people of the most average sort. If you are out to have fun, your hosts will treat you superbly and make you feel totally at home. They may not speak much English, but certainly enough to get by. Besides, you won't need any French to appreciate Jan Madd's talent as a magician, and it won't matter if you miss out on his puns and jokes. Jan Madd is a natural showman and his sense of humor comes across despite the language barrier.

The food is decent and reasonably priced: simple, light fare, just right in quantity and washed down by basic red or white wine. Dim lights, red table cloths, and a staff dressed in black and red, create a theatrical atmosphere, a taste of the main act, which will take place after the meal, in the little theater hidden downstairs. Everything is orchestrated by the charming Chantal, who has more than one string to her bow. I shall say no more except that the watchword she has come up with is *osez rêver* (dare to dream). Go on a Friday or Saturday night for the most romantic atmosphere—be sure to book a table with a view well in advance.

Moulin Rouge
82, boulevard de Clichy, 75018
Tel: 01 53 09 82 82 (phone reservations between 9 a.m. and 1 p.m.)
Price: €89 for 9 p.m. show; €79 for 11 p.m. show (both with half bottle of champagne); €125, €140, €155 for dinner & show
Open nightly for dinner at 7:30 p.m.; shows at 9 & 11 p.m.

Moulin des amours	Windmill of love
Tu tournes tes ailes	You turn your sails
Aux cieux de beaux jours…	To the beautiful skies…

The bright red "windmill of love" at the foot of Montmartre is as unmistakable as the oversized white basilica on top of the hill. As its sails revolve in seductive slow motion, they lure passersby on place Blanche into the city's shrine of lust, the home of Toulouse-Lautrec and French cancan. Once a miller and his wife stood in the windmill's two windows, and there was an enormous stucco elephant in the garden which has since disappeared. So has the glamour, but the Moulin Rouge remains the most famous emblem of the city's nocturnal love life and simply had to go into this book. (Though lining up for a show with 848 co-guests is not my idea of romance. And forget about privacy: there are very few tables for two, and they are not easy to come by. In all likelihood you will be seated assembly-line fashion. Even worse, I was quite disheartened to see that most people turn up in their casual, even sloppy, day gear.

Some even turn up with kids.) What does it matter—you come here for the mystique and a fabulous review. Accordingly, the three menus have been dubbed: French Cancan, Toulouse-Lautrec, and Belle Epoque.

When the Moulin Rouge was inaugurated in 1889, it coincided with the first centennial of the Revolution (along with the Universal Exposition and the Eiffel Tower), and was celebrated accordingly in patriotic tricolor hues. La Goulue, Jane Avril, Mistinguett, Edith Piaf, Yves Montand… so many of the city's glories graced the stage of the world's most famous music hall.

The tricolor is still part and parcel of the show, displayed in a swirl of lace by the 60 Dorris girls as they lift their gorgeous legs to Offenbach's *La Vie parisienne*.

Palais Garnier
place de l'Opéra, 75009
Tel: 08 36 69 78 68
Price: €10–105 for opera; €8–64 for ballet
Call for schedule

If Paris of the 19th century speaks to your heart, you cannot forego a night at the Palais Garnier opera house, the ultimate seat of glamorous romance. Echoing Voltaire's definition of the opera as "the land of fairies," Charles Garnier meant his gigantic sanctuary to be a palace of dreams, girdled by the magic of 3,500 gas lights. He placed it in the heart of Haussmann's new Paris, "the capital of capitals" and linked it to the Palais des Tuilerie by an imperial thoroughfare, the avenue de l'Opéra, then the city's most elegant artery. Haussmann thought that the addition of trees would only spoil it, which is why it is the only treeless avenue in Paris to this very day. A stunning façade completed the monument, a drop curtain of polychrome marble and gilt bronze. As you walk into the opera foyer and up its dazzling staircase, imagine rustling silk and glittering diamonds, the agitated fans, the top hats and tails, the hubbub of the city's gossip. The glamour continues into the auditorium, all red and gold and topped by Marc Chagall's exquisite ceiling, where some of the world's most famous lovers float in ethereal hues—Orpheus and Eurydice, Tristan and Isolde, Tamino and Pamina, and, of course, Romeo and Juliet. From the center of the ceiling hangs a dazzling seven-ton chandelier, shining with 350 lights, the very one that crashed down in *The Phantom of the Opera*.

Today full-scale operas are performed at the Bastille opera house, alas, which cannot boast the miraculous acoustics of the Palais Garnier, but you can enjoy here wonderful ballets and chamber operas such as Mozart's. Make sure to check the program before you come to town. You may even be able to attend a general rehearsal for a few euros. Ask at your hotel.

Theatre du Palais Royal
38, rue de Montpensier, 75001
Also at 17, galerie de Montpensier, 75001
Tel: 01 48 24 16 97
Price: €14, €22, €31, €43
Call for schedule

You will find all the splendid trimmings of the 18th century combined in this bejeweled theater—red velvet, crystal chandeliers, gilt carvings, festoons of roses, and also splendid acoustics and an auditorium of just the perfect size for vocal concerts. These take place on Mondays twice monthly during the season. Music lovers will enjoy this romantic outing in a universal language.

Marie Duplessis, the model for the Dame aux Camélias and Violetta in *La Traviata*, made her last public appearance here on December 12, 1846 (see page 240).

Ste-Chapelle (chamber music)
4, boulevard du Palais, 75001
Tel: 01 44 07 12 38
Price: €18–23; (student & senior tickets about €13)
Open nightly (except in winter) at 7:15 p.m. and 9 p.m.

If you want an uplifting setting for a chamber music concert, spend an evening at the bejeweled Ste-Chapelle. Early in the season, in fine weather, you will also enjoy the glowing splendor of the sun through its stained glass windows.

Note that concerts are often held in many of the city's historical churches. Check listings.

Théâtre des Champs-Elysées
15, avenue Montaigne, 75008
Tel: 01 49 52 50 50
Call for schedule

My favorite concert hall in Paris, the Théâtre des Champs-Elysées, was inaugurated in 1913 on the occasion of Diaghilev's Ballets Russes premiere of Stravinsky's *Rite of Spring*. Nijinsky, who choreographed the ballet and was also the troupe's male lead dancer (and Diaghilev's lover), created an extraordinary and violent *scandale*, which has gone down in history. The audience and critics were outraged by the barbaric stamping, the gesticulations, the "bathrobes" donned by the dancers—in short, by the appalling bad taste. Jean Cocteau, on the other hand, was ravished by "the 9th Symphony of the 20th century." A year earlier Nijinsky had already outraged Paris at the Théâtre du Châtelet in the title role of Debussy's *L'Apres-midi d'un faune*. Dressed in his spotted skin-tight leotard with a bunch of grapes over his genitals, he looked "more

nude than nude," "bestial," and "hideous," according to the press.
More outrage followed in 1925, when Josephine Baker led here the
Revue nègre with nothing on but a pink flamingo feather between
her limbs. Janet Flanner reported that the theater was electrified, but
the next day's *Figaro* called it the "most direct assault ever
perpetrated against French taste."

Music lovers should check out what's playing in this gemlike
theater. The best seats are in the stalls or in the first circle, though the
whole place has great acoustics. Combine this outing with a meal at
the neighboring Plaza Athénée (see page 62). The two landmarks
are contemporaries, and feel like extensions of each other. The Plaza
has a wonderful brasserie, which I particularly enjoy at lunch time,
a wonderful patio garden overflowing with red geraniums (ideal for
a summer outing), and wonderful food, since it is presided over by
chef Alain Ducasse.

Tour Montparnasse and Le Ciel de Paris
33, avenue du Maine, 75015
Tel: (Tour Montparnasse) 01 45 38 52 56
Tel: (Le Ciel de Paris) 01 40 64 77 64

Open nightly until 11 p.m. (restaurant); 1 a.m. (bar)

If you want to end your last night in heaven, make your way to the
bar on the 56th floor of the Montparnasse Tower. Admittedly the
tower is one of the controversial buildings in Paris, but it does reveal
the city's most magnificent panorama. Start out by doing the tour on
the 56th floor, then climb up the steps to the roof (sorry, no elevator
for that stretch). It's incredibly windy, but no other monument can
beat this 360-degree splendor. You'll need something cozy after this,
so make your way back to the 56th floor and head for the
bar/restaurant Le Ciel de Paris. Sink into its warm atmosphere and
soft light, drift away with the melodious piano and float into perfect
bliss as Paris unrolls her sparkling carpet at your feet, seducing you
back, as soon as you can.

EPILOGUE

C'est de ce Paris-là que j'ai fait mes poèmes...
et
J'ai plus écrit de toi Paris que de moi-même:
Et plus que de vieillir
Souffert d'être sans toi

It's out of Paris, that Paris, that I have carved my poems...
and
I have written more about you, Paris, than about myself:
And more than from ageing,
I have suffered from being without you.

—*Louis Aragon*

INDEX